MUSEOLOGY

MUSEOLOGY
Some Cute Points

Dr. D.K. Roy

Publications

KALPAZ PUBLICATIONS
DELHI-110052

Museology : Some Cute Points

Rs. 750

ISBN: 81-7835-410-1

Published in 2006 in India by
Kalpaz Publications
C-30, Satyawati Nagar, Delhi-110052
E-mail: Kalpaz@hotmail.com

Laser Typesetting at: Master Computers, Delhi
Printed at: Salasar Imaging System, Delhi

Contents

Contents

Preface

The material world is the phenomenal perspective where the Man is the creator of his own world. The man underwent a process of change by means of his culture. Thus the material world became a component of total culture within a conceptual framework of material level of culture. In time perspective, each and every achievement defines at this juncture as a mark of progress within a natural order. Thus, a long journey stood as the stages in the process of progression legitimizing the change. As a consequence, the museums are required to come up for demonstration and substantiate the phenomena for common mass of the society to accept and consequently participate in these happenings. In this regard, the museums may be considered as the repository of collected materials. But, the museum is an institution to have an acceptance as the acquisition of objects, study and enjoyment under one roof for disseminating of knowledge and enjoyment of its visitors. According to Kenneth Hudson "Museums are no longer considered as mere store houses or agents of preservation of the country's cultural heritage, but rather as a powerful instrument of education in the broadest sense".

The museum had a long story of its origin with leading legendary. The concept has gone through a process of change. The objectives are varying but the functions remain constant. Though the museums were originally were meant to be use of primarily for specialists, but, today, the museums have some exclusive functions and services to all cross section of people which are easily and nimbly propagated through mass media. As such, it indicates that museums are institutions of forceful and compulsory teaching through non-conventional way. In present situation, the Government of India and the State Government are interested in fundamental education to help the people who have not had access to formal education. Those people are not yet been able to get them educated through written word; substitute methods have to be found for their education through visual aids. Naturally, the museums are come up as the institutions of great utility. According to UNESCO, "Museums in many countries can no longer be considered sanctuaries for the connoisseur or specialist. They are actively engaged in revising exhibition policies and relations with the public at large and play a more important role in general education".

A museum should be structurally equipped to develop its functional potentiality. So, the infrastructure at the initial stage is to carry out the work in conformity with its aims and objectives. First objective of any museum is to keep up the record of uptodate information in the light of past with strong traditional bondage. Second one is to arrangement of meaningful display to organize with the collected artifacts. Third objective is to focus on the diminishing tradition or the artifacts, which are already extinct, or on the verge of extinction. Fourth objective is to maintenance through proper documentation of the collected articles with adequate records. Fifth objective is to set up an applied value of the collection to serve the community at large. As a result, the museum should be developed as a centre of visual education as well as a domain of research for the projection of future prospect. Sixth objective is also to be utilized as the centre for experimental study for revitalization of the diminishing tradition.

Frederic Kenyon has said, " Museums make a man more aware of the world he lives in, of its extension in time and space, of the materials of which it is composed, of the trees and plants with which it is covered, of the animals that have inhabited it from the earliest times, of the activities of man, of his achievements in craftsmanship and art. It illustrates written history and enlarges a man's conception of the possibilities of his race; so it plays its part in enlarging his mind, in multiplying his interests and in making him a good citizen". Sachin Roy says, "This Mirror (Museum) can give to a visitor a reflection of his own self and his culture, and thus stimulate his thought process as also acknowledge of himself. His people and his country in a very wide perspective".

Dr. D.K. Roy

Acknowledgements

At first, I acknowledge and convey my deep gratitude to Dr. (Mrs.) Indrani Basu Roy, Anthropologist, regarding her wholehearted support with all round help in each and every steps of my life. Dr. Shyamal Kanti Chakraborty, and other personnel of Indian Museum, Calcutta deserve special mention for providing me an exposure practically about their professional activities around the museum. I am also very much thankful to Dr. (Mrs.) Ratna Gupta, Anthropologist, for her kind hearted support to improve my expertise. Finally for this production, I convey love with full of heart to my little daughter Shalini that is the actual spirit of mine.

My sincere thanks are due to Kalpaz Publications for their kind cooperation. Specially, I am obliged to Mr. Amit Garg for his encouragement and heartiest cooperation in publishing this book.

Dr. D.K. Roy

1

A Brief Concept of the Museum

Introduction

The chronology of man's progress stands alone on accumulation of knowledge. Mostly, the knowledge as such depends on the education, which can easily be extended by the people. Naturally, to achieve a better knowledge, the museum should have a good scientific exposure for disposition of more reality while the system of understanding and communication is repeated in nature. In historical perspective, the origin of museums is founded as the intellectual approach of the Renaissance (14th Century to 16th Century AD). In this period, the interest for revival of classical culture is channeled by collection of its antiquities with the process of learning, which is provoked by means of inducing invention, modernization and industrialization. Thus, the museum becomes an institution, which must fulfill three minimum conditions. Firstly, it must be enough flexibles for expression of its exhibits, charts, models, etc. Secondly, it must have sufficient educational value that can be easily depicted through exhibitions. Thirdly, the museum should have sufficient content of its own to create popular interest.

As a matter of fact, the concept of museum has undergone a continuous process of change. It refers the museum, which is not an institution of forceful and compulsory teaching; rather it has been taken as a great role of flexibility in question of knowledge for common people as well as the interest, which may even be created by means of it. In this regard, the exposure of the objects is taken as the most important part of any museum for the visitors. On the contrary, the museum is always searching for the betterment of its exposure having the varying degree of realization of the visitors that may be depending on the individual feelings of the viewers. Besides, the awareness of the visitors is also perpetually self-evolving phenomena that are developed by means of museum exposure to its visitors.

Origin and History

The term museum is not a new one. If it is traced back more than 2000 years then we can find the word *museum* which is used in its original sense in the *Alexandria Museum* in Alexandria in 283 BC. This is temple house dedicated to the *Muses*, the goddesses of learning.

In the beginning of 16th Century AD the word *mouseion* came to be used in Italy, more precisely, *museo* in its Italianized form. But, in truest sense, the term museum is derived from the Greek word *mouseion*. The *Mouseion* signifies a sanctuary dedicated to the *Muses*, the presiding goddesses of learning. Thus, the 'Sanctuary of Muses' means the abode where the goddesses of learning and arts are residing. The meaning of Greek word *Mouseion* is simply the seat of the *Muses*, i.e., a temple of the *Muses*.

In this context, it may be said that the *museo* in those days contained small pieces of artistic objects and it was not the place where large or bigger size objects were kept. The object of larger size, especially paintings were place in a long *galleria*, which may be described as the immediate predecessor of the Art-Gallery of 19th Century AD. The *museo* and the *galleria* were two vital pillars of present day museum and the basic difference between *museo* and *galleria* was structural. The contents of *museo* and *galleria* were first exhibited to the public in an Art Museum of Europe around 18th Century AD.

From the Greek mythology we have found the *Muses* who were the daughters of *Zeus*, the Greek Jupiter. The *Muses* were born in *Pieria* at the foot of *Mount Olympus*, that is the mountain of the Gods. They were nine sisters considered as the divinities, which were presiding over the source of all-learning, creative arts, poetry, music, sciences, etc. Thus, the museums all over the world have retained the inherent quality and characteristics of learning in one form or other. So, it may be assumed that the term *Museum* is derived from the word *Musee* that indicates any one of the nine Sister Goddesses who presided over the arts or sciences.

The spirit of curiosity inculcates the growth of collection by means of acquiring different objects. In this way, during the 16th and 17th Century AD, a few Princes and noblemen in Europe were in the habit of increasing personal collections as curio-objects out of a sheer spirit of curiosity and ego-motive. Gradually and gradually these collections took a shape of the museum where the principal aim was to provide some intellectual entertainment confined to a small community of Lords and nobles. Later on, by the patronage of kings and nobles these centres were open to the common mass of the society who desired to seek knowledge and entertainment from them.

The first public exhibition of the treasures may be traced back around 18th Century AD. However, in the middle of 18th Century AD a remarkable intellectual change took place. Primary objective was undertaken to serve the people, both professional and non-professionals and intellectuals in the light of mass education. As a result, the concept of museum underwent a sea change. Confiscation of the private collection became the public treasury and their maintenance had to be paid out of the public fund. In this way, it was essential to raise fund from the public while the work done by museum was useful to the common people.

In the early part of 19th Century AD, again the situation was changed remarkably when revolutionary developments took place in connection with the nature and scope of the museum. Again, in the middle of the 19th Century AD, more stress was laid on the collection of specimens and museum administration, when the main emphasis was imposed over the public involvement. At the end of 19th Century AD a specific trend was emerged as the progress of knowledge by means of new field–the museum. Slow but steadily, the museum came to be recognized as the valuable sources for getting information in connection with the serious study in different fields.

As a matter of fact, the arrangement of world exhibitions during the *Victorian Age* had also influenced the museum. The concept of National or Imperial museums was blooming up to manifest National wealth and culture. It became an ultimate vehicle to express prosperity and glory. Though, later on, this concept was faded out. At last, the effect of two World Wars has germinated a revolutionary development, which took place throughout the world in almost all spheres. The museums find out their new approaches, while the museums started interactions with the public instead of laying main emphasis over the collection of exhibits, more importantly to ensure their involvement.

In this respect for better understanding of the visitors' involvement, a number of surveys were undertaken by the Museologists in cooperation with the Anthropologists, Sociologists and Psychologists. Ultimately, new approaches were developed which can be categorized under three broad categories–the aesthetic, the intellectual and the romantic. These approaches are demanded their own way of classification on the basis of presentation. The *aesthetic approach* is most suited for Arts and Crafts museum especially decorative arts. The *intellectual approach* with a bit of romantic phenomena suits the museums of Natural History and the museums of Science and Technology. The *romantic approach* is the best for Art museum, History museum, etc. But all these three factors, like, as the *aesthetic approach, intellectual approach* and *romantic approach* are desirable for the museums of Anthropology, Archaeology, History, etc. Besides, the basic reason behind that the museum workers became specialized in their working field, such as for collection, preservation, documentation, scientific display, etc. As a result, this meaningful happening took a definite shape to develop a strong base among the four distinct types of museums, which are concerned with Art, History, Science and Industry. Gradually and gradually these four groups of institutions were changed in more specialized types of museums.

At the beginning of 20th Century AD, the museum showed a remarkable growth of its own and main functions of the museums were as follows: collection, preservation and exhibition. In this period the museum was rightly considered as a community centre. It should always reflect some aspiration of the community as such and a unique concern of any museum is the presentation of the specimens in a meaningful way. This concept made an enormous pressure on the museum staffs that have compelled to adopt a new approach in its changing scenario. Later period, more stress laid on educational value of the specimens. Thus, the museums are coming up as the house of knowledge, stimulating the spirit of research and helping at education level in all its phases.

Modern Concept of the Museum

The concept of museum has undergone a big change during the last two Centuries. The modern concept of the museum indicates a suitable place for exhibits, which display the objects for the visitors where they can get mental satisfaction in accordance with their requirements. Modern museum is not only an educational institution, rather it provides recreation by means of its activities, such as display, exhibition, education, research, entertainment, publication and public relations. Besides, many experiments and research, adoption of modern aids for better presentation and representation has given a new dimension to modern museum. Apart from these, the museums have also enlightened with a big impetus to perform their role as a centre of an effective media of non-conventional education. In a better way, we can say that the visual education centre as a synonymous phenomenon of the Modern Museum.

In time perspective, the museums had changed their roles. In this regard an UNESCO pamphlet says that the *Museums in many countries... can no longer be considered sanctuaries for the connoisseur or specialist. They are actively engaged in revising exhibition policies and relation with the public at large and play a more important role in general education.* Gradually, it had been established with definite purposes with well-planned utility and its importance had been realized. As a result, the concept of museum had in the way of a steady change. Finally, we have found various categories of museums, viz. the museums of national importance, State museums, departmental museums, etc.

In addition, the *Division of Monuments and Museums* was a section of UNESCO at Paris. The objectives of this division were to improve the standards of museum-work through international conferences and discussions, technical aids, the preservation from war risks of cultural objects and monuments all over the world. This division published a high standard journal entitled "MUSEUM" which acted as a common platform for the exchange of ideas in concerned museums on an international scale. Again, a technical association known as the International Council of Museums (ICOM) was also established in Paris closely collaborated with the *Division of Monuments and Museums* of UNESCO in 1946. UNESCO felt that, apart from their traditional functions the museums would also be able to improve International understanding. In this regard, ICOM (International Council of Museums) has arranged several conferences on education through museums with the help of UNESCO. Recently, the constitution of ICOM defines the term 'Museum' in the following ways: 'any permanent establishment set up for the purpose of preserving, studying, enhancing by various means and, in particular of exhibiting to the public for its declaration and instruction... artistic, historical, scientific and technological collections.'

Today, the basic contents of the museums evolved a lot, while the functions may be categorized under the following heads, i.e., collection, preservation, interpretation through exhibition and research, education and public relation. Modern museum is nothing but an advanced museum, which presents a story of its contents, impart direct information and stimulate visitors to acquire knowledge through looking at the specimens. So, the modern trend is that the museum must collect, preserve and disseminate knowledge to the people of all cross-section of the society. Naturally, the scope of museum has changed, while educational values of the exhibits are getting more importance. The scope is now well-devised policy to serve the intellectual and scholarly growth of the community as such. This is the backbone of the concept of modern museum.

Nature and Scope of the Museum

The people have realized the importance of the museum where the exhibits are permanently kept for dissemination of knowledge. During the last two Centuries different types of museums have came up with various objectives. Now-a-days, it is being a permanent institution engaged in the service of community at large which is defined as a non-profit making centre.

At present, the museum is defined as a non-profit making, permanent institution in the service of the society and its development. The museum is open to the people of all levels. It acquires, conserves, researches, communicates and exhibits for the purposes of study, education and employment, material evidence of man and his environment. In addition to this definition the following points are essential phenomena, which may be treated as the basic nature of the museum:

(i) to acquire objects as the museum specimens;

(ii) to conserves the specimens;

(iii) to display for communication;

(iv) to make an arrangement of research; and

(v) a clean and good administration.

Above all, different types of museums are found that may be categorized in this fashion. The existences are recognized as the museums of national importance, State museums, Regional museums, Municipal museums, Departmental museums, Site museums, Natural History museums, University museums, Anthropological museums, Folk-Art museums, Forestry museums, Medical museums, Engineering museums, Agricultural museums, Industrial museums, Children museums, Art and Crafts museums, Institutional museums, Personalia museums, etc. and a chain of Science museums. Among this long categorization we can classify the nature of the museums in two ways.

Firstly, on the basis of their *administrative set up*, and

Secondly, in accordance with the *types of their collections*.

On the basis of *administrative set up*, we find six types of museum, which are as follows:

National Museum: These are the museums of national importance where the Central Government is directly or indirectly responsible for its finances and administration, e.g., *National Museum* at Delhi, *Indian Museum* at Calcutta.

Government of India declared four zones under coverage of special status as national importance with various plans and programmes. In this regard, *Indian Museum*, Calcutta is carrying the responsibility of Eastern Zone. Southern Zone is represented by *Government Museum*, Madras. *Prince of Wales Museum*, Bombay is taken the responsibility of Western Zone, and Northern Zone along with Central Region of India is covered by *National Museum*, New Delhi.

State Museum: This type of museums are supported, financed and administered by State Government directly or indirectly, e.g., *State Archaeological Museum*, Calcutta; *Jawahar Toy Museum*, Pondicherry.

Local Authority Museum: These are financed and administered by some local authority, e.g., *Academy of Fine Arts*, Calcutta; *Allahabad Museum*, Allahabad.

University Museum: These types of museums are financed and administered by the University in its' Departments, e.g., *Anthropological Museum*, Calcutta University; *Zoology Museum*, Kalyani University.

Private Museum: Such museums are established under Trusts or Trustee who is responsible for effective use of funds. The administration is directly under control of the Trustee, e.g., *Raja Dinkar Kelkar Museum*, Pune; *Gurusaday Dutta Museum*, Calcutta.

Museum of Business Organization: These types of organizations are established and maintained by business establishments as an extension of their interests, e.g., *Calico Museum*, Allahabad, maintained by Calico Mills; *Samseong Museum of Publishing*, Seoul, maintained by Samseong Publishing Company.

Secondly, the classification is to be made on the basis of their *types of collection,* which are mentioned here in the following ways:

Composite Museum: This is composite form with different wings for specific purposes like research, education, etc. which may also present in various sections like Anthropology, Art, Archaeology, etc. It can also be called as Multipurpose Museum, e.g., *Indian Museum*, Calcutta.

Personalia Museum: It is primarily based on personal collections. Such type of museum keeps various objects related with the memory of someone and his collections, e.g., *Rabindra Bharati Museum*, Calcutta.

Period Museum: This type is nothing but a storehouse of a certain span of time. It can not go beyond that period, e.g., *Victoria Memorial,* Calcutta, which is a typical period museum concerned with Indo-British period.

Technological Museum: It is only concerned with Science and Technology. This museum is interested in preserving and popularizing different technology, e.g., *Birla Industrial and Technological Museum*, Calcutta.

Philatelic Museum: It is the museum of stamps where different types of postage stamps are preserved in consequences of time perspective, e.g., *Philatelic Bureau of G.P.O.* at Calcutta.

Art Museum: This type is primarily for the display of works of fine arts and applied arts, e.g., *Academy of Fine Arts*, Calcutta.

Archaeology Museum: In this type, the collections of antiquities and archaeological remains are preserved, e.g., *State Archaeological Museum*, Calcutta.

History Museum: This type is the centre of historical objects and relics which is secured as the collection of historical evidences, e.g., *Hazarduary Palace Museum*, Murshidabad, West Bengal.

Natural Science Museum: This type of museum is the subject to related science either one or several of the disciplines such as, Biology, Geology, Botany, Zoology, Anthropology, Paleontology, and Ecology. e.g., *Science City*, Calcutta.

Regional Museum: This type of museum illustrates more or less extensive information about the region constituting a historical and cultural entity and sometimes it is also an ethical, e.g., *District Science Centre*, Purulia, West Bengal.

General Museum: This type is nothing but mixed collections, which can not be identified with any one principal field, e.g., *Nehru Children's Museum*, Calcutta.

Other Museum: This type means, when the museum is not included in any of the above mentioned categories, e.g., *Magan Sangrahalaya Samiti*, Wardaha.

As per modern conception, the museums are such a type of institutions where original artifacts and the tangible objects are displayed and preserved. It has been accepted as a centre of education and culture. This institution makes one curious in the human development as well as it increases the knowledge of present period in perspective of the past. So, a complete museum is a means of communication between present and past while it acts like depositories of human knowledge in which objects are preserved, displayed and studied for the people. Naturally, the scope of museum has changed a lot. At present, the educational values of the exhibits are getting more importance. As a result, the scope of the museum is now a well-devised policy to serve the intellectual and scholarly growth of the community as such.

The scope of the museum starts from the very beginning of acquisition of the objects. About the accumulation of the collected items, emphasis is laid on their proper sorting to make inventory, classification and cataloging. To avoid adverse situation, the maintenance of storage of the objects in a scientific fashion and at the same time a well-equipped conservation laboratory become an essential component of a complete museum. Besides, the arrangement of indoor and outdoor exhibitions are much important to develop public relation by means of people's participation. The museum should have a scope for their own presentation unit covering a workshop, photo-lab, and publication division. The scope of research and education are unending process for a complete museum to ensure their acceptance among the people of all accessible corners of the society.

In the post-Independence period, Government of India adopted a new policy where the museum has been treated as a centre of education with special reference to visual education. Different activities in connection with the development have also been taken up to use the museum as a research centre. As a matter of fact, the activities are coming up to enhance the potentiality of the museums, which are mentioned here in the following ways:

(i) to arrange in-service training;

(ii) to introduce museology in University curriculum;

(iii) to set up the service unit for widening the scope of museums;

(iv) to arrange annual museum camp;

(v) to arrange seminars and workshops; and many more other ways as per credentials of the concerned museums when fund raising programme will be more important objective for self-reliance.

Thus, the scope of museum is now a wide range phenomenon for the people of all levels in our society.

Museum Movement in India

In museum world, for better prospect, the coordination and cooperation for the services of the museums became an important part to make a harmony among the institutions. As a result, an international body was established in the year 1946 at Paris to bring well-maintained coordination and cooperation for achieving better harmony among the museums of the world, which is known as International Council of Museum (ICOM). The members of this Council were included the Directors and Curators of different outstanding museums in the world. In fact, the ICOM is an important professional body, which imparts valuable guidelines through its International Symposia, Workshops and useful Handouts on different aspects. Some of its early publications and the journal museum are extremely beneficial for organizational activities. In this context, role of UNESCO is well known in fostering the museums, particularly in case of the developing countries.

The museum as a means of general education is a conscious approach for continuous improvement, which had been started since, between the late 17th and early 19th Century AD. At first, the elementary education with the aid of museum has been gained a strong ground in the Western Europe, which has also slowly and gradually been expanded through worldwide. As a result, the establishment of some great museums in different parts of the world has been flourished due to increasing popularity since then. The first Museum Act of 1845 was established by the Act of British Parliament while the museums began to appear from early 17th Century AD. Some of the great museums were founded in the 18th and early 19th Century AD, which of a few the world's best museums were found in Europe. A few of them are as follows:

(i) Ashmolean Museum, Oxford, 1638;

(ii) British Museum, London, 1756;

(iii) Belvedere, Vienna, 1781;

(iv) Louver, Paris, 1783;

(v) Prado, Madrid, 1819; and

(vi) Altes Museum, Berlin, 1830.

In America, the Museum in Charleston, South Carolina, 1773 and Peabody Museum at Salem, Massachusetts, these two museums were probably the earliest American Museum. The first American Art Museum was the Pennsylvania Academy of Fine Arts, 1805. Besides, Alma S. Wittlin in her book *The Museum–its history and its tasks in Educations* mentioned that several important museums also came into existence in France too. During this period, some anthropologists approached scientifically and led to the establishment of museums. Precisely, the museum movement in that way went on all over the world, while India was not lagging behind.

It is true that the concept of the museum was not new in India. Origin and development of museum movement in India is near about two hundred years old. It may be testified by the early *Alekhyagrihas*, *Chitrashalas*, *Devakulas*, *Viswakarma Mandiras* and monasteries, which did serve the purposes of education as well as healthy entertainment along with various cultural heritages of our own. Probably these were the early documentary facts of museums in our country. In reference to early inscription we also found some evidences of mobile art gallery, which were transported on the road with the help of mechanical devices. Archaeologists recognized the same thing in the same period, at the time of *Kushana dynasty*. But, actual credit of museum development in India goes to the English educated Indian officials of the Asian Royal families and British Indian Companies, who were well-educated British officers and British intellectuals of the 18th Century AD. They studied acutely regarding the Indian literature, Art, Architecture, Anthropology, Geology, Zoology, Botany, etc. and published their research work too. Ultimately they established different Institutions in India for Oriental Studies, viz. Archaeological Survey, Geological Survey, Anthropological Survey, Zoological Survey, Botanical Survey. Besides, some non-governmental efforts were also made to establish the institution likely the Asiatic Society of Bengal, Gokhale Institute of Pune, etc. as the centre of study and research. The first museum in India was established in 1814 at Calcutta, West Bengal. Afterwards, such concepts of museum were spreaded to other important cities like Gujarat, Madras and Bombay. Though the museums in our country are near about four hundred in numbers at present, but that number was only around fifty just before the hundred years from the present day.

The British Museum was established in 1756 when other nine early museums emerged in that contemporary period. Out of these ninth one was the Indian Museum, Calcutta. Seven years before the establishment of Indian Museum another one was started in 1807 at Copenhagen known as 'National Museete', which brought a new dimension for looking at the things. In the same period a Danish botanist Dr. Nathaniel Wallich had his courses from Copenhagen. He was specialized in varied subjects, but unfortunately he had no suitable job. Out of despair he left Copenhagen and finally arrived at Sreerampur, West Bengal under control of Denmark. Dr. Wallich had many ideas and he was inspired by the museum of Copenhagen. The thane's India was under control of East India Co. and as being a Danish citizen he was not resisted by the British in consideration of his contributions, collections of botanical specimens, etc. After sometime he made himself associated with Sir William Carry and other intellectuals of that period. It may be mentioned here that in 1796, Sir William Carry candled first light to establishment of a museum in the Asiatic Society of Bengal. Dr. Wallich wrote a letter to Asiatic Society by stating his number of collections and asked for setting up a museum with his voluntary curatorial work. Incidentally he was offered the post of Curator for first museum in our country, Indian Museum, Calcutta. That very day was 2nd February, 1814. But the museum was popularized through newspapers (1781-82) as Asiatic Museum; sometime it was called as Oriental Museum also. From the days of Asiatic Museum via Imperial Museum to present appellation of Indian Museum the institution had the modest beginning of the earliest museum in Asia.

In short, we may say that Sir William Jones and Dr. Nathaniel Wallich were indeed the pioneers of the museum movement in India since 1784 with humanities and natural history. Their collections took a shape of nucleus of the Indian Museum, Calcutta, and perhaps the greatest multipurpose museum in Asia that was opened in 1814. This movement influenced many Indian intellectuals who wanted to have a greater understanding of glorious heritage covering a period of thousand years or so. This was happened by means of illustrations regarding the India's magnificent archaeological remains as well as the continuation of traditional arts and crafts. Finally, the Government of India took the responsibility for establishment of different organizations. For example, the excellent work undertaken by the botanists like Roxburg and others in the Botanical Garden at Sibpur,

Howrah, West Bengal. Besides, many museums and museum like institutions established with active interest concerning all aspects of India's natural wealth and cultural heritage, which were intermingled to underline both antiquity and richness of culture. This phenomena produced and to strengthen the museum movement in India.

At the end of the British rule, India had shown the development of archaeological museums. Concentration of museological centres at the cities like Calcutta, Bombay and Madras had been observed since from inception of big multipurpose museums. Gradually it had been focussed for the need of a better distribution of museum potential of the country. The first attempt was a kind of an overall appraisal of the museum foundation in India was undertaken by the Museum Association, London. In this connection, S.F. Markham and H. Hargreaves were entrusted to make a comprehensive survey of museums in Indian sub-continent. This survey report was published in the year 1936, which create an effective impact on the need of overhauling and modernizing museum service in India.

In pre-Independence period, we have found the enactment of the *Treasure Trove Act* in the year 1878 at the time of Lord Lytton who helped a lot at large number of museums to develop their coin collections. Apart from this, some clauses of *Ancient Monument Preservation Act*, in the year 1904 has been passed since the period of Lord Curzon who also favoured the growth of museum collections. The Archaeological Survey of India, since its inception in the year 1861, has been maintaining and nourishing various museums with numerous numbers of antiquarian remains, which have yielded from excavations. Museum Branch of Archaeological Survey of India has been formed since the year 1947. Thus, some other Survey Offices also thought its necessity and established museums to illustrate their works and the result of their field work and research work.

In post-Independence period, museums got a big impetus and it cannot be denied that the museum movement received a tremendous inspiration and encouragement from various levels, especially from the government. The importance of the museums is in need for acquiring knowledge, which is also act as an effective media to have the education. This type of educational set up was first highlighted by the formation of the Museum Association of India, as a wing, rather we can say adjunct of the Indian History Congress at Benaras in 1944. Besides, other eventful step may be called as the report of the Museum Expert Survey Committee in 1956. This report materializes the subsequent formation of the Cultural Advisory Board of Museums by the Government of India. As a result, a remarkable upsurge in the Indian Museum Movement is witnessed in the year 1965, which was accompanied by the understanding of importance of the museums as instruments of social and cultural advancement.

Finally, the museum workers in India involved themselves in exchanging their ideas with the leading museologists of international repute who joined the UNESCO Seminar in connection with the Development of Museum in South East Asia as well as the meeting of the International Council of Museums. Both the gatherings of the delegates held for the first time in India at New Delhi during 1965. In this regard we can recapitulate that the UNESCO expert on museology, Mr. P.S. Rawson undertook a study tour of India in 1964. He has written a report entitled "India–Museology", published by the UNESCO in May 1965. He recommended, "that there be instituted a Government Museums Commission, with a function analogous to that of the University Grants Commission, and with a Secretariat of appropriate size. It should maintain the closest liaison with the University Grants Commission over the museology course".

In this perspective, several novel experiments gave new dimensions and importance of museums enhanced considerably. A number of museum camps are organized under direct patronage of the Ministry of Education, Government of India under leadership of Dr. Grace Morley. There are all can be desired for improvement of museums in general and upgradation of the skill of museum personnel in particular. The most important trend is marked as the development of the museum coming out as an educational and research institution. This new form of museums are offering ever-increasing community audience by means of professionally organized programmes including concerts, lectures, theatres, dance, films, and short courses for the people of all ups and downs corners of the society.

2

Structural Part of the Museum

Museum Building

The museum building in India as well as abroad had the monumental exteriors with palacial and ornamental interiors that indicate themselves as the symbols of culture rather than the centres of culture. In course of time the concept has undergone a considerable change to provide adequate facilities of regular activities along with other affairs of museum administration instead of ornamentation. It has been observed in many cases that the existing museum buildings were not specially designed for museums. Today, the museum building should be functional with a friendlier atmosphere. The visitors will come to share their hospitality and enjoy the whole during their visit in the museum. Now, we can assume the ideal conditions for building of a museum where we do have the freedom of site selection as well as the planning of museum building.

For an ideal situation, a site selection is the first task to erect the museum building when primary consideration should be of present requirements with future expansions. It should be easily accessible from the main roads and must have enough space in and around the proposed building for ensuring sufficient natural light and continuous ventilation. This space gives a good atmosphere and natural setting by creation of a garden or park or any other suitable steps. Besides, the museum building should have enough open space around it, for considering the future perspective. The climate control is a major task for museum, which can be possible at the time of initial planning of museum building, and it would be easiest possibility to accelerate the functions of preservation and conservation of the specimens. Inspite of it, the building must serve as a comfortable, delightful and attractive place for the visitors.

The planning of a building would be successful, when it is not to plan for the existing collections only, rather the collections to be made in future also. Existing collection will be the influencing factor for creating different rooms of various forms and sizes for making needful the exhibitions and other related services of the museum. The rooms for other services are also required apart from regular galleries, exhibition rooms, which should be considered as the covered space for maintaining the economic and social aspects of particular purposes of the museum, like as theatrical performances, lectures, concerts and so on. It is very much necessary that the museum authorities and architect should work in close cooperation. This joint venture is required for developing perfect style of building where interiors of the galleries and other related rooms should be architecturally pleasing with a full of functional efficiency.

The building area may be divided into two broad categories, *public area* and *service area*.

Public Area

This area is a composition of an *enquiry office*, the *galleries*, an *auditorium*, and *library*.

Enquiry Office–This space of the museum should be situated in entrance to the main hall to provide all the information and required guidance to the visitors.

Galleries–The planning of a gallery is solely depending on the type of collections, the volume of the rooms and the height of the ceiling. The gallery wall is the most usable space for display in the museum. The colour of the wall must be lighter in comparison with the floor for getting reflection of the light from wall to wall and visually it makes a lot of difference. The electrical fittings should be concealed on the walls and ceiling. But, the lighting fixtures may be hanged from the ceiling. The ceiling should be painted with light colour or white for getting a clear light reflection as much as possible. The floor must be smooth and clean to keep it as easy washable and the colour must be darker in comparison with the walls for absorption of light rays from the reflection of walls. Inside the gallery; natural ventilation is necessary for air circulation. So, a high level windows on one side and a lower level windows or doors on the other side creates a natural cross ventilation. It is advisable to arrange air-conditioning system considering the financial position of the museum administration. Besides, another important aspect is the planning of a *relief area* between the galleries. Naturally, to maintain this relief area rather we can say blank area that is necessary to keep up the interest of the visitors. A continuous looking at the objects create tiresome and naturally they will get a short gap to avoid stress and strain by means of that relief area.

Auditorium–This space should be organized with a projection room, which is necessary for illustrated lectures, as well as film projection. The stage of performance with necessary accessories is also another structure within the auditorium that can be appreciated for modern auditorium and it is also suitable for multipurpose activities, including various occasional cultural performances.

Library–This space should be arranged with a separate stacking room and a reading room. Well-organized and well-maintained library is essential for modern museum. The reading room requires enough light along with sufficient space for sitting.

Service Area

The service area is required for the *Office of Administration and Technical Staff, Preservation-cum-Conservation Laboratory, Workshop, Storerooms, Air-conditioning and Electrical Plants.* For an ideal area management of any modern museum, only forty per cent of the total area is being used as service area.

(i) ***Office of Administration and Technical Staff:*** This space is consisted with the rooms for office staff including higher level of administration as well as separate rooms for technical staffs of the museum. The area should not be more apart from the museum galleries.

(ii) ***Preservation-cum-Conservation:*** This space should be well-organised as a modern laboratory, which will be near to the workshop in one hand and storeroom on the other hand.

(iii) ***Workshop:*** The workshop area should be well-coordinated with different sections of the museum along with the preservation-cum-conservation laboratories.

(iv) ***Storerooms:*** The space for storeroom is considered as the few well-protected rooms with protection and proper ventilation as well.

(v) ***Air-conditioning and Electrical Plants:*** This area should not be attached to the galleries but not apart from the workshop and laboratories. This particular place of the museum is more critical as because all sections are in need of power connections, which are provided by the infrastructures of this space.

Apart from these two areas (*Public area* and *Service area*), the *Common area* is also necessary in museum building. The common area should also be easy accessible to the visitors, which may be mentioned here in the following ways.

(vi) ***Toilet and Cloakrooms:*** This area should be directly accessible from the main areas of the building where the provision is to be made for both of the visitors and the staff. The arrangements must be clean, neat and well maintained and well equipped with sufficient rather than a mere provisions. This area should also provide safe drinking water.

(vii) ***Staircases and Corridors:*** This space requires a wide enough area for making smooth as well as noise-free movement of the crowd. Besides, a normal crowd with easy traffic of their movement around the museum should also be maintained in this fashion for considering the safety measures of the museum.

Building Structure

Every museum building has its own problems, mainly for human comfort. The structure of building along with its necessity itself depends on its location, orientation and climatic zone. Most of the buildings are made for human occupation. But, the museum is occupied by valuables, irreplaceable, rare objects and specimens of different disciplines along with the multifarious models of human beings. Naturally the building for the museum should be comfortable for human occupation as well as it should provide a healthy environment for its precious collections and protection as well. It is true that only by construction of an excellent building structure is not enough for museum building, rather it requires the creation of a favourable climate inside the building by controlling the external and internal determinant factors. Museum building alone makes the task of preservation-cum-conservation with a great deal, which is easier and more economical. Considering the different climatic zone the style of building structure should also be different by alterations of essential components of the museum building, such as *Walls, Roof, Ceilings, Floor, Windows, Ventilation, Relief area* and *Courtyards.*

Walls

The walls are important measure to control temperature, solar radiation, ground radiation, drought, and dust. These are acting as a shield receiving the rays of the setting sun. The museum building should also be protected by adjustable sun-breakers, which is necessary to manipulate the length of such walls. It is desirable to have a heavy masonry wall on the west side. Above all, the thick walls are necessary for museum building. But, east and south walls can be of light construction, if sun-breakers or overhangs protect it. In general, thick walls with small windows are good for hot-dry conditions when days are hot and nights are cool. Again, cavity walls are considered as an effective measure for blocking out heat transmission. Inside the building, the treatment of the walls makes a lot of difference to a gallery. For example, an undistorted wall space is the most usable space in a gallery; if the windows are above eight feet high then the wall space below the windows is free for exhibition purposes while the electrical fittings are not located on the walls. The walls are also act as good backgrounds for free standing objects. It should be painted with plastic emulsion, which is easily washable as well as to be kept clean while the colour should be lighter than the floor for getting reflection of light.

Roof

The roof is functioning as a shield of the building from direct radiation as well as different natural hazards. Primarily it is in need to have a protection from high radiation, so thermal insulation can be provided for roof protection. Besides, the roof should be covered with white or near white paint for reflection of radiation. For durability of the roof, at least 5 inches thick RCC slab with 3 to 4 inches lime-concrete layer or mud-concrete layer is sufficient effective. Apart from these, it should be kept in mind that the roof might be a strong floor of next upper floor.

Ceilings

This is the interior layer of roof. In the traditional constructions, the height of ceilings were provided from 15 feet to 25 feet in combination with small escape windows with high level of wall for the rising heated air of the room. For various reasons a little high window are not opened regularly, naturally this extra height of the windows does not seem effective for this purpose. Now, the general opinion is that the height of the ceilings should be 10 feet to 15 feet with some provision of guarded ventilators, which can be satisfactory. In fact, the ceilings should not be ornamental, rather it should be white or of light colour to reflect as much light as possible.

Floor

It is to be remembered that the flooring should not absorb any dirt and dust. The floor should be easy to keep clean and should easily be washable. It should never be slippery. The colour of the floor should not be lighter than the walls, better to maintain dark colour for the floor, which will help not to reflect light on the exhibited items and showcases.

Windows

The windows should be faced with wind direction, which must have the placement as cross-ventilation. The opening of the windows should not be bigger in the hot-dry zone. Hot-dry zone is characterized by high air temperature (often exceeding body temperature), dry air and dry ground. As a result, we can see high intensity of direct solar radiation heat dries the air, which affects plant life, and dry-ground reflects solar radiation. So, direct and reflective solar radiation can be prevented by means of smaller windows opening. Another character of tropical climate is hot-humid zone, which is characterized by moderately high temperature, moist air and damp ground when cloud and vapour act as a filter and the ground does not heat up easily. Moisture with moderate heat favours the growth of vegetation, which in turn reduces reflective solar radiation. In that case the windows should have bigger opening than the windows of the hot dry zone, but smaller in comparison with the window's openings in cold climate. West and south side windows should be protected from solar radiation. All windows are to be protected from high summer sun, except on the north. South windows may be more broad openings but it requires an arrangement of a possible screen to the lower part while the upper part keeping clear. Eastern windows are in need of exterior sunshades in summer only. West windows should have adequate screens or shutters. North windows are seeking only protection from the wind in winter. As a matter of fact, throughout the year, the doors and windows should require to maintain the control level of humidity as in-doors and out-doors environment. In fact, the windows should provide protection against dust.

Ventilation

Natural ventilation is a prime necessary for a room in a normal condition. A continuous replacement of the mass of internal air is required by means of external air, which should have a clear and easy air-traffic in a constant fashion. Openings of the room must be arranged with some provisions that maintain easy flow of natural air currents in between internal and external airfield. The normal approach of achieving this phenomenon is the arrangement of windows and other small openings, known as ventilators. High windows on one side and doors or lower windows on the other opposite direction give rise to a cross-ventilation. The cross-ventilation is a very good management of air-traffic in the ventilation of a room. For better preservation it is advisable to maintain air-conditioning machine, which can also be able to provide desired room temperature with appropriate humidity throughout the seasons.

Relief Area

This is an important place of any museum, which act as a link space for making a proper arrangement of the series of galleries, where to keep up the visitor's interest. Mode of presentation along with the colour schemes of the galleries varies from one gallery to another where the visitors can feel boredom. So, this area will give some relief and it requires a good planning to build up this place after two or three galleries where the visitor's eye may have some rest with the natural surroundings and get relief after continuous looking at the exhibits of the galleries. This area may be provided with something relaxable to the visitors, which may be arranged with some seats with lobbies overlooking a little garden or balconies overlooking the landscape, etc.

Courtyards

This enclosed area is desirable to retain heat in winter and to allow rapid radiation of heat and cooling of the house in summer evenings. It can be provided with garden, lawns, fountains, and sprays, which can able to prevent excessive accumulation of heat in summer. Courtyard planning is a necessary activity for a museum building and it also helps to maintain overall atmosphere of the museum building in different aspects.

Lighting

Lighting is the highest priority of display mechanism for any type of museum. There are two concepts about museum lighting, i.e., artificial lighting and natural light. Illuminating engineers and scientists are preferred complete artificial lighting while museologists are in favour of natural light especially for the materials not affected by daylight. Particularly the ultra-violet rays' contents of sunlight and fluorescent lamps and the heat of tungsten lamps have to be taken care of. Naturally the source of light should be as far as possible be hidden from the objects as well as from the visitors. Basically, we can define two kinds of lighting system, namely, natural lighting and artificial lighting. But, either the provision of artificial lighting or natural lighting and of mixed lighting is a deciding factor for designing the galleries. In addition, it may be assumed that the lighting system should be dependent on easy availability of products and materials which can easily be procured indigenously and that may influence the cost-benefit relationship in terms of illumination system of the museum.

Properly controlled natural light is the best suitable for presentation of true colours. But, it is subjected to qualitative and quantitative changes of the display due to intensity of light rays and selection of proper angle of light rays, which can alter the colour range of the objects. The artificial light has the advantage of reaching the most interior places for illumination and it is easy to install and control. Intensity and angle of light rays of artificial light never changes due to season and weather though it can be fatigue to the eyes. In fact, the quantity and quality of light rays should be considered for the museum galleries in terms of contrast, glare and colour effects in relation to total illumination of the room. Strong contrast by lighting is tiring and confusing to the visitors. Again, single directional contrast gives a sharp looking, which is not right way for the museum, so the lighting from both directions with predominance of light from one direction makes a successful lighting. It is quite acceptable that the objects should be seen with brightest way and not through glaring light. In this regard, proper controlling of light source is required to produce diffused light rays for avoidance of light glare.

Colour of objects tends to be changed under the influence of light, for example, blues and greens material look brightest in daylight and dull under incandescent light. Actually, the sunlight contains a high proportion of colour spectrum, which cannot found in artificial light. But, artificial light can be produced in a great variety of colours by means of blending with different filters for producing appropriate and desirable colours. Naturally, the museum lighting is in need the artificial light, which may be useful by blending with appropriation of mixtures for creating effects as of natural light. As a matter of fact, the orientation of the galleries as well as the storage areas of museum should demand the protection of natural light and controlled fashion of artificial light in a well-maintained combination of sources where the objects must be displayed without glare along with protection. This has to be an important consideration while the museum display mechanism is concerned.

In museum, three forms of lighting-system are useful, such as, natural light, artificial light and mixed lighting, which are simultaneously effective for planning of museum building and its galleries. Natural light is effective in room lighting for human ease while artificial light takes major part of lighting on the objects to produce highlights and shadows to bring out texture and three-dimensional forms of the museum artifacts. In lighting, the gallery should be bright and the objects must be distinctly visible in reference to application of light in proper way. The objects should be brighter in comparison with the background. Amount of light should be uniform to avoid the development of patchy bright and dim areas. These are all basic precondition of museum lighting.

Natural Lighting

Natural lighting is nothing to control sunrays according to desire. Windows are usual sources for getting fresh air and natural light. These windows may be placed in walls of museum building in various ways.

Side Lighting

The gallery is lightening up by side lighting when windows are located on sidewalls. The windows may be at a high or normal level that should be dependent on requirements of the gallery. High windows are effective while more wall space is needed. Unilateral light can be produced on one-side windows whereas the windows on two sides give bilateral lighting. However, windows may cause a possibility of contrast with bright openings and at the same time dark walls with difficulty through glare and reflection, which can be avoided with the use of adjustable blinds.

Ribbon Windows

When the windows are formed a continuous band above the eye level on one side of the gallery then it is known as ribbon windows. This type of windows can produce a very good and uniform light if it is placed on the north side. This band of windows may be extended to the ceiling for avoiding dark wall band. It should be well supplement with artificial lighting to light-up wall below the windows, and it may be accepted as the best method of introducing natural light.

Sun-Breakers

Sun-breakers is also used for natural light. It should be used outside windows to avoid excessive sunrays and to control glare. It is simply concrete slabs acted as the fins at an angle outside the windows, which does not allow direct sunlight and reflects it by means of its fins. Sun-breakers allow subdued sunrays.

Corner and End Lighting

It indicates a long window from floor to ceiling at the end or corner of the long walls and called it as corner lighting. But, end lighting means the end window on a short wall of a rectangular gallery from one end to the other end of the wall. It can be produce good light, which give enough wall space for exhibition and sufficient natural light while the glare can be cut off by simple curtains or adjustable venetian blinds.

Side Lighting at High Level

It is simply a side light at high level, which may be covered by false ceiling. It may be noted here that the false ceiling should be at that level where the bottom of the window is not visible in the galleries. The ceiling is penetrated with metal or wooden grid panel in this fashion when light rays reflect and allow the diffused natural light into the galleries for cutting its glare. It may also be combined with artificial lighting by providing fluorescent light above the grid panels giving diffused artificial light in combination with natural light for creating descent lighting in the galleries.

Sky Light

It is another lighting system, which was used a lot in the past. In this fashion more light falls directly on the floor instead of being directed to the walls where it is needed. Disadvantage is the source of light, which is visible and gives glare. Naturally use of diffusing glass or louvers can reduce the glare.

Lantern Light

This system is modified form of sky light where the top of lantern is not glazed only sides are glazed. It is better method in comparison with the previous method. Though the height is reduced in comparison with skylight which is still needed a considerable height to control reflection.

Inverted Lantern

This system is more advantageous than other ones. The height of the light is lower but source is not visible. Direct light falls on the walls and on the objects but visitors are in shade.

Artificial Lighting

Artificial lighting is available in two forms, direct and indirect method of artificial lighting system. Direct artificial light is mostly used for lighting the artifacts. But room lighting is required indirect artificial lighting.

Fluorescent Light

Fluorescent lamp is not suitable for straight way use in the gallery and showcases as because of the UV-rays sensitive materials, which may loss, their original qualities. But, luminous efficiency of fluorescent lamp is 2 to 5 times higher than that of incandescent lamps. Again, it is cool in comparison with incandescent lamp. So, it can be used satisfactorily for galleries and showcases with indirect manner of lighting.

Spot Light

It is good enough for projecting objects directly but completely destructive for the paintings. This projection lamp is favourable due to its adjustable character and dramatic effect.

False Sky Light

For general lighting of the galleries, artificial light arrangement as false skylight is an excellent performance. It is the combination of fluorescent lamps and incandescent lamps and the light-fittings are fixed above the frosted glass-panels. Basically these are the processes, which eliminate traditional roof openings though the effect is the same. The height of the galleries is lowered down for fixing the skylight in the ceiling. It is useful for general lighting of the galleries.

Louvered Light

This system is developed in a various forms of fluorescent and incandescent lamps. The light rays throw downwards diffusing them by means of louvers.

Louvered Ceiling

The ceiling is suspended and it is made with crossed strips of metal or plastic with rectangular units. Total fittings give an entire overhead grid through which light rays from the source passes at an angle. This panel light comes in a semi-indirect way on the room, while the objects can be lighted directly from lamps that are projected through the grid.

Trough Light

This system is surface mounted fixture either covered with lenses or glass or open. It has a flexible mechanism for tilting the fixture for desirable direction of the light. It is direct artificial lighting but it also gives a good indirect light.

Troffer Lights

This system is an arrangement in the ceiling as panel luminairs. The troffer is a unit, which is fitted in the channel as per requirements. The lights are covered with special directive lenses that can control the light rays at an angle over the wall or other desirable surfaces. The troffers are simply box-like units arranged as per necessity or in long trough like units distributed end to end. Advantage is the control of light rays, which can be focussed; projected parallel or spread and the beam may be thrown to the place where it needed.

Cove Lighting

Coves are narrow shelf concealing light sources. It is indirect artificial lighting system of the galleries when the fixtures are suspended. Cove-ceiling lighting give us uniform light by reflecting the light to ceiling.

Suspended Fixtures

Suspended fixtures are found as the ceiling panels or rectangular, or square or circular types of lighting system. These types of shades have long, narrow channels to conceal light source in their rims. It can work with both the incandescent or fluorescent lamps. It is indirect artificial lighting and most important feature is the lateral distribution of light, which gives relatively high brightness of ceiling with ornamental appearance.

3

Functional Part of the Museum

Administration

It is assumed that the administration plays a vital role in any kind of organization. A proper administration can widen the scope of museum with the help of modern management system. Previously the administrative policy of the organization was to look after the sections or different wings separately with an attempt of evaluation in connection with the activities. Nowadays the modern management acts in different ways for understanding the exact position of the administration. In fact, the condition of different wings of the organization is considered as an integrated whole for evaluation of different activities. In museum administration, the modern management system intends to push away the non-productive sections for achievement of aims and objectives in a better way. Besides, the museum workers should be well-behaved persons as well as they are used to use their brainpower as much as possible. Naturally, in museum administration, it is important one to develop their managerial skill for better administration in museum management.

In the administrative field the term as POSTCORB is popular enough to the people engaged in modern management system. Each letter of this term denotes a separate identity with a proper appropriation in administration, such as Planning, Organization, Staffing, Training, Synergy/Co-ordination, Reporting and Budgeting.

Planning

The planning is a vital phenomenon of the organization. It is mainly involved with the activities of the organization and its administration. Two types of planning are found in administration, such as *non-plan* and *plan*. The plan programme of planning is nothing but a full-length-complete programme with justifications or new proposals along with a projected expenditure. The non-plan programme under planning is simply the committed expenditure of existing or on-going programmes. It includes regular expenditure, cost of repairing, renovation expenses, etc.

Organization

It is the structural part of administration of an organization. All tangible items are considered as the inevitable part of museum administration. These items are the museum building to all other material resources of the museum.

Staffing

It is also important part of administration to find out efficient and effective staff that stands for hard works with sincerity and honesty.

Training

In-service training programme is very much necessary step to gear-up work culture among the staff of the organization. This training helps to develop museum personality.

Co-ordination

It means the sections of the organization are functioning properly and the results are coming up in a harmonious way.

Reporting

It is useful to keep up records uptodate with the facts and figures of the organization.

Budgeting

This part is too much necessary part for any organization. Budget analysis speaks alone the whereabouts of the organization, whether anything is going wrong or right. Any prospect or evaluation work regarding organization can easily be estimated by the budget-study/analysis.

Budget

Original-cum-traditional definition of budget is a sack of its content. At present, it is a financial statement or a detailed programme of expenditure that is to be put before the authority. The budget is the annual financial statement of official account of expenditure of the organization. Mechanics of actual budgeting may be divided in the following heads.

Actuals

It is concerned with total funds, rather it can be said as exact expenditure of the programme.

Budget-estimate

It is a preliminary step before detailing of the budget expenditure. The classification of plan-out-lay for framing it with a possible estimation of expenditure which is required in this phase.

Revised Estimate

An acute revision is necessary in this phase for allotment of money in different heads under budget-estimate. The revision of classified money of different heads required in details for budget-estimate that is essential work to have accuracy in revised estimate.

Reappropriation

It shows ups and downs of the expenditures of the programme. Therefore, the funds of the organization may balance the gaps at the time of necessity by controlling the expenditure of different sections. It means the easy flow of fund, which often goes high from low level of expenditure. It is too appropriate for overall budgeting.

Flow of Funds

The expenditures of different sections are maintained by the flow of funds. It is an effective device to control the system of reappropriation.

Rent

It is a kind of privilege, which may not be seen but understandable conspicuously. It exists in the form of prestige, power, influence, etc. The rent is an important factor, which always makes the budget higher for establishment of their importance.

As a matter of fact, the budget is only a better arrangement of expenditure pattern of organizational resource within a specific limitation. It is dynamic too instead of static in state.

Security

Security is a separate facet of museum administration. The word 'security' comes from the term 'secure', which is indicating free from danger and to remain safe. The administration is looking at the security from two corners, i.e., *types* of security and *degree* of security. The types of security are depending on the physical condition of the museum in appropriation with various devices. Degree of security shows the quality and quantity of security measures taken by the administration.

Types of security in museum are divided in four heads, *elements of conservation, visitors, theft,* and *fire.*

Elements of Conservation

Except fire, five elements are found as natural danger, which can affect the museum specimens. These elements are, the light, rain, temperature, dust and the humidity, which are active in many ways for damaging the specimens. Many steps are taken by museum worker to control these elements of natural danger. A wide range of measures are undertaken by use of appliances, chemicals, etc. to fight against natural decay in consideration with the nature and characters of the specimens as well as the factors responsible for natural decay.

Visitors

A large number of visitors in the museum are nothing but a crowd. Therefore, crowd control is an important work in the security system. It may be tackled with the help of organized and trained staff along with some modern gadgets. However, the easiest way is to develop people's awareness in one hand and to decentralise the crowd in different ways on the other. In museum security the illicit traffic control in and around the museum is an important task, which can help the security system of the museum. So, easy traffic-system for crowd control within the museum will be helpful for maintaining security system.

Theft

The alarming system is a necessary prevention for the protection against theft. It requires a continuous research and development for increasing efficiency. As a result, many sophisticated *Electronic Intrusion Detection-cum-Alarm* systems are available today. These modern alarm-systems are consisted with these following parts:

(i) Different type of sensors/detectors.

(ii) Process control units.

(iii) Audio and visual units.

This modern device is useful to provide information in time for security personnel. Though, it cannot replace human elements, still it is worthy as the guards can resume the facts and figures after fast detection of vandalism. In fact, shorter detection period ensures more probability to resume the items. Otherwise, a longer period of detection is simply a resistance to the success. If the counteraction is required to get back the exhibits then a joint venture is to be made with the police of our country and abroad.

Fire

It is a worst enemy of the museum. Most of the fire-massacre happens due to electric short-circuits and it may also be found as many other reasons. Three types of fire control steps are adopted by the museum worker, such as *prevention, detection* and *extinction.*

Fire Control

Prevention

Prevention is routine check-up of the areas of electric wiring and other fire susceptible zones around the museum.

Detection

Detection is an alarming device to inform fire-danger in details. It is available in two types of equipment, thermal and smoke detector. *Thermal detector* is working with thermostatic principles of physics. *Smoke detector* is too much sensitive equipment with two kinds of technical differentiation. One is *Ionization smoke detector* and other one is *Photoelectric smoke detector.*

Extinction

Extinction is the last step of fire-control mechanism. In this part it is much necessary to understand the destructive power of the fire. Naturally, the types of fire may be classified in the following ways:

1. *Class A type:* Fire from ordinary combustible materials, e.g., wood, paper, textile, etc.
2. *Class B type*: Fire from chemicals and inflammable liquids, i.e., oil, grease, camphor, etc.
3. *Class C type:* Fire massacre from electrical installation.

As a matter of fact, the extinction mechanism is allowed in responding the types of fire. It is maintained by following the characters of four basic techniques of fire extinction; (a) *Blanketing and cooling*; (b) *Cooling and drenching*; (c) *Blanketing and excluding oxygen*; and (d) *Deficient oxygen.*

The principle of fire extinction is to create as deficient oxygen, which is demanding a tool, i.e., the *fire extinguisher.* The fire extinguisher can minimize the damage with extinction of fire on the basis of its capacity. The following types are common fire extinguishers available in the market.

Foam Type

This type is working with a chemical reaction between the *bicarbonate of soda* and the *aluminium sulphate.* The bicarbonate of soda is a foam-stabilizing agent and both of these ingredients are water-soluble chemicals. This extinguisher is an effective measure for Class A type of fire, but not useful in the fire from oil or electrical installation.

Soda-Acid Type

It is exclusively used in Class A type of fire. It also works on the basis of chemical reaction between *acid* and *soda water*. This soda-acid type extinguisher produces a powerful stream of water with a considerable inside pressure.

CTC Type

It is filled up with a liquid of *carbon tetrachloride*. At the time of use, this liquid is vaporized into gas form by heat contact of fire. It is effective for Class B and C type of fire. However, it is not recommended due to toxic effect of its carbon tetrachloride gas.

Carbon Dioxide Type

The solid state of *carbon dioxide* is used here. However, it comes out in gas form to the fire to put it off. It is very simple as well as useful for three types of fire as Class A, B, and C type.

Dry Type

This kind of extinguisher is filled up by dry chemicals. Two types of dry chemicals are used in these extinguishers. *First one* is prepared with *bicarbonate* base in the form of dry powder. Generally it is useful for Class B and C type of fire, but also helpful to Class A type. *Second one* is manufactured with different types of dry chemicals excluding the bicarbonate powder. It acts by adhering to heated surfaces to make a coating on them. It can be used with equal efficiency for Class A, B and C type of fires.

Proper maintenance of the fire extinguisher is an important task to have the best performance. It must be kept in easy accessible place. Periodic recharging is an absolute need as per recommendation by the manufacturer as because the extinguisher does not remain effective indefinitely.

Degree of security is primarily depending on the security personnel and secondarily on the equipments. It is true that the man behind machine cannot be overlooked in security control system. It is required to develop efficiency of man engaged in security control. Efficiency of security personnel should be gear up by multidimensional training, like as, (i) parades; (ii) control of traffic; (iii) *lathi* and weapon training; (iv) art of observation; (v) functionaries of modern gadgets; (vi) first-aid, etc.

Apart from these phenomena, the establishment of antiquarian laws is another measure in security control regarding the antiquities of man. During the British rule, Government of India had formulated several acts for protection of monuments and other antiquities and also for the preservation of this heritage. Earliest act was *Bengal Regulation Act, Act No. XIX. in 1810.* In the same line *Madras Regulation Act, Act No. VII in 1817* was taken to protect the misuse of public buildings by private bodies. First *Indian Museum Act, Act No. XVII in 1866* was passed for the establishment of a public museum and a body was corporated by the name of the Trustee.

The *Treasure-trove Act* is functioning as the safeguards for protection of the antiquities. Still, this *Act in 1878* is existing as it was in the past. According to this act, the treasure means any object of 100 years old or found under the soil and more than Rs. 10/- is value of the object. The District Collector is the Treasure-trove Officer and he can acquire treasures directly by paying to the owner or the finder/collector by paying the actual value of the recovered items plus 1/5th of such value. *Ancient Preservation of Monuments Act in 1904* was mainly concerned with the preservation of monuments. Indian legislature passed *Export Antiquities Act in 1947* to prevent antiquity export without proper approval and authorized license from the government. After a few modifications in 1958 a comprehensive act was passed to protect the treasures in our country and it is still governed.

Fakes and Forgery

Fake is something imitation and forgery is intention to make or imitate falsely to defraud the people. Copy work is not forgery rather it is appreciation of art and sometimes for religious activities with a good intention instead of evil purpose. In truest sense the forgery is the fabrication of any creation with a specific motivation for making fool and attitude to deceive the people. Any specimen may be a fake one if it tries to mislead the people. So, a fake object always brings confusion between artificial and original one.

Identification is a systematic step of the scientific conclusion and inferences. The scientific and aesthetic methods have been adopted for identification of fake objects. The scientific method is simply the step by step approach of different techniques, such as the use of *black and white photographs* for detection, the micro-chemical analysis of pigment for age detection of the paintings, to use of *X-ray photography*, the utilization of *ultra-violet rays* for getting a difference of wavelengths, etc. for accurate identification. The *magnifying glass* and different types of *microscopes* are common equipments to observe minute structures of the objects. Various types of physical test and chemical analysis are necessary work for metal identification. The rock specimen is required *mineralogical* and *petrological* examination for detection. It may be concluded that the scientific methods are unable to help us in some cases. In this situation we should have to depend on our own *experience* and *aesthetic senses*. The aesthetic method of identification is much effective for fake paintings and drawings. It is a combination of certain *sense-techniques* acquired by man with his *experience*, training of *visual observation*, *constant touch with the subject*, *devotion* and *dedication*. This method helps a lot at the time, when the scientific method fails to understand fake items.

Identification of Gems and Semi-Precious Stones

A large number of minerals are found in the world. But, only twenty to thirty varieties are counting as semi-precious stones and gems or precious stones. Especially the gems are not available more than ten varieties from total minerals. The precious minerals should be the gems after possession of the following three characters:

(i) it must be beautiful with colour, luster and transparency;

(ii) hardness in question of durability; and

(iii) rarity, i.e., how much rare it is in the world.

Basically the mineral testing is a destructive analysis. But, it is true that the gem testing should not be destructive at all. So, considering the situation a few measures are taken up for gem identification.

Specific Gravity

The specific gravity testing is very much useful for gem identification. Specific gravity or 'G' of the precious stones are not above 4 [G is 4], only *Zircon* and *Garnet* is higher than four are. In this test different kinds of fluids with known varying specific gravity are used to find out 'G' of the gems. In this process the gems are dipped into fluids one by one, because it follows the Pascal's Law of Buoyancy for identification of 'G' of the minerals. Of course, it is a rough method of gem identification. The finer method goes with Archemedes Principle where the water is only way for identification. The specific gravity is to be noted here by an experiment that how many times it is heavier than water.

Hardness

The hardness of the gem is estimated by scratching. In Mho's scale of hardness is able to measure up to ten (10) standard. For example, *Talc* is soft and standard is one (1) but the *Diamond* is hardest one with ten (10) standard.

Colour

The gem should have a star-effect, or chatoancy or cat's eye effect, which helps to identify it as the precious stone.

Magnetic Property

The method is based on magnetic property count of the mineral, which is required a laboratory with some sophisticated machines for identification of gems.

Optical Property

The refractive index or RI of light is an important property for identification of minerals. This property can be tested with the help of refractometer. For example, the velocity of light passes through *Diamond* with RI of 2.4 and RI of *Glass* is 1.6. Again, the *Ruby* and the *Saffair* are fall in the category of 1.7 RI.

Isotropism

The light with its nature at the time of passing through the minerals is the study of isotropism. The minerals, especially gems should be isotropic or anisotropic. The *Diamond, Garnet* and *Spinel* are isotropic minerals where the light passes in all direction. In case of anisotropic minerals the light cannot pass through, rather the light is dispersed. The *Glass* is isotropic material. But the glass is not mineral as because it has no crystalline structure.

Identification of internal property is essential to make difference between synthetic and natural gems. The *Corundum* is basic mineral for the Ruby and the Saffair. The Emerald and the Aquamarine, both these gems are developed from the *Beryl* mineral. The synthetic Corundum is same in all way to natural one, such as physically, chemically and optically. Under a microscopic observation we can find out some bubbles of gases and minute grains of mineral in case of natural gem, which does not exist, in synthetic mineral. But synthetic one is also showing a few bubbles. This bubble of synthetic gem is much clear due to the application of modern technology at the time of production.

Dark-field illumination microscope shows the difference; for synthetic one has some gas bubbles but the natural gem shows minute mineral grains and a portion of liquid in the cavity of gas bubbles. In natural minerals the straight growth lines are found but the growth lines with carved mark are developed in the synthetic minerals. In synthetic minerals these lines are formed in layer upon layer, which may be seen through bare eye. It may be mentioned here that the flux-fusion method is applied for production of synthetic minerals. In the group of precious stones the Coral is not mineral. It is an organic material and may be tested in addition to dilute hydrochloric acid solution. If the Coral reacts in contact with diluted acid solution then it may be assumed that this Coral is original one. The Pearl is also an organic material and may be tested in the same way of its originality.

Additional Method

The light has an interesting character to produce a range of visible colours. It depends on the wavelength of light rays. It may be stated that the minerals are able to retard the velocity of light. The velocity of light should be retarded after introduction of short wave of light to the minerals. It means the shorter wavelength should be longer wavelength of light after passing it to the minerals and developing visible lights with colours. It is known as fluorescence. American Diamond or cubic Zerconia has much fluorescence than Diamond. Under ultra-violet rays the Diamond shows some colours like blue, white and transparent. But American Diamond shows yellow and transparent only. Ruby shows dazzling red and Aquarian shows bright green. But Saffair produces no colour. Another simple method of identification is the use of Dichroscope. It is an instrument for detection of anisotropic minerals. The instrument indicates two separate light rays in case of coloured anisotropy minerals.

Simple Process of Elimination

1. Sense of light and sight, how it looks on.

2. Touch and feel it. The gem is kept in a room for sometime. The gem will get the room temperature quickly which may be felt by touch only; otherwise it is a glass piece.

3. The minerals should be smooth which may also be felt by hand.

4. Hafting is only device for feeling heaviness of the stone. For example, American Diamond is two times heavier than Diamond.

5. Refractive index of Diamond is very high. If it's face is placed toward the light then the light never passes from the backside. But the Ruby and the Saffair can pass light from the back.

In may be concluded that all of these activities are also required to identify museum specimens. The adoption of these devices is useful to have first hand information regarding the specimens for acquisition.

4

Documentation

The specimen of the museum is simply an object unless it conveys some meaning in association with certain information. So, much more useful information in connection with the specimens are necessary phenomena for a museum. The arrangement of these information are required a specific process of record keeping system. In fact, the record keeping with a systematic arrangement is helpful for identification, stock verification and conservation work of the specimens. Thus, the record keeping system as a whole is also known as documentation. But actual documentation starts from the collection of the object as a specimen.

Acquisition and Identification

The acquisition and the identification, both the terms are very common to the people concerned with the museum. The acquisition is to get something by acquirement and the identification is the establishment of identity of the object. In general, the acquisition comes before identification, but sometimes it may happen reversely as per demand of the situation. So, everything is depending on the nature and types of collected object or the object to be collected.

Simply, the acquisition is a process of collection, which may be classified in the following ways:

By Loan

The exhibits of one museum are taken as loan by other museum for a fixed period of time. But, this kind of acquisition is not popular among the museums.

On Exchange

The museum is acquired the specimens in exchange of own specimens with other museum. The exact face value or price of exchanged objects is not necessary to be equal in amount. The acquisition register keeps a record as permanent loan regarding the specimens on exchange.

As Gift

The specimens are collected as the gift from any institution or individual that wishes to donate without applying condition. The acquisition register keeps a record with a mark as 'G'.

Through Purchase

It is a popular way of collection among the museums, especially art and culture, folk-culture, ethnographic/ anthropological museums. This process of acquisition is to be made by purchase of the objects from local market, from the individual, out of fieldwork, etc. The acquisition register is maintained with a mark 'P'.

Excavation/Exploration

The excavation is an important process of acquisition for Geological, Archaeological and Anthropological specimens. After excavation, a large number of site museums were developed near to archaeological site. The exploration is the popular process of acquisition for science museum as well as Anthropological Museum. In this process, most of the specimens are acquired on the basis of proper scientific manner to disseminate knowledge for the visitors.

In fact, acquisition is the collection of specimens with something meaningful and identification by visual observation. The documentation is an end part of acquisition and identification. The documentation of the specimen is taken up by following the steps, such as photography, measurements, weight, colour, texture, material used, functions, name, chronological sequences, etc. with a proper record. The supplementary work of documentation is maintained by the preparation of card index, to use of computer, video-filming, still photography and microfilming.

Archaeological

Archaeology is the study of antiquities. It is the science of earlier history for understanding the Nations and its people from the evidences of buildings, burial places, implements, utensils, ornaments and artifacts of the period of a few or no written records. First part of Archaeology is dealing with *prehistoric antiquities* and other part is concerned with the *artifacts of historical time period*. The Archaeological specimens in total are classified in the following groups, such as Palaeolithic implements, Neolithic Celts, Inscriptions, examples of Architecture, Sculptures, etc. Most of these antiquities are coming up through excavation by means of vigorous fieldwork.

Excavation had been played an important role in Archaeology since before 18th Century AD. General Pitt-Riverse of Great Britain, since 1827-1900 AD, had been introduced the principle of three-dimensional recording system in excavation work. The methodology of that system was a record management device by accurate plans and section-drawings along with detailed drawings; description of excavated sites; and immediate publication of the report. In 1944-1948, Sir, Mortimer Wheeler projected this recording system in India with some significant developments. Today, much more technological advancement has been adopted in the methodology of excavation work.

Archaeological remains are kept under a shade near excavation site for identification, documentation and preservation. Most of the artifacts are either sculptures or some portion of sculptures. This shade near excavation site is surrounded by natural setting and known as the sculpture shade. Gradually it becomes a site museum with some necessary transformation. We can find thirty-one site museums and thirty sculpture shades in India till the year 2000. These structures are all under direct control of Archaeological Survey of India.

Archaeological specimens are required a concise knowledge for acquisition and identification. Precisely it may be summarised in the following points for collection as the specimens:

(i) Any coin, sculpture, paintings, epigraph or other work of art or artisanship.

(ii) Any article, object or thing detached from a building or cave.

(iii) Any article, object or thing illustrative of science, art, crafts, literature, religion, customs, morals or polities of former ages.

(iv) Any article, object or thing of historical interest.

(v) Any article, object or thing declared by Government of India, by notification in the Official Gazette, as an antiquity which has been in existence for not less than the hundred years.

(vi) Any manuscript, record or other document, which is of scientific, historical, literary or aesthetic value and it, has been in existence for not less than seventy-five years.

Anthropological

Anthropological specimens are dealing with the genesis of Man and his inhabitancy in different regions. Anthropology is the Study of Man in all aspects and especially behavioural patterns of human beings. It is nothing but a holistic study of humankind. At present, the Bio-cultural Anthropology engulfs the first part of Anthropology or Palaeo-anthropology. Bio-cultural Anthropology is scientifically definable process of human evolution with proper perspectives. In fact, it is an integrated history of human evolution along with his cultural development.

A continuous history of human habitation with artifacts from Lower Palaeolithic Age, Middle Palaeolithic Age, Upper Palaeolithic Age, Mesolithic Age, Neolithic Age, Chalcolithic Age, Iron Age, to Modern Age of today still exists with evidences in Indian Sub-continent. The evidence of earliest hominid is found here as Ramapithecus who was the inhabitant of eight to twelve million years BP (Before Present). Unfortunately the evidence of human skeletal remains is very poor in our country. But, a large number of stone tools from stone-tool-industry are coming out from different places as the clear evidences of early man's habitation. Besides, a rich cultural continuity with wide variations is depicting a big canvas of material cultures in India.

Another part as the Social-Cultural Anthropology is dealing with Ethnography, Ethnology and other sections of study in connection with social behaviour of the Man. The Ethnography is concerned with individual culture with a descriptive and non-interpretative study. The Ethnology is the study of one or more culture with a scientific analysis. It is an interpretative approach to study culture on the basis of comparative analysis.

It is more important to remember that the anthropological specimens are demanding detail documentation from the very first stage of acquisition. The specimen conveys the scientific view of regional bio-cultural variation with a complete cultural mosaic. The items are required to be documented in association with a special reference to richness and diversity of culture patterns. The anthropological item alone can present a complete story of humankind with a proper perspective.

In anthropological museum the items are concerned with fossil remains and many more cultural artifacts. These items are required to understand human evolution and their associated culture. The fossil remains should be collected through excavation. The acquisition of cultural artifacts to be made by means have either through fieldwork or by purchase from the local market. One thing must be kept in mind that the anthropological specimens should be documented in details from the very first stage of the collection.

A continuous history of human habitation from Lower Palaeolithic Age to Modern Period still exists in Indian Sub-continent. Earliest evidence of hominid is found here, namely the Ramapithecus who was the inhabitant of eight to twelve million years BP. Though the evidence of human skeletal remains is very poor, but a large number of stone tools prove a clear evidence of human habitation. Besides, a big canvas of material culture is the evidence of our rich cultural continuity. So, it may assume that the acquisition of anthropological specimens should be documented in association with richness and diversities of cultural patterns. These specimens should convey the scientific view of regional cultural variation in one hand and a complete cultural mosaic on the other. As a matter of fact, the anthropological specimens are the evidences of man's existence with the story of its content.

Geological

The geological specimens are always to be replaced by new ones as because no one specimen is perfect. These specimens are grouped in two different classes, such as *terrestrial* and *extra-terrestrial.* Extra-terrestrial items are further classified in the following sections, *Meteorites, Tektites* and *Asteroids.* The Meteorites comes from other planets and the Tektites are found from the moon. Both of these specimens are available on earth's surface as a clear-cut result of accidental findings. But the Asteroids are to be collected by man from outside of the world. The Terrestrial specimens are simply different portions of the Earth, which can also be divided in three following sections, such as *Minerals, Rocks* and *Fossils.*

The mineral is a natural occurring of inorganic material with a definite chemical composition and atomic structure. It is available in six forms, i.e., stable, unstable, crystals, gemstones, thin sections and polished sections. The rock is the natural aggregate of minerals. It is found in a great bulk without any fixed form of its structure. A simple difference between the rocks and the minerals is in comparison with their fixed forms, though the rock may also be a composition of one mineral. The rocks are found in six classes, *viz.* coarse grained, fine grained, polished blocks, unconsolidated samples, bore hole, coarse section and thin section. The fossil remains are completely different types of terrestrial item. Simply it is an evidence of past life, which was preserved in rocks.

Geological specimen requires a specific expertise and sufficient knowledge of identification for the acquisition of the items. Geologist collects the specimen through fieldwork and good items are obtained after removing of the weathered portions. These weathered portions are deposited due to continuous action process of deterioration on earth's surface.

Record Keeping

In case of museum specimens, a specific process of record keeping system is a part of documentation. It is no doubt that a systematic arrangement of the records of museum objects is extremely helpful for storage, identification, stock verification and its maintenance. Thus, the record keeping system of the specimens is known as the documentation as a whole.

First Phase

At first, the specimen demands an entry to the *Accession Register* with following informations, such as, Serial No./ Accession No./Name of the Specimen/Local Name/English Name/From whom it was purchased or collected/How it was collected/Place of Collection/Price/Remarks, etc.

A Multipurpose Museum is required to maintain a *General Accession Register* for two reasons, one is to know exact number of the specimens and other one is to increase the scope of the museum. In abroad, it is popularly known as *Central Accession Register* and operated by the Documentation Unit of the Museum.

After first entry to General Accession Register the specimen is to be received by the Sectional Head for a new entry in the *Section Register*. The Sectional Heads are liable to receive specimens for their own sections. The specimens are sorted out with acute identification as well as more specifications to keep up a record of each specimen. These elaborate informations are recorded in a book known as *Classified Register*.

As an example, the specimen gets an entry by G–n in General Accession Register, thence it goes to Section Register as G–n/A–n and, finally reached the Classified Register with a mark as G–n/A–n/An–n, 'An–n' may be denoted for Anthropology and specimen number in n, which means a numerical status of the specimen.

Apart from these, a few other Registers are also maintained accordingly. The *Loan Register* is opened to maintain uptodate movement of the specimens. The *Transit Register* follows every movement of the specimens from one section to other within the museum. The *Exchange Register* is used for incoming specimens in exchange. These articles in exchange are registered and further it should be recorded in General Accession Register as permanent loan. Besides, a specific sign mark is required as an indication in General Accession Register for outgoing specimens in exchange of new ones. The *Written-Off Register* is demanding a clear-cut record of the specimens, which are no more required in the museum due to natural decay or any other reasons. The objects of this Written-Off Register should be strike out from General Accession Register, Section Register and Classified Register to keep up latest stock position of the museum and this process is called as *deaccession*.

Second Phase

In this phase, the documentation is being considered as the identification, in addition, the tag-label is attached with the specimen. Identification of the specimen would be in trouble without this tag-label. Considering this situation the specimen is marked directly on its surface by *Accession Number*. If the tag-label is lost then the specimen is easily identified by this Accession Number via General Accession Register.

Third Phase

This phase is exclusively assigned for the preparation of index card. This card shows the exact location of the specimen, especially where it is displayed or kept for storage. In addition more informations are also recorded in this card. Backside of this index-card is utilised for black and white photograph of the specimen and the negative number is marked below this photograph. A large size index-card is a necessity to accommodate more information in connection with the specimen and it is known as *Research Reference Card.* This card is designed with some additional columns and the sketches of different components of the specimen. In some cases the index-cards are prepared in three sets. Basic philosophy behind this triplicate index-card is 'quick retrieval'. The arrangement of these cards are found in the following ways, such as:

(i) Geographical base;

(ii) Basis of functional role;

(iii) On the basis of community or any other.

Recently the people are feeling that the accumulation of informations is not useful until we have any quick retrieval system. In fact, the index-card is an adoptive mechanism in relation to quick retrieval of the informations. Besides, the Computer is playing a big role in the process of documentation, which is now inevitable phenomenon for a modern museum.

Storage and its Maintenance

The storage is a place for accumulation of goods or tangible objects, which are preserved for use in time. The items of the museum are special type of goods demanding more care in every moment. Naturally, the museum store is something different in comparison with ordinary storage. Here, the items are being reserved systematically with proper classification, care and protection. The items are also required to have easy accessibility to all staff for regular check up. Besides, the museum storage should maintain a proper environment and a careful handling of the specimens. There is no hard and fast rule regarding location of the storage. It is solely depending on Curator's discrimination. A few points have been mentioned below in connection with the storing of museum specimens:

(i) *Fragile* object requires cautious handling.

(ii) Objects made of *gold* ought to keep in a safe custody.

(iii) The *silver* items are stored within air resistant wrap for its sensitivity to weather.

(iv) The *copper* objects are also to be kept within a wrap in safe to avoid corrosion.

(v) The *iron* articles are preserved in the storage under moisture free condition to avoid rust, which causes permanent damage.

(vi) *Organic* materials are too sensitive to climatic condition. So, it requires regular cleaning as well as chemical treatment. For this type of material the storage should be well ventilated for protection against fungal infection.

(vii) *Leather* articles should be placed with oil-free and grease-free in condition.

(viii) *Wooden* objects are stored in dust-free zone of the storage.

(ix) The *textile* items are kept by rolling it on the PVC pipe or aluminium rod. But, the clothing is requiring a special care to avoid any folding or diagonal stress on it.

(x) The storage pattern is different for *paper-sheet* items. Small pieces of paper documents are kept in storage after lamination or encapsulation. The bigger ones are stored in between cut-mount boards. A wooden box is used for storing eight to ten cut-mount boards of same size. *Paper-pulp* objects are kept within a polythene pouch along with some dehydrating agent and low doses of insecticides.

Periodical check up is a necessary work for the storage of any size and maintenance of the list of recorded items is another activity. The Storage Record List is required to prepare by room-wise, row-wise, showcase-wise, shelf-wise, etc. It is very much important for knowing about the exact position and location inside the store regarding the preserved items. The following points are helpful for maintenance of storage.

1. It must have an easy access for proper classification, labeling, etc. for maintaining the stock of specimens in a clear way.

2. An inventory list is required and that should be kept shelf-wise. It helps in verification, identification and for the purpose of security of the specimens.

3. The objects should be handled carefully to avoid over-handling and dropping-down the floor.

4. The storage of a museum is demanding appropriate furniture for the specimens. Selection of furniture is not possible unless some one is not aware about the new products, which are coming up in the market regularly. Naturally, somebody should have a regular touch with commercial producers of the market. It will activate the zeal for developing as well as modification of the furniture in appropriation with other accessories.

The verification is a binding factor of the documentation and the storage. It is a needful job for maintaining uptodate position of the specimens. The verification is to ascertain accuracy of the total holdings along with their factual condition through physical observation. So, it is helping in four ways, such as;

(a) to correction of the errors to arise by human factors;

(b) to overcome time lag in documentation of the specimens;

(c) to rectify erroneous aging of the specimens to keep safe from confusion; and

(d) to avoid complication arises due to shifting of the museum items.

The adoption of verification card ensures to get rid of unnecessary complication at the time of verification operation. This card is found in different colour code for easy handling. For example, the verification card or *verified card* is red and the white is *not verified* card. But the content of these cards is same. A few yellow cards are kept to find out removal cases of the specimens. This yellow card is important to know why, when, where and expected date of return in concerned specimen. This yellow card and the Transit Register, both are supplementary to each other.

Three rubber stamps are used in verification operation, such as 'Verified', 'Missing', and 'Rejected'. A note is to be kept in the blue card for surplus specimen with a mark as SUR–1 and it is indicating the specimen is not recorded in the Accession Register. Certainly it is a temporary measure in verification work as because nothing will surplus in final stage of the verification.

The surplus or blue cards should be adjusted with the cards are not been verified. Still some cards may be left as surplus, which will go to the Accession Register for current entry. Not verified or white cards will be marked as 'Missing' by rubber stamp. The verified or red cards will be marked by 'Verified' stamp. Some of the specimens are found as damaged condition. These are in need to write-off from the Accession Register with a record in the Written-Off Register. So, the red cards regarding these damaged specimens will be stamped by 'Rejected' mark.

In short, the process of verification can be arranged in the following ways.

V C (Red Cards) + N V C (White Cards) + S C (Blue Cards) = *Ought to present in the Museum.*

V C (Red Cards) +————————————+ S C (Blue Cards) = *At present stock of the Museum.*

————————————+ N V C (White Cards) +———— ————= *Missing from the Museum.*

V C (Red Cards) + N V C (White Cards) +———— ——= *Total Accession Number in the Register.*

[VC = Verified Cards; NVC = Not Verified Cards; SC = Surplus Cards.]

5

Display Mechanism

Modern display mechanism is a process, which requires a planned approach that can be divided into two steps, such as, a proper planning at first and then its execution. The planning starts right from the museum building then lighting and gradually it passes on towards designing of show cases, colour schemes, reference materials, accessories, and so on. In fact, all efforts are coming out as a principle of display techniques.

Principles of Display Technique

The term 'display' is commonly used in commercial activities. But in case of museum object, it is calculated application of aesthetics with a graphic representation in three dimensions for visual appeal and appreciation. In fact, the museum display means indications of information, which has some bearing in connection with the artifacts–to identify, signify, discover, reveal, disclose, present, exhibit, show, designate, specify, notify, impress, inform, symbolize and to keep up the record for further investigation as well as documentation of heritage. The arrangements of the objects in a space or composition of the objects in the perspective of three dimensions, show cases for security, preservation and looking well, appropriate lighting, combination of texture, colour-scheme, and scale of exhibits are the main concerned aspects regarding the principles of display techniques. Finally, the maintenance of a proper balance along with the harmonious flow among the objects and also the selection of appropriate perspectives are the basic principle of display techniques of museum specimens, which may be pointed out by means of following aspects.

Composition

This step is very much important measure for arrangement or layout of the objects in the museum hall for display. Composition is the strength of display. It is simply an arrangement, which should be able to attract and hold the attention of the visitors. It is very much clear that every object has a typical size, shape, texture, colour and tone, which is affected simultaneously by the size, shape, texture, colour and tone of each and every other objects particularly in composition for the display arrangement of the museum specimens. The physical arrangement of the objects required to create an environmental influence where the visitors can enjoy it, as an example, the difference can be found when we looking at a showcase bound picture instead of open display of that same picture. So it should accentuate, emphasize and focus the attention of viewers. But it must be kept in mind that the object should be more important than surroundings. In fact, the object must be full in view with characteristic features in association with good-looking appropriate surroundings.

Light

Apart from direct influences of light, the shape, size, texture and colour of the object can not be enjoyed, such as, the light brightens the objects, which can make a clear view of the objects and builds an atmosphere. Intensity of light should be sufficient but must not be glaring. Sources of light should not be visible to the visitors. Objects must be brighter than the surroundings and subdued light is the most effective, which can be developed by use of indirect and reflected light rays.

Texture

Texture of the object should be considered according to its nature. Texture of the art-object must be brought out in comparison with the texture of the background and that background texture can be treated as simply the background. Naturally, here is a cute question of interplay between object and its background. For example,

Rough and Smooth–Smooth bronzes against rough textiles.

Light and Heavy–Heavy sculptures against lightwood.

Shiny and Dull–Shiny silks for dull terracottas.

Clear and Opaque–Clear glassware against opaque textiles.

Loose and Tight–Loosely woven textile for closely woven and embroidered clothes.

Jewellery is shown on the background of soft silks and velvets. The softness of the background accentuates the hardness as well as richness of jewellery. Texture of the textile should be a good background of sculptures and woodwork. Most interesting interplay is that the softness of textile diverts the mind from soft to hard surface of wood and stone. Again, smooth glassware impress more with rough textures of textiles or any other surface, which bring out the smoothness of glass. In the same way, smooth background of polished wood is very much effective by use of delicate and soft textiles.

Colour

Colour is another appealing factor for display. The background colour should compliment and enhance the colour and beauty of objects in presentation, and that background presents matching and contrasting the colours in comparison with the objects. Besides, some utilitarian devices like pedestals, platforms, fixtures, etc. may or may not be identical with the background colour in order to characteristics of the objects. Apart from the visual effect, the colours can also be used for the creation of illusions of the space and distance. For example:

- Blue and sheds of blue shrink back the background.
- Red and sheds of red and yellow advance in space.
- Neutral colours like grey, etc., stay in positions.
- Light colours reflect light and give brighter appearance.
- Dark colours need extra lighting as they can absorb light.
- Red and yellow attract attention.
- Blues and greens are soothing to eyes.
- Light colours are responsible to shrink back.
- Dark colours are always in advance.

Scale

Scale of the object in comparison with the space of the gallery is a worthwhile consideration. Small objects in a big showcase or a huge gallery with small scale of objects that will get lost proper aesthetics value of display. Rather, it has to be displayed with a proportionate background along with a proper scale of showcase, which should be balanced as well as in proportion with the gallery. Similarly, some huge sculptures in a crowded gallery should required isolation for proper display that makes it beautiful. In fact, the display with maintenance of a scale is mainly required to develop a pleasant atmosphere for the objects and its visitors. The principle is to be applied in consideration with the circumstances instead of the following any rigidity. It is basically depending on the artistic sense, which will undertake such works of presentation with full of aesthetics.

Preparation of Exhibition

From the very beginning the important functions of the museum are always to prepare exhibition along with collection and preservation of the objects. It also implies that the preservation is not only limited to use of chemicals, rather it also keeping the objects in good condition by saving from different hazards as well as to prepare for exhibition in a safe mode.

In case of museum objects, it is very much necessary to have the responsibility of prevention and controlling the use of any hazardous methods by the designers, where he should guided by the Curator's knowledge for maintenance of its safety. It may also be found that in many times, the requirements of preservation and presentation of the objects are contradictory. Naturally, in this situation, only museum Curator can handle the matter with experience and the concept of aesthetic sense.

It is well known that all types of lighting are not beneficial to the museum specimens from the preservation angle. Particularly the textiles and the paintings are sensitive due to ultra-violet radiation in presence of fluorescent light and the effect of radiation are also to some extent present in presence of the incandescent lights for bleaching out the colour pigments of paintings. Same thing may also happen in case of natural lighting unless it is diffused, reflected, or otherwise controlled.

The museum specimens can be protected from these hazards if the Curator or other museum personnel scrutinize various methods of display and to take proper care for preparing the objects for display in advance. So, more care is needed at the time of planning for display of the museum objects. A simple planning is ensuring the objects against any damages that can save the artifacts to a great extent.

Simple Preparation

Small items need to be fixed on a base at first, which can hold the object securely. So, it should not fall at the time of any types of movement. In case of small figurines and sculptures, a suitable groove is necessary in the base that can hold the object. It should also be secured by holding the same with wooden wedges. This preparation may be known as the base and pedestal, which facilitate holding of the same when the objects are lifted or carried. Thus, the objects are prepared for exhibition as well as to minimize touching and rubbing of the specimens that can protect the artifacts as well. Large items especially standing sculptures can be fixed with additional support on the backside against the object from which the object can rest and the movement of the object would be prevented by the same way from toppling.

Paintings for the exhibition are required to be mounted and the edges of the mounted paintings are also protected for damage. Glass framing of the paintings is much more effective regarding the protection. For better display uniform size of mounts are necessary and it is also convenient for standardizing the frame size.

Textiles are prepared by an arrangement of given the edging of cotton tapes, which can be fixed or nailed to the frame or wall panel for display with proper care. Edging is to be provided with loops or rings for hanging the same with ease in a rod. Delicate textiles may be stitched on a strong background of *markin-cloth* for facility of folding or spreading even in a table case for purpose of display. Costumes should be displayed on padded hangers.

Paper items especially manuscript pages may be held securely by fixing it in between the tape-strings that fixed by wrapping. A piece of glass-sheet with smooth edges or a transparent plastic sheet can also be put over the manuscript pages to hold the pages in place.

Finally, in order to save the items from dust, the showcases should be used for display. Large objects cannot be put under the showcase, where frequent cleaning with appropriate brushes or vacuum cleaner is more effective. Many alternatives are found for safe display of museum objects with increasing awareness of the problems, which are unending process of museum presentation.

6

Presentation

Museum Display

The word 'display' is a favourite term of commercial activities. It is always commercial because display is neither ornamentation nor decoration rather propagation. In museum world, the term 'display' is denoted by the word 'presentation' which means to present a view with some technical manner for better information. It is a direct representation of calculated application of aesthetics of the object for visual appeal and appreciation. In fact, the presentation or the museum display is an essential function of the museum continuing over the years long with changing concept of the museum. In time perspective, the mode of museum display has been evolved since from the beginning. Still, the importance of presentation remains unchanged.

Museum display is a method of thinking and working together with the help of symbols, signs and available resources. Chiefly, it is an adoption of various technical aspects coming out of different disciplines for making fruitful result. Simply, it is a continuous process maintained by trial and error method by means of available technical supports. It should be kept in mind that nothing is ultimate in presentation of the museum object.

The presentation is an unavoidable phenomenon for the success of a museum in relation to its popularity. It can be measured in terms of the museum gallery where the objects are displayed to keep up the minds of its visitors. The objects of a museum can be best remembered if they attract the attention of the visitors due to their distinctive presentation when the question of rarity and importance of the exhibit does not arise. So, the museum display is the 'spokesperson' of a museum where the visitors should get an impression about the objects with their mind set up for further remembrance. From that stand point it may be understood that the display mechanism requires a definite approach of presentation with proper consequences of the objects, which is reflected as a sequence in the story.

As a matter of fact, the museum display is simply a good composition with a successful objective. Proper composition can build up a complete story of its content to make an impression about the museum. So, basic objectives of the museum display may be mentioned here in the following ways:

(i) We should keep in mind that how much it is enjoyed by the visitors.

(ii) It should be maintained a harmony to avoid monotony of viewing.

(iii) Presentation should be planned and deliberate for specific information.

(iv) Museum display should be attractive with more knowledge within a fixed framework.

(v) It would be able to develop people's participation, rather more involvement of the visitors in development of the museum.

In case of museum display, the simplest and most commonly found approach can be termed as 'open storage approach'. In this approach, all objects are installed without any sequence as such. The exhibits are placed within the easy notice of the visitors. So, they can look into total collections within a limited time. Besides, some curiosity and interest grow with the guide lectures, which are supplemented through identifications, descriptions and explanations. Another approach is termed as 'illustrative approach'. In this approach the arrangements and display are to illustrate ideas or concepts about the objects. It consists of labels, captions, charts, diagrams and sketches. Next approach is known as 'functional approach'. Here one object or a group of objects is displayed to explain function, adaptability and durability of the objects. This approach is fully supported by the photographs.

Factors Responsible for Display

Museum display is a complex phenomenon, which is dependent on various responsible factors for its success. It requires a proper planning at first then its execution. Thus, the planning for display starts from the construction of museum building to lighting, gallery layout, and design of showcases, colour schemes, reference materials and accessories. These factors are either directly or indirectly interrelated for making successful presentation. So, these factors may be accepted as the responsible phenomena for successful display of the museum objects.

Museum Building

The building of a museum should be pleasant looking exteriorly and the interior should have enough space for working. A good balance in between exterior and interior is necessary to build up a congenial atmosphere for the visitors. The building area is to be essentially divided into two broad divisions, i.e., public area and service area. The service area is meant for office administration and the place for technical staff. The public area includes all other places accessible to the visitors.

Lighting

Light is indispensable for the exhibits. But, most of the specimens are affected by day light, except a few. The artificial light is very easy to control and install. But, the constant exposure of artificial light is fatigue to human eyes. In this situation the scientists and illuminating engineers are in favour of complete artificial lighting system while the museologists are encourage the natural light for museum specimens. As a result, a combination of natural and artificial lighting system is well accepted for illuminating the specimens for museum display.

Gallery Layout

This factor demands a pre-planned work for getting exact length; breadth and height of the gallery correspond to the sizes of the specimens. A partitioned space has to be reserved at the side of the gallery entrance, which is covering brief information about the gallery. This space is known as *reference area* or *introductory area* as it provides at a glance information regarding the particular gallery. Such a place is actually a representation of the respective gallery with photographs, paintings, sketches, inscription, etc. Besides, a clear way should be kept in between two galleries for easy traffic of the visitors.

Design of Showcases

Different types of showcases are to be made for the museum, which are solely dependent on the gallery layout.

Colour Scheme

Colour matching is an effective device to influence human mind. For that reason it is an important work of application as the colour scheme for display. In fact, colour matching is the selection of necessary colour for making the object prominent. This process is known as colour scheme of museum display. Though the artist's help is solicited in that respect, but the curator is main responsible person to select the colour schemes by means of trial and error method.

Reference Material

These are all supportive materials focussing main emphasis over the main exhibits. These materials show a wide range of variation from the display board-to-board pins, posters, photographs, etc. It is an inevitable part of display to develop a complete story of the exhibits.

Accessories

Different kinds of equipment as well as gadgets are necessary for the museum gallery to create a special effect in connection with museum display of its exhibits. The accessories regarding the museum display are as follows: slides with automatic slide projector, motorized revolving stand, translite box, video unit, audio-visual unit with a complete computer backup, etc.

Basic Components

Presentation of museum objects requires a congenial environment influenced by the spaces to be utilized. It can be classified with three basic components, namely, *planning an exhibition gallery*; *principles of museum presentation*; and *design inputs of exhibition.*

Planning of an Exhibition Gallery

The *space* is an important consideration for museum exhibition. Naturally, the available area will be a limiting factor for selection of the number of exhibits. If the number of exhibits is already finalized for display, then one has to find out adequate space for accommodation of the whole lot of the objects. The space has to be found out in adjoining gallery if the gallery-space is not sufficient. So, considering the situation, a layout preparation is required to unifying the spaces for the purpose of display. It should be remembered that the purpose of display will maintain in such a way that there is a natural break in terms of its different sections which will not show disharmony among the exhibits.

The gallery space is in need a proper *lighting*, and the lighting of the space is another aspect influencing the exhibition gallery. Nature of exhibits will be the determinant factors for selection of lighting. For example, stone sculpture can be illuminated by natural light, which will not at all be suitable for delicate objects like painting, manuscripts, etc. Again, for painting and other delicate objects, diffused and reflected natural light or indirect artificial light is advisable for gallery.

Selection of objects in relation to space and lighting can also be considered as the feasibility of forming an impressive theme. In this regard, a few objects should be selected for their importance including their artistic merit. This phenomenon creates a good understanding of the theme, which will be much better than exhibiting a big lot of objects similar in nature. In general, the large number of displayed objects may also be responsible for development of unwanted space problem. Besides, it may also be boredom to the visitors for viewing the exhibits repeatedly in a short gap.

Furniture is also required proper planning and designing to provide suitable places for display. Chiefly, the showcases, pedestals and panels are minimum requirements of the gallery according to the nature and condition of the exhibits. For example, small and delicate paintings, manuscripts, clay figurines, etc. should be displayed behind the glass whereas valuable exhibits like jewellery must be kept in lockable showcases. Again, new and strong textiles are to be exhibited by hung in standing showcases but flat table showcases should be provided for comparatively weak and old textiles. Display panel is required for two-dimensional objects like framed paintings. Apart from these it should be kept in mind that the built-in-locking device for any museum furniture is strongly advisable. In comparison with the commercial exhibition the museum showcases should be designed that way, which can be easily opened, rather handled without aid of skilled staff like carpenters, as because the museum furniture needs frequent cleaning.

After finalizing the gallery spaces, the necessary step is the selection of the objects. After that, the gallery planning is to decide the mode of display. A gallery layout is very much important for placement of furniture, which is fully dependent on the mode of display. Finally, a scale-model is also required which often helps in judging the proportion of showcases, besides to ensure the movement as well as circulation of the visitor's traffic in terms of available gallery spaces for exhibition that is also required for space management.

Principles of Museum Presentation

Design of museum display is primarily dependent on the exhibits. We know that any kind of objects possesses a specific volume and mass. So, the objects can be divided into two sections, two-dimensional and three-dimensional objects. Two-dimensional objects are showing only length and breadth. But, three-dimensional objects have the length, breadth and height or thickness. As a matter of fact, if volume of the objects within the gallery space makes a balance in a specific manner, then it can produce a good presentation. So, it is a proper design display, which is guided by some principles of art. The main principles of presentation may be summarised in the following ways:

Space

The scale of objects and the display space have a direct relationship for museum presentation. The objects should be displayed in accordance with the space available for display. Small objects in a large showcase as well as small showcase in a large gallery should affect the space balance. Similarly, large and tall objects in the crowded gallery or narrow space will develop strain for viewing to the visitors and they will simply to feel boredom. So naturally, for maintaining space balance, the scale and size of the objects as well as the distance of viewing should be well coordinated. Automatically, the *scale* of the object, *surrounding* place and the *level* of viewing should be maintained for well coordination. The best level of viewing has to be decided by trial and error method. But, it is good enough to avoid presentation of an object, if it is not being displayed at proper level along with proportionate space.

Texture

The characters of many objects are exposed by their textures, especially in case of textiles, and surfaces of many other objects. In truest sense, the nature of the object is revealed and captured by means of its textures. It can be visible with the help of lighting as well as background. For example, the smooth velvet with appropriate colour is not only protective for jewellery but its contrast accentuated the rich character of beautiful jewellery. On the contrary, the Bronzes and Terracotta exhibits will be best displayed against the textured cloth, especially *khadi* (hand-woven thick textured cotton cloth) or silks. As a matter of fact, the interplay of textures and their background should help in revealing the true nature of the objects.

Colour

It is another eye appealing factor, which has a psychological impact. Combination of pleasing colours is much attractive in comparison with garish combinations. The background colour will help to retain their character and it should reveal the colour of objects. For example, an object or white marble or white metal can be best seen against maroon or blue backgrounds rather than white ones. Principally, the colour is used to accentuate objects and not to make an attention or attraction of the background. So, the colour contrast should not too much bright, rather it must be pleasant. It should be kept in mind that the pedestal, the blocks, etc. have the same colour as of the background or of walls where the objects are displayed. Besides, the visual effects of colours can also be able to create illusion of spaces and distance. For example, blue and shades of blue recedes the background. Again, the space looks larger while red and yellow are used in their all shades. Neutral colours like grey, buff and cream stay in maintaining the same position of the space. Light colours with soft tones reflect light while dark colours absorb light and so it needs extra or highlighting for effective viewing. Red and yellow shades are hard colour infuse warmth while blue and green shades are soft colour for creation soothing to eyes. Thus, the shades of different colour play an important role, which has a good deal of psychological impact.

Scale

The scale or size in measurements of the objects is also a considerable phenomenon of the space for display, which has a direct interactional relationship between object and space. As an example, small objects in a large showcase or a small showcase in a large gallery are not seen in general as it gets totally lost of display principle. Similarly, narrow spaces or crowded gallery will cause strain for viewing large and tall objects. In case of painting with intricate details should be hung at the eye-level for avoiding the strain of viewing and in the same way, a flat objects with minute engravings should not be placed low that one has to bend for its observation. In this regard, the scale of the object and the distance of viewing are required a well coordination. So, the scale of object along with its surrounding space and the level of observation should be most important as well as considerable phenomena. As a matter of fact, the best level for viewing of a particular object has to be decided after some trial and error method in reference to available space. Compromise is not suggested at all, it is better not to display if it is not in proper way.

Composition

Arrangement of the objects are required to have a perfect layout, which should have a proper placement of its varying scales in the space for making an interesting composition. Such an arrangement, whether two-dimensional or three-dimensional objects, the main focus of composition is display. The purpose of composition is defeated; if it is not carried out effectively rather it fails to have visual appeal. Though the exhibits of varied forms, textures and colours are displayed in one space; still it requires an arrangement in such a way to make out some distinct characteristics of the exhibits. So, the museum objects should be arranged to bring out a few characteristic features of the exhibits within a preplanned framework of the given space. This arrangement is the composition to create an impact that should capture, accentuate and focus the attention of the viewers in order to increase their curiosities. It should be kept in mind that the museum exhibits should not be either hidden or shadowed in the composition. Besides, other factors are also to be considered as the supportive components such as scale, colour, texture and space for making a good composition without shadowing the presentation of museum exhibits.

Design Inputs of Exhibition

Exhibition of museum objects is another essential part of presentation while it should have an aesthetic appeal to the viewers. The specimens should impress the minds of the viewers. The exhibits should be able to induce visitors to know more about the specimens for increasing their own knowledge. In this regard the following points may be considered as the basic objectives of design inputs for museum presentation:

(i) The exhibits should impress the minds of the viewers with aesthetic appeal.

(ii) The visitors should be inquisitive to know more about the exhibits.

(iii) The specimens should disseminate some specific information by means of its presentation.

(iv) The design inputs of exhibition should provide intellectual relaxation by means of space management, easy traffic and visual appeal.

(v) Maximum utilization of that unique opportunity, which should be made by imparting informal education rather visual education with great care and thought in the exhibition.

Different design inputs are required for making a successful exhibition. Some important inputs may be mentioned here, such as, lighting, selection of specimens in relation to space, balance between the proportions of exhibits and furniture for display, colour scheme and use of reference materials, etc. Above all, the perspective of presentation should be planned and well coordinated to impart a theme around the exhibition.

The planning of gallery layout is required after selection of the specimens. The arrangement of the exhibits may be made in different ways in which the objects can be arranged and grouped. It can be arranged according to their locations, periods, styles, or subject matter, as per preplanned schedule that should be prepared in advance.

The placement of showcases should be considered in relation to space of exhibition to be used for display of the furniture. A few objects are to be placed in standing showcases while other can be displayed in table showcases. Apart from these, large and free standing objects are to be fitted by use of pedestals, again a few of such objects can be arranged in a group and sometimes in a common platform. For example, the specimens like textiles can be arranged in standing cases as well as table cases. Under display techniques, the cases of different forms and shapes should be used to avoid monotony of viewing. Diorama is being commonly used for natural history specimens, which may not be interesting if it is not presented in a gallery with full of Dioramas in combination with a few other presentations. So, a museum gallery is required to have a few individual objects, some standing showcases for a group of exhibits, a few table showcases and dioramas to create interesting combinations of exhibition technique.

After selection of the theme of an exhibition, the replicas of original specimens along with some photographs are required for an arrangement of that exhibition when the original ones are not available. Besides, the cast or replicas of objects, photographs, maps, charts are often needed for giving references to find out the exact information in addition to labels.

An isolated space or corner should be arranged with informative materials for the purpose of giving the proper orientation to the exhibition. This introductory area may be arranged near to the entrance of the gallery. This reference area/introductory area will help in preparing the minds of the visitors and they are introduced by supplying the background information regarding the theme of the exhibition. Required information may be supplied to the visitors before or at the time of entering the gallery by distribution of folders and catalogues.

Labels are very much guiding materials for the gallery. In gallery exhibitions the labels can be divided in three categories. The *general introductory label* is used for disseminating background information of the theme of the exhibition and objects. The *sectional labels* are also providing information of particular section of the exhibition and objects. The *individual labels* are used for a group of objects and individual object covering brief information in connection with the particular object. But, it should be kept in mind that these labels should provide brief information for avoiding the consumption of larger area in comparison with the objects.

Finally, nothing is ultimate in question of presentation. At present period, the museum presentation is required to develop a complete environment from which the object comes or its environment instead of display individual object.

Preparation of Reference Materials

Reference materials are required items to support the presentation. These materials depict a clear background of the specimens at the time of display. These items vary widely in the form of replicas, drawing and paintings, photographs, etc. Only a few items have been illustrated here in brief.

Mould and Casting

The *mould* is simply a cavity in which something is to be shaped. The *cast* is a product to be shaped by the mould. The replica is considered as an exact copy of original one. In fact, the *replica* is the product of casting through the mould. Mostly, the original specimens are not easily available due to many reasons. In this situation, the casting is only solution to have the replicas of original one.

The size of the objects varies widely from a small one to a big size either two-dimensional or three-dimensional in the form. For a big size object, the mould also demands a big size to produce a big size cast. But, this size creates many problems in handling. So, the big size mould is divided in the small pieces for proper handling. After casting the small pieces of casts are rejoined to produce a large size cast. This type of composite mould is known as *piece-mould*. A few moulds may be prepared for a single use to produce one cast only. This type of mould is known as *waste-mould*. So, the preparation of mould is an important task to have a good cast. The clay is required for *clay-mould*. The plaster of Paris is used in plaster mould. The *rubber-mould* is prepared with the materials like the *latex-rubber*, the *vulcanized rubber* or the *silicon rubber*.

The clay is a harmless material to the original specimen. The sticky and sand-free clay is used in clay-mould. This clay is directly applied on the object to prepare a mould of it. But, most of the cases replicas are used to make a mould instead of original ones.

Plaster of Paris is only item to prepare plaster-mould. It is easily available in the market with two qualities, *Country-Plaster* and *English-Plaster*. The Country-plaster will take 20 to 30 minutes for getting a hard condensation. But the English-plaster is demanding only 10 minutes to get the hard in condition. The plaster *piece-mould* is divided in the following parts as the *small piece*, the *cover piece* and the *mother piece*. Such piece-mould is prepared in two or more pieces according to requirements. The reinforcement work with iron rods is required for strengthening the mould as well as cast of large size.

In the preparation of rubber-mould, the latex-rubber may be applied directly over original specimen. But it is not at all preferable due to strong grasping power of latex rubber. It is a special kind of problem for rubber-mould, which is also found in case of vulcanized rubber. So, both of these materials are not suitable for direct use over the specimen for preparing the mould. But the silicon-rubber is the finest variety of rubber with less sticky and strong grasping power. It can be easily used to original object directly for preparing the rubber mould. The silicon-rubber can produce all minute structures of original specimens accurately. It is very expensive material with a quality of unquestionable durability. It is available in the paste form. It demands a catalyst, which is to be mixed with the silicon-rubber paste in proportion of 2 gm. catalyst with 100 gm. of silicon-rubber paste. After completion of mixing, the paste is ready for preparing the mould. The ready paste is applied directly over original object by a brush. The material is very soft. Naturally, a hard-grip of plaster-jacket is required to hold it properly after preparation of the mould.

The releaser is very important material for avoiding sticky and grasping problem of the mould. The releaser is used for getting correctly and having a satisfactory result in casting operation. It is a kind of soft material rather a separator making no harm of the surfaces. The materials for the use as a releaser vary widely due to different qualities of the mould and cast. The French chalk is a good releaser for clay-mould and clay-cast. This French chalk is also efficient releaser at the time of clay casting in a plaster-mould. A *solution of soap* is a correct releaser for plaster-mould and plaster cast. The soap solution is a mixture in proportion of *water* 100 per cent with 4 per cent *coconut oil* and 2% *sunlight soap*. This mixture is boiled till the form of air bubbles and it proves that the solution is ready to use as a releaser. Only coconut oil is a good releaser for rubber moulds especially latex-rubber. The releaser is not essential for silicon-rubber mould. But, the coconut oil as a releaser is good enough for silicon-rubber mould if it is required by the situation.

The discussions are already made regarding the clay-cast and the plaster cast by use of moulds of different materials. But, the fiberglass is a complete different type of material. It is hard, remarkably durable, and lightweight. But this material is too much expensive.

The fibreglass material is available in two forms, such as the *fibreglass mat* and the *fibreglass surface mat*. Fibreglass mat is coarse-grained material and the fibreglass surface mat is fine grained to get finer details of original object on a final product as the cast. A *fixer* solution is used in fibreglass casting. This solution is a mixture in proportion of *resin* (G.P. Resin) 100 per cent with *Accelerator* 2.25 per cent and 2.25 per cent of *catalyst*. Firstly, the resin is fixed with the accelerator then catalyst will be added in proportionately. The fibreglass surface mat is placed on the mould in addition to fixer. Next, the coarse-grained fibreglass mat with fixer is placed upon the first layer of fibreglass surface mat. The fibreglass cast is demanding two or more layers of application. It must be kept for 10 to 12 hours at least for drying up the materials. The releaser must be applied on the mould before placement of the first layer of fibreglass surface mat.

The releaser is an important requirement for fibreglass casting. It is the *PVA chemical* in liquid form. The chemical is available in powder form, which after boiling in water turns to a liquid state. This releaser can produce a single cast from the plaster-mould. But, the same releaser can produce many of fibreglass casts from the mould of vulcanized-rubber. In case of rubber mould, the *spirit-lacquer solution* is also another effective releaser. The spirit with lacquer in equal proportion is the combination of *spirit-lacquer solution*. This solution is also another effective releaser for silicon-rubber mould. The silicon-rubber mould is highly efficient to produce a large number of fibreglass casts from a single mould. A mixture of *mason polish* with *turpentine oil* in same proportion may also be a good releaser. At the stage of final production, the fibreglass cast is painted with *oxide colours*. Oil colours of *SL quality* are most preferable choice.

Drawing and Paintings

In truest sense, the drawing is rendering an impressive appearance to express the object with their substances, to represent hardness/softness, lines and masses, design and the interrelationship of the whole. In short, the *line*, *form* and *rhythm* are most important aspects of a drawing work. A clear conception of the subject is necessary before to start drawing. In fact, the rough line becomes a sketch and the rough sketch becomes a picture.

The drawing board should be kept straight up. One has to sit with drawing board to keeping upside at away from the arm's length. Give our arm full play, so that we can draw from the shoulder while we should get freedom on our line. Drawing may be made step by step.

- First thing is to get a clear idea about the form.
- Next, we need to draw with accuracy.
- Finally, the drawing is completed with details.

In drawing, delineation is essential part, which is represented through simple line. It catches the form, but without attention draws many more lines from which we should select outline that is too essential in delineation. Rhythm is produced by the interplay of fast and slow lines, stiff and flowing lines, strong and weak lines, and of forms, all in proper relationship to the subject. A straight line is fast while a spiral or bent line is slow. The use of lines with varying speeds is important in drawing textures and substances. To maintain accuracy in drawing is also important for making a lively expression. The details in drawing should come out through lines of different nature with creation of shades. The artist can only express light and dark in proper proportion by controlling each shade in relation to the whole.

For oil painting, we should use linen or a good grade of cotton canvas or canvas board. The grain of canvas is a matter of preference but too absorbent in a ground is not recommended. The drawing should be started with charcoal. The application of a fixative is required to keep up free from colour mixing after a satisfactory charcoal drawing.

It is always best to use an easel, inclined forward to prevent shine or reflected rays from striking the canvas. We should use brush as much as possible for oil painting. It should be kept in mind that dark shade is to be painted first and gradually comes in light shade. For multi-colour or polychrome painting the palette is required to arrange systematically:-

1. On the left side–Blue, French Ultramarine, Burnt Sienna, Golden, Yellow Ochre and Alizarin Crimson.

2. In the centre–Zinc White.

3. Next to White on the right side–either Vermilion or Cadmium Red and Light Red.

4. Next line–Viridian Green, Lemon Yellow, Cadmium Yellow and Light Yellow.

To use of purified linseed oil is necessary for oil painting. To use of turpentine oil alone is not recommended since it reduces brilliancy of the colours. But, this oil produces good result with the mixture of linseed oil. The mixer is in proportion of 50 per cent turpentine oil with 50 per cent linseed oil. This mixture can maintain the brilliancy of the painting as well as to keep up the fluidity of the oil colour. Besides, this mixture does not take slow drying period in comparison with the 100% linseed oil or poppy seed oil.

In general painting, the colour is applied with reasonably loaded brush with a minimum quantity of oil.

Technically, any colour can be made by mixing of primary colours such as *yellow, red* and *blue.* Each of secondary colours, *orange, violet* and *green* is made by mixing of two primary colours on either side of it. Mixing of primary and secondary colours produces intermediate colours, *yellow-orange, red-orange, red-violet, blue-violet, blue-green* and *yellow-green.* The complement of each colour is directly opposite it or the mixing of secondary and primary colours. The mixtures of complements make *grays.* Colours containing a greater proportion of yellow or red are considered as "warm"; conversely the colours containing a greater proportion of blue are "cool". Besides, many things are required in oil painting that would be achieved by self at the time of painting.

Photography

Photography is a very successful media of communication. It is a scientific process wrapped with aesthetic sense. It can produce an unquestionable truth with incredible accuracy. The photographer shows the world what he sees. He never produces documents or duplicates of reality. He interprets, give images instead of picture. Modern technology is effected surprisingly in the methods of photography. Now its, application is so vast and widespread that it is an indispensable part of our life. The knowledge regarding simple techniques of photography is mentioned here for young scholars.

The photographic process can be divided in two ways, i.e., photo-taking and photo-processing. Photo-taking includes 'mechanical operation' in handling of cameras, 'knowledge of physics' in controlling of light and finally the sense of composition to select the frame. On the other hand, processing comprises 'knowledge of chemistry' which can help to develop the images and the sense of composition is also necessary here.

The camera is a light-tight box with three important controls, i.e., aperture, shutter speed setting and focusing. Aperture or 'F' stop setting is the opening behind the lens through light passes and denoted by 'F'. Bigger 'F' stop number produces smaller opening; so that lesser quantity of light is allowed. Similarly, smaller 'f' stop number increases opening to allow more light. Shutter speed adjusts the exposure time, i.e., how long the shutter will remain open to allow light to fall on the film. Speeds are calculated as 1/60, 1/125, 1/250, etc. of a second. Focussing is required to make a sharp image. All the cameras are depending on this system, although a wide variation is commonly observed.

Knowledge of 'Depth of field' is most important phenomenon for photo-taking. It is a zone in which the subjects can move to and from the camera and remain in sharp focus. The span of this zone increases when:

(a) The distance in between the subject and the lens increases.

(b) Aperture decreases by setting bigger 'F' stop opening.

(c) The focal length of the lens decreases, i.e., using Tele-photo lens.

Therefore, adjusting the said factors the depth of field can be increases or decreases.

Another important aspect is the composition. It is a sharp format produced by the photographer's capability to synthesize own knowledge, creativity with expression and the communicative factors in a single frame. It depends absolutely on aesthetic sense of the creator.

The negatives can be graded into the following three groups in general.

(a) Contrast negatives, which contain all images very clear and distinct with high contrast. These types of negatives are formed by over-exposure and over-developing and the size of grain will be increased.

(b) Normal negatives are always good. It is a resultant of correct exposure and perfect development. Here, the grain will be finer in nature. It produces maximum tonal variations with details even in the thinnest part (i.e., *shadow areas*).

(c) Flat negatives are formed due to under-exposure and under-developing of the exposed films. In this situation, there are no details in shadowed part of the film; the negative will appear very thin.

The following table will definitely useful to know the possible cause and effect on fault-findings in black and white printing:

Effect	*Cause*
1. Prints may very contrast and it may very dull.	1. Wrong selection of paper grade.
2. Prints are dark and lack in details.	2. Prints are over-exposed. Exposure time to be correctly determined by the test bits.
3. Prints are brownish and lack in details.	3. Processed with too short exposure and forced development, i.e., weak/used/oxidised developer.
4. There is brownish grey colour all over or in corners of the prints.	4. Silver stains persist over the prints. Prints have not been fully immersed in fixer/hypo.
5. Prints have yellowish colour in white portions.	5. Processing has done by very weak fixer, i.e. used hypo.
6. Prints become yellowish after a month or two.	6. Prints were not properly washed or stop-bath (chemical solution to stop reaction) was not followed.

Negative preservation is necessary task for photography. A wooden box is required to preserve them properly. Negatives should be placed in polythene wallets, which in turn may be systematically stored in the wooden cabinet. If possible a register may also be maintained for the negatives. The silica-gel crystals are to be kept inside cabinet for absorption of moistures. It can be concluded that the knowledge and skill regarding photography is essential for museum work.

7

Stabilizing Factors for Deterioration

Preservation

The term *preservation* means to keep up safe the specimen, especially in case of the museum specimens. It is an action to prevent, to stop or to retard deterioration. In this context, the *restoration* is another term, which indicates the treatment of object with necessary corrections and alterations. The *preservation* is primarily supplemented by *restoration* work to prevent or to slower the speed of deterioration. Naturally, the *restoration* work is an attempt to check the deterioration and the preservation, which is an unending process to maintain the health of object with a sound physical and chemical condition. As a matter of fact, a continuous process of *preservation* and *restoration* is the basic concept of *conservation*. The *conservation* is nothing but a reconstruction or representation of an original one in its own form with proper preservation to retard deterioration.

In present situation, the preservation work can be differentiated in two ways, such as *preventive* and *curative*. The *curative preservation* is too much sophisticated approach with various modern techniques that demanding modern laboratory with professional workers. But the *preventive preservation* work is a simple approach to find out the causes and factors responsible for deterioration. It is mostly taken up as the preventive aspect of degeneration with some kind of restoration work.

The museum specimens show a wide range of variation in accordance with the nature and its form. These specimens are classified in two groups, such as the *organic objects* and *inorganic objects*. Organic objects are especially made of wood, ivory, textiles, papers, etc. and inorganic objects are coming out from the metals, stones, fined-clay, etc. Apart from these, a large number of objects are available as composite artifacts. These are the combination of organic and inorganic materials.

It is an unavoidable phenomenon that all items are subject to natural aging and decay. In this condition it is inevitable to control the causes of degeneration for retarding the speed of deterioration. So, in this operation to examine the properties of materials is a necessary work. In fact, after thorough examination of the objects the factors are coming out as the responsible for deterioration, this will helpful for preservation work.

Types of Deterioration

The damage incurred by man is known as *man-created deterioration*. It may happen in the following ways: mishandling, negligence, injuries, accidents, and fire-massacre.

The agencies of *natural causes of damage* can be divided in two sections, such as the *external agencies* and the *internal agencies*. The external agencies are mainly responsible for creating structural problem of the objects and known as auto-deterioration. The control of auto-deterioration demands a complicated modern scientific approach. But, internal agencies are easily manageable by the help of preventive preservation and restoration work. The internal agencies are activated under influence of external agencies.

The main causes of deterioration due to external agencies are depending on these following factors:

(a) Climatic conditions and environment which will be included as the clusters of the *climatic condition, temperature and humidity, climate control, and environment*;

(b) Light; and

(c) Bio-deterioration.

Climatic Condition and Environment

Climatic Condition

Literally, it means the weather characteristics in a specific region. Extreme summer, monsoon and winter are critical weather condition in any specific region. These three seasons are showing high degree of fluctuation in the climatic condition in India. Ecological set up of a region is also responsible in showing climatic fluctuation to a considerable level. In short, the *climate* is used to illustrate the condition of a region in presence of the factors like as the *sunshine, precipitation, humidity* and the *temperature*. The altitude, latitude, surroundings, and proximity to the sea and the mountains govern all of these factors. It is easily and acutely observable with variations in a particular area is known as *microclimate*.

The climatic condition of the museum indicates microclimate of a limited area of the city or even of a building itself. The microclimate of the museum building is forming under influence of its orientation, surroundings of vegetation, fountains or ponds, thickness of walls and the materials used in its construction. In addition, the space, opening and the provision for ventilation are showing a clear effect in response to sunshine, precipitation, humidity and temperature in the area of museum building. As a matter of fact, the *microclimate* of a museum is the climate in a confined space as the building, or a room, or a showcase. This space is treated as an immediate environment of the museum specimens rather it may be said as the microclimate of the museum.

Most important factors in the climate are the *temperature* and the *relative humidity*. These two factors are very much active in maintaining an equilibrium in the atmosphere and also responsible for the climatic fluctuation of a place.

Temperature and Humidity

The temperature is a reflection of the strength of heat energy. It is measured by the scale of *Centigrade* or *Fahrenheit* and known as degree Centigrade or degree Fahrenheit. The humidity means the presence of moisture in the air. It is expressed in terms of relative humidity. *Relative humidity* (RH) is the ratio of moisture present in a unit volume of air.

More scientifically, the relative humidity (RH) indicates the amount of moisture required to saturate same volume of air at the same temperature.

In the mathematical form:

Relative Humidity (RH)

$$= \frac{\text{Amount of moisture (...)}}{\text{Amount of ... saturate (–)}} \times 100$$

$$\text{Therefore, RH} = \frac{Mvt}{Msvt} \times 100 \text{ (v and t constant)}$$

[M = Moisture amount, Ms = Moisture amount in saturation, v = Unit volume of air, t = Temperature]

The moisture-saturated air is unable to absorb any more water particle in the form of vapour or moisture. In fact, no more water vapour means the atmosphere is fully saturated with moisture. This saturated atmosphere is showing hundred per cent (100 per cent) *relative humidity* (RH). In this situation, if we introduce more water vapour above the 100 per cent RH then the condensation will take place. Again, zero per cent (0 per cent) relative humidity RH means the absence of moisture in the atmosphere. Relative humidity (RH) 15 per cent is indicating dry condition and the moist condition of a place is showing 75 per cent relative humidity (RH).

In fact, a unit volume of air can absorb more water vapour at high temperature and less amount of moisture under low temperature. Naturally, the RH will decrease at the time of temperature is coming down or dropped but the moist condition will decrease. On the contrary, RH will increase by responding the high temperature but the presence of moisture amount will increase and to be the moist condition. So, RH is to be controlled in a place by the manipulation of temperature.

Climate Control

The Museologists have recommended an ideal climate after completion of a considerable number of study in that respect. The relative humidity (RH) of a standard situation ranges from 45 per cent to 60 per cent RH. Again, the temperature is prescribed as within the range of 68°F to 76°F or 20°C to 24°C. This information may be achieved by the study of climate throughout the year. A plotted record of temperature and relative humidity (RH) acquires the data in a record sheet. The study is to be continued throughout the year in a regular way. A machine is required for this study as a tool known as *Thermo-hygrograph* for counting the temperature and RH. The ambient condition of climate will come out after analysis of these recorded data. If it has been recommended by the Scientists and Museologists for the museum specimens then, it must be preserved in the range of 40 per cent RH to 60 per cent RH with maximum permissible variation of 5 per cent RH.

A crude way of climate control is the arrangement of humidifier for getting moisture and dehumidifier to arrest the humidity. Another crude but simplest way is to keep up proper ventilation for natural control of RH. In this way, it would be better in addition to placement of *exhaust fans* in opposite windows. The chemical application may be altered with a few chemicals that will be able to absorb moisture in a great extent, such as *silica gel, calcium chloride, dry wood,* etc. The silica gel absorbs moisture from wet air and giving it off in presence of dry air. Self-indicating silica gel or *silica gel blue* can collect the moisture 30 per cent of its own weight and changes the colour. The change of colour indicates the absorption of moisture. The colour is regenerated in original blue in presence of 120° F to 130° F temperature. For working condition, the silica-gel crystal of 500 gms. is sufficient for one cubic metre of enclosed space. The best way of climate control is to use of continuous air-conditioning system. It is an expensive device but effective too. The machine of this device is known as *Climatizer* or Air-condition machine.

Environment

The environment is a surroundings of the objects within the atmosphere. Many gases are available in the atmosphere. But, a considerable quantity of gases like, *sulphur dioxide, chloride, ammonia,* and *nitrogen oxide* exist in the air causing damages to the objects externally. This kind of damages can be prevented with an introduction of enclosed condition. This enclosed condition of the objects is the *microenvironment,* which is found in the showcases, boxes, etc. The space inside the cases may be controlled easily to prevent the causes of damage of the specimens.

Besides, the particulate matter is another factor in the atmosphere for developing environmental pollution. This particulate matter is a combination of four factors likely the *soot*, *dirt*, *dust* and *lint*. The *soot* is basically a little quantity of black carbon with some other materials. The *lint* is simply a fine and small piece of straw. The carbon-filter is only effective tool to arrest the soot and the lint excluding other pollutants. Only preventive step for *dirt* and *dust* is to keep up the place clean regularly. The organic material is much susceptible to 'particulate matter' in comparison with the inorganic material. But, the aluminium oxide can absorb quite efficiently the gases likely sulphur dioxide, nitrogen oxide, etc.

The showcases are not suitable for big size and unusual shape of archaeological stone structures. Generally this type of specimens is also displayed on open space. Naturally, some kind of salts may be deposited over the specimens. Gradually the salts are penetrating the stone objects by its *capillary action*. Many capillarics are existing in the stone and developing more in due course of time. In the capillary action, water rises up from the bottom due to turgor pressure and to make a contact with the deposited surface salts and the gases of the atmosphere. A chemical reaction is made and practically some white depositions are found over the stone objects. This white deposition is known as *efflorescence*. Repeatation of this reaction is a cause of cracking with a clear destination of destruction. The *polymer coating* is a good enough measure to check this chemical reaction. But the use of *silicon rubber* as the coating is the most effective one for protection against efflorescence. This measure is taken by paint technique over the stone objects. The *calcium carbonate* is a good preservative especially for mural work, though the sulphur dioxide gas of air reacts on it and the calcium carbonate is converted into different compounds. After a completion of chemical reaction between calcium carbonate and sulphur dioxide a new compound is developed, which is known as the *calcium sulphide* that reacts further with other chemical ingredients of the air. The calcium sulphide itself is heavily destructive chemical agent for mural work. So, it is proved that the most active reagent for chemical reaction is the oxygen and the moisture. Both of these factors are sufficiently available in the air. Naturally the *sealing* is the best technique to avoid air contact. The *wax film* is also good enough as the sealing agent. This process is known as *waxing* and it is also an effective measure for many cases but not suggestible in all cases.

The bronze is an alloy product of copper with tin. The copper can produce another alloy as the brass to be mixed with the zinc. So, the copper is common metal in the alloys as the bronze and the brass. In atmosphere the copper reacts easily with the chloride. As a matter of fact, the copper in presence of air, moisture and chloride can be converted to *cupric chloride* and *hydrochloric acid* after chemical reaction. Further, this cupric chloride comes in contact with oxygen and moisture of the air for further disintegrating in the form of chlorine and oxides of copper. This nascent chlorine is converted to chloride again with a repeatation of the reaction. This chain process of chemical reaction is going on with a result known as *green corrosion*. This corrosion is dangerous for the objects. This may be prevented with the wax film as a coating to check this chemical reaction.

Light

The light is an important agency for destruction, yet the properties of objects are also determinant factors under light rays. The influence of light also depends on its nature, source and intensity of rays. Nature of rays is found as the visible light rays and invisible light rays. The light comes out from the natural source and the artificial source. Finally, the intensity of light is measured in two ways–the *duration of exposure* and the *quantity of rays under exposure*.

The light rays are electromagnetic energy with a property of radiation. Some kind of radiation is sensitive to human eyes and contains visible rays. But, a few rays are not sensitive to human eyes and not visible. Laws of electromagnetism explain that the energy is inversely proportional to the wavelength of light rays. So, the higher energy produces shorter wavelength of light rays. The visible spectrum of light rays is in between the wavelength range of 400 nm [1 *nanometre (nm)* = 10^{-9} *metre (m)*] to 700 nm. The wavelength below 400 nm is known as ultraviolet rays and longer than 700 nm is infrared rays. Both of these infrared and ultraviolet radiation or rays are invisible to human eyes.

Organic materials in comparison with inorganic materials are more susceptible under light radiation. The wavelength of light rays below 500 nm is sufficient for deterioration. The light rays in between the wavelength range of 300 nm to 500 nm are responsible for photochemical degradation of the objects like as the leather, textiles, papers, etc. Ultraviolet rays cover the range of 300 nm to 400 nm while violet and blue rays are in between wavelength range of 400 nm to 500 nm radiation. It is relevant to know that a high temperature with dense humidity enhances photochemical reaction to the objects by radiation.

The photochemical reaction through light rays is influenced directly under assistance of some external factors like as the humidity, temperature and oxygen of the atmosphere. The specimens susceptible to light demands protection by adoption of three steps in the following ways :

(i) less intensity of light over the specimens;

(ii) minimum period of exposure on the objects; and

(iii) elimination of photochemically active rays from the radiation.

A minimum light as 15 lux (*lux is the unit of illumination*) is necessary for illumination of any object. This illumination level is sufficient for viewing satisfactorily. A few objects, such as oil paintings, basketry, etc. can tolerate more intensity of light. The light continues up to 150 lux as the safe limit for photochemical deterioration. But, the maximum limit for illumination level is recommended as 50 lux for sensitive objects, such as the coloured textiles, miniatures, watercolour paintings and similar works of art.

Bio-deterioration

It happens for the presence of *insects* and *microorganisms*. High humidity level promotes fast growth of those biological factors. So, to control humidity level is the simple way of prevention. Besides, more steps may be taken up for controlling bio-deterioration. Application of chemicals is the most popular measure against biological factors for damages.

Insecticides are common chemicals for killing insects. But, a few chemicals are functioning as repellants instead of killing. The following points should be kept in mind before the use of the insecticides or the repellents:

(i) The chemicals should not transmit any colour of its own or of its solvent to the specimens.

(ii) The chemicals would not affect adversely as well as the durability of the objects must not be neglected.

(iii) It must be non-toxic and non-irritant to the human being.

The chemical treatment is to be done by *spraying technique* or *by touching method*. A *spraying gun* is required to spray the liquid chemical on the object. A *painting brush* may also be used to paint over the specimen, which is known as *touching method*. *Non-touching method* of treatment is *fumigation*. Here the chemicals are applied in the form of vapour or fume around the object. Popular fumigation equipment is known as *Thymol chambers*.

The termite is a dangerous type of insect. Out of many, only two types of termite species are common to the museum workers, such as *dry rot type* and other one is *common termite*. This dry rot type variety is much dangerous in comparison with common termite. Common termite is not that much harmful. It makes a link within the ground only, without intention of damage or further attack. But, dry rot type makes contact with the object directly for destruction. Effective insecticides for termites are available in the market with brand name as *Termax* and *Aldrine*. These chemicals under dilution of 1 per cent to 2 per cent are sufficient to control termite invasion. A prior consultation with experts is required regarding the operation.

The *microorganisms* like *fungus*, *algae*, *bacteria*, *lichens* and the *moss* are commonly found in museum. The fungus is a serious threat to the museum. It is a parasitic plant with microstructures, which grows rapidly under humid condition. The growth rate is very high at the time of 70 per cent relative humidity RH. The fungus spore floats in the atmosphere under dormant condition. The growth of these dormant spores germinates as soon as the RH and the temperature arrive at favourable points. The stagnant volume of air forms a pocket in the room. This air pocket is favourable for fungal germination. This growth can be retarded only by air circulation in a proper way. Naturally, an arrangement of proper ventilation is a simple preventive measure against unwanted fungal growth. The fungicides can also be used in affected areas to remove fungus. Effective fungicides are *thymol*, *ehtylene oxide*, and *formalin*.

Sodium pentachlorophenate (brand name is *Santo brite*) and Sodium orthophenylphenate (brand name is *Topane W.S.*) are good chemicals to kill fungus. Paradicholorobenzene (*PDCB*) and *Thymol* are used as fungicides. The *carbon disulphide* is also an effective chemical for fumigation as like as Thymol. But, it is inflammable. So, it is required to be mixed with carbon tetrachloride (1:3) to form a mixture solution, which would be non-inflammable. Such a mixture solution is too effective for textile items.

The preservation is the process, which never stop. A few more things have been discussed along with the conservation part.

8

Stabilization of the Existing Status

Conservation

The *conservation* means a protection on environment and it is a continuous process of *preservation* and *restoration*. In fact the *conservation* is a synthetic approach of physical sciences with excessive delicacy. It requires a planned management of natural resources with some principles, which have been mentioned here in the following ways:

(i) All treatment should adequately be documented.

(ii) The structural and decorative falsification should be avoided.

(iii) The process of conservation should be reversible and the artifacts can be returned to its pre-treatment condition even after a long lapse of time. But, in some cases, this process of reversible action is not applicable, e.g., lamination, use of synthetic adhesives, impregnation, etc.

(iv) The consequences of aging should not be removed from the original materials.

A complete knowledge of chemistry and physical properties of the specimens is useful for conservation work.

The knowledge regarding historical value of the object and available material resources for this work are also important. In addition of all phenomena, the practical exercises on conservation work may be categorised as follows: *Cleaning; Mending; Strengthening; Renewing;* and *Preserving*.

Cleaning

It is first step for practical exercises on conservation. All superficial dirt and dust would be removed with the help of a small soft-hair brush or a small pair of bellows. In case of sticky and over-hanging dust on the object can be handled with running water to remove it. This kind of water treatment is basically depending on the nature of the object. It may also be summarised in the following points:

(a) Use of water is limited unless the object is hard and good in condition.

(b) Water can be used safely on metals but thorough drying up is required before any treatment.

(c) Stone objects and painted pottery should not be cleaned directly under water unless the items are varnished or waxed in proper way.

(d) Not painted pottery, stone and glass items may be washed with water by soaking technique. In this technique a piece of cotton, sponge or soft brush is required for brushing repeatedly with continuous change of water under careful handling of the object.

(e) To use of water should be restricted on the object of plaster of Paris.

(f) Water is not suitable for ivory items.

(g) Woven fabrics may be washed with water except the fabrics under bad condition or old.

A mixture solution is more appropriate cleaning agent instead of plain water. A common solution is the mixture of *benzene* with *petrol* or *alcohol* (1:10). But, the oil painting should not be treated with this solution. Only the mixture of *alcohol* with *water* or *hydrogen peroxide* (1:1) is effective cleaning agent for old oil painting. Another two kinds of cleaning agents are helpful when the *benzene-alcohol* or *petrol mixture* fails to remove dirt and dust. First one is the solution of diluted *acids* or *alkalis*. Second one is the mixture of equal part (1:1) of *acetone* with *pyridine* in 50 per cent of *water* (1:1) solution. It should be noted that the cleaning is required to keep up patience of observation to have better result.

Mending

The mending is the addition of new materials for re-fixation of broken or loose parts of the items. The cement or adhesive plays a vital role along with its selection for mending work. It is in need to remove old cement or adhesive carefully and completely for re-fixing the parts of the objects. But, an unknown cement preparation may cause further damage. To avoid this problem a few common matching of adhesives are mentioned here in the following points:

(a) Glue for wooden objects.

(b) Celluloid cement for the items of glass, porcelain, quartz and flint.

(c) Plaster of Paris for pottery and stone objects.

(d) Fine stone dust and the solution of sodium silicate for stone objects.

(e) A mixture of country-made cement, i.e., a combination of fine-grained sand with fine clay, is the good matching for fire-baked clay or terracotta items.

(f) The wax and some of its combination (mixture of bees-wax with carnauba wax or paraffin) is very good fixing materials for ivory objects.

Strengthening

This is a process to increase durability of the object. It is obvious that the handling of old object under fragile and delicate condition is practically impossible without causing damage. So, the strengthening is an important work for museum specimens. The process as the impregnation is a one of the most important step to strengthen the object. A few reagents show good result in impregnation work, such as the melted *Paraffin*; melted *Bees-wax*; *Celluloid solution*; *Linseed oil*; and *Plaster of Paris*.

Renewing

This activity is responsible to make the item valid again or restoration of the object. Besides, the missing parts may be resumed with newly constructed one as it was before. The matching of material is inevitable for renewing the missing parts. In fact, the affected objects should be renewed with matching materials to revive original look of the specimens.

Preserving

Aim of this work is to decrease the speed of degeneration of the specimens. The factors responsible for deterioration must be detected at first hand. Nextly, it is in need to explore a way out with available resources. Lastly, the effective measures must be adopted to retard the speed of degeneration. It may be concluded that the preservation requires a well understanding of the specimen's condition and the remedies should be with easy availability. It is a non-stop activity, which seeks constant research on it.

Practical Exercise

Simple *practical exercises* on the specimens of different materials are mentioned here in the following headings :

Wood and Bamboo

Both the materials absorb water particles and make damp. This dampness may be responsible for damage, which should be removed. It requires a few days and a cool place should be arranged for drying up the materials. This process is known as *seasoning*. The object after seasoning may be washed or soaked with *celluloid solution* or *vinyl-acetate solution* or *liquid paraffin*. This treatment is in need after seasoning as because of the natural foodstuff (starch, etc.) are found inside of the material that can attract insects. For the protection against insects the material may be treated with *crude creosote solution* by paint technique and *carbon disulphide vapour* by fumigation technique.

The specimens under insect infection must be treated with *carbon-disulphide vapour* by fumigation. If it fails to destroy insects completely then *creosote solution* is required for direct application on the specimens by paint technique. *Crude creosote oil* is dense and black in colour. This oil is not suitable for direct application. For better result it can be diluted in *kerosene oil*. This *creosote solution* is able to keep up original colour of the specimens. The proportion of the solution is in the ratio as (2:1), i.e., two volumes of *kerosene oil* and one volume of *crude creosote oil*. The specimen consumes seventy-two (72) hours after creosote treatment to make it complete dry.

The *shellac solution* is another popular preservative. It is a simple protection against insects. Any kind of specimen can be painted with this solution. The coating of this solution also produces a luster effect on the surface of the specimens. A substitute of *shellac solution* is also available in the market as ready-made *synthetic resin solution*. The *shellac solution* may be prepared in the following ingredients, *shellac crystals*; *methylated spirit* and *mercuric chloride*. The strength of *mercuric chloride* varies from 1.5 per cent to 2 per cent as per requirement.

Shellac crystals................................20 gms.

Methylated spirit............................100 cc.

Mercuric chloride........................... 2 gms.

This composition is 20 per cent *shellac solution* and the concentration of composition varies on the basis of requirements. For example, 10 gms. of *shellac crystals* in same composition is known as 10 per cent *shellac solution*, which is most appropriate for the items, made by bamboo-splits.

The woodcarvings may be coated with *varnish* or *linseed oil* for better result. But, most effective measure for woodcarvings is *ascu treatment*. This treatment can protect against destruction by insects, algae and fungi.

Grass, Reed and Cordage

The specimens like as the basket, mat, bag, etc. are commonly made with grass, reed and cordage. In course of time, all of this material would be brittle in condition.

These items may be cleaned by brushing and blowing. But the specimens under fragile condition must be treated with *petrol* by the help of soft small brush or a piece of cotton. The objects of these materials should be strengthened for increasing durability and it must be prescribed after cleaning and brushing. So, these items must be strengthened by *wax* paint, especially the *bees-wax*. In some cases the items may be processed under *diluted creosote solution* (creosote oil 1 Vol.: kerosene oil 4 Vol.) for preservation. Finally, all of these specimens must be painted with the *shellac solution* of 2 per cent to 5 per cent concentration considering the nature of the items.

Fabrics

A common phenomenon of the fabrics is the problem of *disintegration*. This problem may be divided in two ways, i.e., chemical and biological disintegration. *Chemical disintegration* is caused by oxidation and the sunlight takes active part to make it faster. *Biological disintegration* is the resultant of bacterial and fungal infection.

The fabrics of fresh or good in condition can be cleaned by brush or washed with *soap in warm water*. At the time of washing, the rubbing action should be avoided. The fabrics may be soaked in the mixture solution of *benzene* with *petrol* (1: 4) before washing. The specimen must be for free from hard stains through washing. If some hard stains are still prevailing on the specimens then the use of acetone as a good reagent that is able to wipe-off it completely.

The solution of *turpentine* with *methylated spirit* (1:10) can remove the hard stains. The *methylated spirit* alone can dissolve the stains. In some cases the *oxalic acid* produces very good result. The *oxalic acid* (10%) may be allowed to remain on the spots or stains for three to five minutes to erase out the extra hard stains. Lastly, the fabrics must be washed with *warm water* carefully. After washing the specimens should be placed in a warm room for dry-up slowly.

Old fabrics are found in fragile state. It must be dipped in the solution *benzene* with *petrol* or *alcohol* (1:4) for cleaning. This process is one type of dry-cleaning and it is unavoidable for old fabrics. Reinforcement is necessary job for old fabrics. Naturally, a solution of *alum* with *gum arabic* may be used to reinforce and freshen-up the colours of these old specimens.

In case of the fabrics in extreme fragile condition should not allow undertaking any kind of movement for cleaning and preservation. This situation must be handled with a *special type of solution* and the *tissue paper*. This *special type of solution* is a mixture of 10 gms. *glue* in 500 cc. *distilled water*, which will develop a *special kind of adhesive*. The *glue* materials may be dipped in the *distilled water* for twenty-four hours in a same state. After that, the mixture solution may be heated for dissolving the residue particles of *glue*. This *glue solution* must be mixed with 2 cc. of *formalin*, which is formed as a *special type of preservative adhesive*. It must be applied on the specimen immediately after preparation and a *tissue paper* should be pasted on it to make a firm grip. This reinforcement work is required to dry up thoroughly for completion of strengthening work. Nextly, a solution may be sprayed on it for preservation work. This solution is the mixture of *naphthalene* or *camphor* that is dissolved in *lysol*. This *naphthalene* or *camphor* solution should be sprayed over the old fabrics after reinforcement. After this treatment, the specimen should gain more resistant against bacterial and fungal infection.

Book, Manuscript and Paper

Common enemies for any sort of paper items are as follows; white ants or termites, cockroaches, silverfish, etc. Out of these enemies more dangerous one is the bookworm. The bookworms (Silverfish, Lepismas, Anobium Panasicum and Corrodentia or Book lice) are generally found in the area of darkness. All these can grow rapidly inside a room if they are left since for a long time. In this regard a few steps may be taken as helpful measures for the books:

(a) Dusting is required as a regular task. Because, less dirt and dust invites less bookworms.

(b) Exposure of sunlight either direct or indirect is required at least for a short period of time. A long exposure of sunrays will do the paper brittle in condition.

(c) To use of *phenyl* as repellent should be restricted by spraying on the sides of the books.

(d) The books should be treated with some insecticides. Only three types of insecticides are effective for the books under preservation work.

The first type of insecticides is the combination of,

Corrosive sublimate .... ½ oz.

Carbolic acid .... ½ oz.

Methylated spirit................. 1 pint.

This insecticide mixture solution may be painted with a brush to the covers of the books, both inside and outside. This treatment may be made twice a year for getting a good result.

Second and third types of combinations are in the following proportions.

Rectified spirit .... 1 gallon.

Mercuric chloride .... 1 oz.

Phenyl .... 1 oz.

and,

Corrosive sublimate .... 50 drachmas.

Creosote oil .... 60 drops.

Rectified spirit .... 2 lbs.

These two types of combination solution of insecticides are much helpful to use in the joints and in between every ten or fifteen page of the damaged books. A little quantity of these insecticides can be added to the paste of book binding as a preliminary work for preservation.

A solution of *benzene* with *alcohol* or *petrol* (1:4) is very much effective for affected books. The *oxalic acid* is helpful to remove reddish patches on the paper and it may also be considered as the protection against fungal infection. The *citronella oil* is helpful for dry-leaf material to resume softness as it was before. The *carbon black* or *graphite* may be rubbed over the inscription on dry leaf to restore it before use of *citronella oil.* If it is failed then the *carbon black* or *graphite* may be mixed with *cellulose acetate* solution to put it on the dry-leaf material for revival of the inscription.

A *gelatinous* material is needed as a fixing agent to the *parchment paper.* This parchment paper with fixing agent may be pasted below the soft leaf or any paper items for the reinforcement work. For old and damaged specimens, this paper with gelatinous material or solution is performing as the work of strengthening the items. This gelatinous solution is nothing but a mixture of the *gelatin* with *acetic acid* and *vinegar* (1:1:1).

De-acidification is an important task for any kind of paper items. Normally, the solution of *calcium bicarbonate* with water or *calcium hydroxide* with water (1:4) can produce a good result for de-acidification work. But, in some cases the solution of *barium hydroxide-tetrahydrate* (2%) in *menthol* base is required to use directly on the paper documents to neutralize acidity or to prevent acidity.

Paper documents must be assembled together for storage in a safe custody. But the sizes of the documents may not be found as same or equal. In this situation, a few extra papers (bigger or equal in size) are required for storing. The documents are added to extra paper for making equal size to store it properly. At present, readymade boards in acid free condition are easily available in the market. So, de-acidification problem is not at all a problem to day. The acid free boards of equal sizes are able to solve the problem of packing and storage of paper documents.

Encapsulation is the recent method for preservation of paper documents. It is a process of sealing in between two separate *poly-plastic films.* In general, thin *polythene films* of 0.04 mm thickness can be used for encapsulation. The border sides of the films must be sealed with the help of ultrasonic rays. To use of *polyvinyl films* or *PVC* films is very recent development in encapsulation work. This film or PVC film of 0.08 mm to 0.125 mm thickness is used for preservation work considering the nature of paper documents. A high frequency electric current is required for sealing of the PVC films. This process is completely reversible and the documents may be released in its original form by a simple cut-off the seal or joint of PVC films. It is a cost-effective process in comparison with the process of lamination. The lamination does not provide the reversible facility.

Leather

Automatically, the leather item will go towards disintegration in course of time. The reasons for disintegration may be recorded in the following ways :

(a) Oxidation is an important cause influenced by light and heat.

(b) Acid reaction is another reason of disintegration. The leather item absorbs *sulphur dioxide* from the air and sometimes it remains from the time of erroneous process of tanning. Gradually this *sulphur dioxide* in the presence of atmospheric ingredients is converted to *sulphuric acid* after chemical reaction.

(c) Uncared process of tanning is another reason.

(d) To use of inferior quality dye is also a reason for damage.

Cleaning is a primary work and regular use of a solution for dressing is also a preliminary preventive measure for leather item. This process is helpful to prevent air contact as well as the sulphur gases. Besides, this treatment will lubricate the leather tissue to be in soft and smooth condition. This solution is commonly known as *dressing solution* and it may be made in the following proportions of the ingredients.

Bees wax .... 7 gms.

Lanolin anhydrous .... 100 gms.

Cedar wood oil .... 14 cc.

Hexane .... 170 cc.

Old leather items are tremendous fragile and brittle. So, a common dressing solution is not at all suitable for old items. Special types of solution will effective for old and brittle items. This special solution is the mixture of 60 parts of *alcohol* with 40 parts of *castor oil.* A soft brush is used to paint this solution for increasing durability of the item.

Ivory, Bone and Horn

Ivory is more steady than bone and horn. Incrustation is main problem of the ivory items. It may be cleaned by an application of diluted hydrochloride acid (5%) [5 parts of hydrochloride acid and 95 parts of water]. The specimen may be washed repeatedly with water after the use of diluted acid. This washing is needed a continuous change of fresh water till the acid remains on it. But this process is not suitable for old ivory item. So, in that case a brush is only usable for cleaning up it thoroughly.

Ivory specimen requires a room for dry up it properly. This room must be a zone of free air circulation with a protection against the exposure of sunrays. It is known as *dry zone*. The specimen is treated with a solution by the help of a piece of cotton or sponge through the sponging technique. After dry-up it properly, the specimen will be treated with a solution. This solution is a mixture of equal parts of *acetone* and *rectified spirit*. Final processing of the ivory specimen is impregnation, which will be more successful with application of the wax or *venyl-acetate*.

In case of bone item a brush is useful for cleaning. After cleaning the dirt and dust the specimen may be painted with *shellac solution* of 2 per cent to 3 per cent strength. But the *mercuric chloride* 0.05 per cent may be added to *shellac solution* to increase preservative power of the solution. The number of coating is depending on the basis of requirement. But, the previous coating of *shellac solution* should be dried up properly before use of next coat of the paint. The horn material does not require any treatment except cleaning and dusting. A proper wash with warm water is sufficient treatment for horn made items.

Pictures and Paintings

This section may be classified in the following categories:

Mural Paintings (Tempera and Fresco).

Painting on Plaster.

Painting on Wax.

Oil Paintings.

Drawings.

Tempera

In any kind of tempera painting the colour pigments requires an adhesive medium, such as the glue, gum, and white part of egg. These mediums are basically organic substance and susceptible to infection. For this reason different factors can deface the paintings. Tempera painting may be treated with *diluted ammonia solution* to remove lichens from it.

A proper cleaning with extreme care is necessary for conservation of the tempera work and it requires brushing gently with the mixture solution of water and *alcohol*. Besides, the paintings may come up in its original form by simple brushing with the help of a soft brush. After cleaning the affected paintings are painted with a mixture of *benzene petrol* (1:6) solution.

The salt in atmosphere takes an active role to deface the paintings. Adding a transparent coating of celluloid solution (1%) over the tempera paintings may prevent it. But, direct use of celluloid solution is not suitable rather it requires an appropriate medium to paint over the paintings. This medium is a mixture solution of *acetone* and *amyl acetate* in equal parts.

Fresco

This kind of wall painting demands very careful attention at the time of cleaning and dusting. The following three steps necessary for maintenance and preservation of fresco. Firstly, to use of very soft brush is suggested with serious attention to wipe-off dirt and dust. Secondly, a piece of soft cotton is employed for the purpose of sponge-technique treatment in addition to the *alcohol*. Finally, the surface of the painting requires a coating of *paraffin-wax mixture*. A soft brush is enough for application of the liquid *paraffin wax*.

Painting on Plaster

In this case the specimen is handled with a soft brush for removing loose dust. Nextly, a piece of soft cotton is soaked in the mixture solution of *benzene alcohol* (1:4) to remove dirt and dust by sponge-technique. This process is equally suitable for both the specimen with varnished surface and the painting with unvarnished surface. It may be noted that the specimen with unvarnished surface demands two or three coat paints of *celluloid solution* (10%) for strengthening the item. The varnished surface of plaster painting is normally coated with a *paraffin-wax mixture* for strengthening it.

Moreover, it may be said that the coatings over the paintings are also an agreement of preservation work.

Painting on Wax

Cleaning is the only treatment for this type of specimen to make it clean. The surface of this item requires a gentle rubbing with a very soft piece of cotton soaked in water or *alcohol* to wipe-off dirt and dust.

Oil Painting

It is a combination of many materials, such as canvas, pigments, mediums, varnishes and chemicals.

Chemically the canvas is cellulose material changing its dimension under influence of moisture.

The glue and other materials of oil paintings are responsible to attract fungus as well as insects under moist condition. The pigments are chiefly the minerals in different forms, which perhaps absorb the moisture. The volume of the pigments changes after absorption of the moisture.

The varnish is a good protection, but, in course of time, the varnish from vegetable resins is obtained optical saturation. In consideration with all these factors the oil paintings should not be treated without a prior examination. Again, a complete record of all activities should be kept with in written form along with photographs for having a feed back in future.

The mark of cracking is the first sign of decay. It happens quite often in many old paintings. In course of time the canvas is expanded but oil colours or dry paints on it do not allow this expansion. Automatically the cracks appear due to unwanted stress on the canvas. Serious damage by cracking is known as the *flaking of colours*. These flakes are gradually takes a cup like structure and that is called *cupping*. Main reason is simply negligence of the painter.

At the time of painting it should be kept in mind that the colour requires a specific period of time for dry-up properly. If the painter does not allow necessary time-span for drying-up the layers of paints, flaking will appear in course of time. The adhesive can play an important role to get rid of this problem. However, the most important phenomenon is to know the responsive capacity of adherent to adhesive. In fact, the adherent and adhesive should be in the same group.

It may be stated here that insufficient knowledge of painter may causes more damage. A new support of the canvas is an extra lining, which is a necessary measure to check the damage in oil painting. If the canvas is required to change with new ones then flake transfer is inevitable. The flake transfer is the work of a high esteem of accuracy and precession. In this operation, most vital ingredient is adhesive, especially chemical adhesive as the *thermoplastic resin*. This chemical adhesive is not responsive to the moisture. The flake transfer is known as *thermoplastic resin process* that is required a condition of high temperature and a vacuum pressure table. It is most sophisticated technology and the technique is much expensive as well as complicated too. However, the organic adhesive or organic resin adhesive is not at all suitable in comparison with this modern flake transfer technology rather it attracts insects too. The varnish loses its transparency in due course of time. Old varnish is turned yellow in colour. A dissolving solvent is necessary to remove this opaque-yellow varnish. Oil paint will regain its transparency after removal of old varnishes. This solvent can dissolve the varnish without disturbing the paint. Old varnish can be wiped-off and new varnish need to be added on it for preservation.

Drawings

In this item discolouration is a big problem. It happens because of the action of sulphur compounds available in the atmospheric surrounds and these compounds deposited on the white lead pigment of drawings. As a result, gradually it is converted to a dark coloured *sulphide* after having a chemical reaction in due course of time. In this situation the use of *hydrogen peroxide* is good enough to change the dark *sulphide* in a state of white *sulphate*.

The plain water is not at all suitable for drawings especially for watercolour paintings, charcoal drawings, etc. The effective reagent for drawing is *ethereal solution* or *alcohol*. This reagent is applied to the drawings with a small soft brush for clearing it without further damage.

Siliceous Materials

Clay

The clay is a basic component of siliceous materials in any form. Chiefly, it is a combination of aluminium and silica with varying proportion of other ingredients. Other ingredients are the compounds of iron, calcium, manganese and many vegetable matters. The clay composition is a mixture showing wide variation. However, it has a common property of plasticity in wet condition, which would be hard after baking. This property of hardness will be soft again in presence of water when the baking temperature was below 600°C. But the hardness is sustained when the baking temperature is above 605°C and no more character of softness will come again in addition of water.

The clay items are available in different types with varying characters. So, the varying characters are depending on the types of clay. Only two reasons are found behind these differences–the proportional composition of ingredients in one hand and the difference of baking temperature on the other. The colour of the items relates to the baking period. However, the change of colour at baking temperature can be prevented in addition of the *kaolin* in a considerable proportion. As an example, the white clay remains white as it is in the porcelain. In fact, any item of clay is the *ceramics*. Therefore, the siliceous materials can be divided in two groups, *ceramics* and *glass*. In general, the *ceramics* are available in the following names, earthenware, terracotta, stoneware and porcelain.

Earthenware

The earthenware is the product of ordinary clay under the range of 1125°C baking temperature. The items are looking at natural buff-colour though a few objects are found in dark shades. The production is porous in nature and not able to hold water for a long time unless it is glazed or coated with non-porous materials.

Terracotta

These items are also made with natural clay under the range above 1915°C baking temperature. All are porous material with reddish colour. These materials are popularly used in a wide variety of utilitarian vessels and different form of sculptures.

Stoneware

The material of stoneware is hard and vitreous. For this reason the stoneware is quite efficient to hold water for a long period of time without being glazed. It is a special type of blended clay demanding the baking temperature at the range above 1285°C to achieve its characters.

Porcelain

This material is the result of a special preparation of clay composition with *kaolin*. It requires the range above 1350° C baking temperature. However, the colour is unchanged as white after baking due to presence of kaolin. In porcelain material, the clay composition along with its glaze is fired together for baking. As a result, it becomes too hard and vitreous.

The glaze is an important part of porcelain items. It is nothing but a coating of minerals to develop a glassy surface-layer around the ceramic piece. This layer is free from chemical reaction and looking very good shiny surface. Besides, this layer makes the item waterproof and vitreous. The glaze material should not be the range of higher melting point in comparison with the firing temperature of the body. The flux is required to melt the glaze properly in glazing. Two types of flux material are available in the market as the *lead* and the *soda*. The colour of the glaze is fully dependent on the metals in the form of *oxides*, or *carbonates* or water-soluble *salts*. The shades of colour are also varying in the proportional composition of these *metal oxides* or *carbonates* or *salts* with glaze material and its flux.

Broadly speaking the clay items are divided in three categories in the following groups: *fire-baked, sun-baked* and *unbaked*. The distilled water is necessary for washing the fire-baked item to be free from loose deposited salt. Nevertheless, the sun-baked item is not suitable for direct use of distilled water. Therefore, in this situation a piece of pulpy blotting paper is required to wrap the specimen. This blotting paper must be soaked in distilled water before use as a wrapper. The item under wrapped position is keeping undisturbed for a few hours to a full day for cleaning. Unbaked items need a warm condition for treatment as cleaning. It would be better to work near a furnace with bellows properly. A piece of wet blotting paper is confined to the item by sponging technique under warm condition.

Glass

This item requires no treatment for preservation. A simple wash with soap-water is sufficient for glass items. Sometimes the items produce good response in addition to *diluted sulphuric acid* (1%) for cleaning. After cleaning and washing with clean water the items are in need to dry-up with a piece of clean warm cloth.

Metals

Copper, Bronze and Brass

The copper is an ancient metal with its alloy as the bronze and the brass. The bronze is alloy of copper with tin and the brass is the product of copper with zinc. The copper and its alloys are required to wash with hot running water. Nextly, the items are washed with distilled water and to dry-up properly. Finally, a coating of *celluloid solution* (2%) is necessary to paint over the object for preservation.

The incrustation problem is a common factor for the items made with these metals. The *caustic soda* (NaOH) solution (2%) is a popular reagent to remove incrustation. Further, the *citric acid* solution (2%) may be used in case of heavy deposition as incrustation. Sometimes, the corrosion is found in the form of green-patina. It is thin, hard, and green enamel like appearance on the specimens. This green-patina is coming out as a layer due to chemical reaction in presence of gasses in atmosphere. This layer is basically the *carbonate, chloride* and *sulphide* of the metals, such as copper, bronze and brass. Considerable level of corrosion can be cleared by use of cold and diluted sulphuric acid solution (5% to 10% concentrations as per requirement). The cleaning, washing and dry-up of the specimen should be done accordingly.

Lastly, the specimen is in need to cover up with a coating of preservative solution. A thin layer of wax is a good remedy for this work. Apart from this, a mixture solution of *paraffin wax* in the *benzene* solution (5%) is also an effective solution for preservation. But this solution is required to use with alternative coatings. Another two types of solutions are also helpful for preservative coating. First one is *venyl-acetate* solution (2%) in the *toluene* (1:2) and second one is the mixture of *celluloid solution* (2%) with equal parts of *acetone* solution (2%) and *annyl-acetate* (2%) solution (2:2:2).

Lead

This metal is most popularly used in the antique objects. A common corrosion of the lead is incrustation or it can be said as white deposition. Atmospheric ingredients in contact with this metal can produce basic *carbonate* of lead, after a chemical reaction. Further reaction occurs in contact with *oxide* in the form of a white deposition on the object.

A little corrosion due to incrustation may be controlled by use of diluted *acetic acid* (10 parts of acetic acid and 90 parts of water, i.e., 10%). Repeated use of diluted acid is suggested to wipe-off the incrustation with the help of medium hard brush. The object should be soaked with diluted *acetic acid* (10%) for a few hours in case of heavy incrustation. The brushing is to be done at intervals until the heavy white deposition is erased out completely. Nextly, the object should be dipped in the diluted *caustic soda* (NaOH) solution (1%) for neutralizing the acidity. The acid free object demand acute washes with fresh and boiled distilled water till it is free from *alkali* as because the alkali reacts on lead. This process can be monitored by the *phenolphthalein*, which can change at pink colour in presence of alkali, but remains colourless under alkali free condition.

At least seven days are necessary for dry-up the object under a clean-undisturbed-atmospheric environment. Finally, a coating is to be made on the object for preservation. This coating is the solution of either *venyl-acetate* solution (2%) or hot *paraffin wax* as in the liquid form. A medium hard brush is sufficient for this operation.

Silver

The silver is a well-known metal. This metal is soft and not ups as to the level of wear and tear of daily use. Alloying it with other metals solves this problem. The copper is most important ingredient to a large extent for coinage and other purposes.

The corrosion on silver-alloy object come up as the deposition or coating of silver chlorides due to atmospheric reaction. The silver item shows slight surface tarnish or discolouration due to oxidation and showing grey, brown or black in colour. Many silver-alloys are covered with thick green crust misguiding it as the bronze item instead of silver. This green crust problem can be easily solved by a soft pad of cotton wool or a semi-hard brush or simply by fingers with a gentle friction. But, the embossed or engraved surface demands another technique. However, a semi-hard brush cans wipe-off the incrustation in addition to diluted *ammonia* (NH_3) solution (10%). Thorough washing and a proper dry-up of the specimen are suggested after removal of the incrustation. Lastly, a coating is required for preservation. The preservative solution as the coating is either *celluloid solution* (2%) or *venyl-acetate solution* (2%).

The corrosion due to oxidation shows discolouration of the object. This situation is controlled with the help of *formic acid*. Affected specimen is to be kept in a porcelain pot and the *formic acid* (5%) is poured into it. This porcelain pot is necessarily being heated for an hour under low temperature. After that the object is to be taken out from the acid-filled pot for washing it thoroughly with distilled water. The specimen is to be dipped in diluted *ammonia* (NH_3) solution (20 parts ammonia and 80 parts of water, i.e., 25%) after a thorough wash. The specimen requires a further wash and dry-up before preservative coating. This preservative solution of coating is either *celluloid solution* (2%) or *venyl-acetate solution* (2%).

This treatment is sufficient for slight corrosion. In case of heavy incrustation, the strength of *ammonia solution* should be increased to the strength of 50 parts of *ammonia* in the 50 parts of water.

Gold

Pure gold is soft metal. A small proportion of silver, copper, bronze, etc. are mixed with this metal for making hard and usable in condition. Basically, these impurities are responsible factors to make the gold tarnish or discolouration of the surface. This problem is solved simply by wash with soap in warm water. A soft brush or a piece of cotton may be used in the period of washing.

If, this simple wash is not enough to remove gold tarnish, then the solution of ammonia (10%) is required with the help of a piece of sponge. The cleaning by sponge technique is enough to wipe-off the silver-chloride deposition as gold tarnish. The incrustation of calcium carbonate or calcium sulphate is to be released in addition to *hydrochloric acid* of 50% dilution in water in the ratio of 10 parts diluted *hydrochloric acid* (50%) in 90 parts of water. Moreover, the black stains are to be removed with the help of *nitric acid* of 50% dilution. Finally, the gold item is required a compulsory treatment with *ammonia* (10%) solution after acid treatment.

Iron

This metal is too much susceptible to outside agencies and rapid deterioration is shown in comparison with other metals. The agencies for deterioration are as follows :

(a) Moisture of the environment causes rusting over the iron.

(b) Oxygen and carbon dioxide in the air are most harmful for the iron object.

(c) Common salt (NaCl), i.e., sodium chloride is derived from the earth and it is an important agent for deterioration.

The rust is common erosion to this metal. It is the mass of iron oxides. A high degree of corrosion due to rust may cause the degenerate of the surface and look like a few small brownish moist beads of chloride compounds along with the oxides of iron. This condition is treated with a wire brush.

But, in some cases the *caustic soda* (NaOH) solution (10%) of boiling temperature is necessary to apply on the object and rubbing with the brush. This application of *caustic soda* solution (10%) continues till the complete elimination of chloride particles and rust. The object may be cleaned with diluted *nitric acid* solution (10%) for lime incrustation before use of caustic soda solution. In the last phase of treatment the object needs plenty of clean water for thorough washing. After complete removal of caustic soda solution the specimen should be kept in a dry warm place for dry-up it properly and it should be coated with a preservative solution as quick as possible.

The iron object is coated at least twice with anti-rust solution or preservative solution. The effective solution is the mixture of *paraffin wax* and the *benzene solution* (5%) in a combination of (1:2). The object may also be dipped in hot melted *paraffin wax*. The coating of *shellac solution* (20%) is also used in iron object. Lastly, the *linseed oil* alone is a good preservative for the iron objects.

9

Prospect

Education

During 19th Century AD the museum was the place of permanent exhibition of its collection. But, a drastic change has been taken place from 3rd decade of present Century (19th Century) regarding the function of the museum. It has been decided as an attempt to present a coherent story of its contents, impart direct instructions and stimulate the visitors at the same time for learning through observation and experience.

Late Sir Asutosh Mukherjee was one of the first Indian to emphasize the educational role of museums in unequivocal terms. Speaking on the occasion of the Centenary of Indian Museum, Calcutta, on 28th Nov. 1915, Sir A. Mukherjee said, "I have no desire on the present occasion to enter upon an exhaustive discussion of the true functions of a museum in relation to the community at large.... It is now generally recognized that a museum is an institution for the preservation of those objects which best illustrate the phenomena of Nature of Works of Man, for the utilization of these in the increase of knowledge and for the culture and entertainment of the people".

The formal educational institutions of our country are disseminating knowledge formally under a specific structure.

The formal institutions like the schools, colleges and universities are dealing with the homogeneous group of students. In case of the museum the knowledge is departing to the heterogeneous group of visitors. It is true that the museum is functioning as a non-formal education centre. But, it is not sufficient to understand regarding the role of education. Here, the system of education is completely different in comparison with the formal educational institutions. The education through the museum starts from much audio-visual assistance in connection with three-dimensional original artifacts of its own. The specimens or artifacts are displayed in association with many reference materials for better illustration. It conveys a message to the visitors; rather it is information through original artifacts with some supportive materials or reference items, such as posters, photographs, charts, labels, maps, etc. In the museum, many blank spaces are reserved intentionally to avoid monotony of viewing the objects. The objective behind the blank space is that the visitors can learn, relax and enjoy exclusively the environment of the museum and at the same time they should remember some information. In fact the visitors should have a positive impression regarding the exhibits, which is acquired by them through non-formal way of education or to learn by *visual education*.

Today the concept of museum is changing very fast where the system of *visual education* is getting top priority in the role of museum. Thus, the museum is now being a *workshop*, where things are done; a *school*, where things are taught; an *academy* of higher learning and a place for *cultural enjoyment*. The visitors can feel a free atmosphere from the monotony of everyday life, hard work and personal anxieties. This place is suitable for exhibition and display of the objects where the people can achieve their mental satisfaction. It is being considered as a community centre. It should have some reflection of aspiration level of the community along with their surroundings.

A popular proverb is to be mentioned here as "one physical look is better than to refer 100 books". It is obvious that the scope of collection is much wider in the museum and the visitors can use the chances of observation by physical verification of the specimens. The specimens are acquired and displayed for the people to develop their interest and knowledge. In this regard the museum is getting an extra advantageous position as the centre of visual education.

In time perspective the museum is changing their priority and thinking about an approach to disseminate more knowledge to the people. This approach is more enhancements regarding the presentation of the object instead of much collection. This presentation is simply a link between the specimen and the visitor. It is a unique concern of present day museum. The basic objective of this link or presentation is education by means of specimen to show, to exhibit and to display in a meaningful way for the visitors. This education is visual education followed by the principle of communication between the museum and its visitors. Communication denotes a process of purposive interaction. It is depending on the medium as a factor to be it successful. In fact, the presentation of the museum specimens is solely dependent on the process of communication in a proper and better way.

The museum exhibition is the end part of display of the specimens and starting point of visual education. It is an intellectual relaxation as well as to disseminate knowledge to the visitors. Thus the museum exhibition is an excellent scope to impart non-formal education. Here, the placement of the objects are required to be planned with a great care along with some aids, like as the lighting, space arrangements, colour schemes and well coordination of all aids. In addition, the replicas, photographs, labels, captions, etc. as the reference materials are needful to build up a complete story. For non-formal education of the museum, the label is inevitable part. The label can be categorized as the *introductory label* for a brief introduction or background of the exhibition, the *sectional label* is necessary for information regarding the objects of a particular section, and the *individual label* for more specific information of the object or a group of objects. But, it is important to remember that the labels should not be occupied large areas of exhibition instead of brief information in a short space. At present, the specimens are displayed with an environment where it is depicted with a story of its origin and its development. It is a perspective based exhibition while many modern museums are doing their best. This technique of exhibition is continually undergoing a change for achievement of more and more knowledge in concise form to disseminate among the visitors.

All efforts in connection with the museum activities are ended in a good public relation. It is the degree of goodwill and some kind of understanding achieved through different activities undertaken by the museum. In this regard we can remember the meaning of democracy, i.e., by the people, of the people and for the people. Naturally, the museum is always ready to accept people's contribution; so, it is by the people. The museum has a social responsibility to satisfy all cross-sections of the people with their vivid interest; so, it is of the people. The museum is taking different programmes with full of responsibility to satisfy their visitors; so, it is for the people.

However, in consideration with public relation the role of museum is to some extent guided by the demand of their visitors. Thus, the public demands are fulfilled by taking up some programmes for development people's awareness regarding rich cultural heritage to daily life. Besides, the museum is also a tourist spot in its own right. From this point of view the museum is acting as a motivating factor with a passive role of education for the tourists in many ways, such as socio-cultural, economic, environment, cultural heritage, etc. It is also a resourceful centre for tourists in many things.

As a matter of fact, a good public relation is simply an asset to a museum for achievement of its objectives. In this connection, the role of education is ensuring direct help and it can be said as the visual education when the museum is concerned. The museum education or visual education is flourishing by taking up some popular as well as useful programmes for the people, likely as the short-courses on our heritage; the short exhibitions with lecture demonstration, workshops, seminars, etc. These are all effective measures for gaining people's faith and good understanding regarding many things in connection with the museum. It may be concluded that the museum is an institution of visual education with all efforts where the visitor's position is looking at a focal point.

Research

The research is an endeavour to discover answers of the problems intellectually and practically by adoption of scientific method in the universe. It would be directed toward the solution of a problem based on observable experience and empirical evidence. Research demands accurate observation and description. So, the research must be carefully recorded and reported and may be summarized in the following ways:

1. A statement of the purpose of research, which is to be made in the form of formulation of the problem.

2. A description of the study is to be presented.

3. The techniques of data collections should be justified.

4. Analysis of collected data and illustration.

5. Interpretation and report writing is the end part of research.

The research is a collective term of a scientific method, which is denoting many processes of the science. It consists of systematic observation, classification and interpretation of data. The research methods are found in six primary forms and all others are merely variations of the same forms:

(A) *Induction* is the expansion of knowledge from particular fact or facts to a general principle or rule.

(B) *Deduction* is the reduction of knowledge from a general rule to a particular fact.

(C) *Historical* method is a backward movement of knowledge to trace the previous cause or causes of a phenomenon.

(D) *Comparative* method is the analysis and comparison of two contemporary phenomena and it is always undertaken in order to discover new facts.

(E) *Structural* method is a study of *what a thing is*, what are its outlines and significant features. This study may be considered as the anatomy.

(F) *Functional* method is the study of the processes with their causes, that is, '*how*' and '*why*' of a thing or fact. It may be considered as the physiology.

The *sample* is an essential part of research work and the sampling is a short-cut alternative of the study. A sample is a smaller representation of a large whole and selection process of those samples known as *sampling*. In research work, the *observation* is another essential aspect of the study.

General characteristics of observation may be made in the following ways:

- to observe physical activity;
- it would be selective and purposive;
- it makes direct study;
- a few dominant features must be recorded;
- to observe functional activity; and
- to establish cause and effect relationship.

Next part of the research study is *editing*. It is the first step in *data processing* and *interpretation*. Interpretation may be considered as the central part of research process and it is a search of research findings in broader meaning. In fact, the meanings and implications of the study become clear through interpretation. Final part of the study is *report writing*.

Primarily, a research report is concerned with orderly presentation of information in association with a table of contents, sections or chapters, bibliography, etc. The *articles* generally do not require original research and it is to be circulated for awareness generation of the people concerned to the topic. It is more concerned with coherent argument without sub-section headings. The *research monograph* is a report covering fairly large research project on a single subject. It is usually longer than an article but shorter than a book. The *dissertation work* represents a specific idea, which is to provide a systematic discussion on the subject or topic with purposeful establishment of a view of formal discussion. Naturally, it is a detailed report on the subject of the study that was undertaken. A *thesis* is a too long dissertation work, which is written on the basis of detailed research work. It is commonly regarded as a coherent report of research study in its origin of the problem while both the process and the results are given accordingly. It includes preliminary parts and reference sections in similar to the form of a *book*. Academically, a thesis is superior in comparison with a dissertation. Lastly, a hypothetical model of report writing is being placed here under three sections, *preliminary sections*, *text* or *context*, and *reference material*.

Preliminary Section

Title Page

This page makes a concise and adequate description of the title of the research study. It is a way to convey the meaning of matters precisely. It should be typed in all capital letters.

Acknowledgements and Preface

A preface includes the reason behind the selection of that topic. If the researcher has opted to discuss the significance and nature of his/her research in a subsequent chapter, usually in 'Introductory Chapter', then he/she may only use the page for 'Acknowledgements'. The *Preface* and *Acknowledgements* are usually signed by its writer.

Table of Contents

This page appears after the Preface and Acknowledgements. It provides an outline of contents of the report. The first page should not be mentioned in the contents as because it is the title page. Similarly, the page as 'table of contents' is not reflected in the table of contents.

List of Tables and Figures

A separate page is required for the list of tables and figures, which are to be, followed the table of contents.

Abbreviations

The abbreviations may be used to avoid monotony of writing as typing lengthy terms in full. It should appear before the main text.

All pages in the preliminary section are numbered at the centre position of the bottom with lower case Roman numerals (e.g., i, ii, iii, iv,...).

Text or Context

Introduction

Statement of the problem must be clear in nature and its importance would be mentioned properly. Illustration of historical background along with the significance of the problem is also appropriate appreciation to introduce the project to its reader. The *Objective/Purposes* of the study indicates enough background to make clear understanding to the reader. It is necessary to establish worthfullness of the problem. *Review of literature* presents background information of the present study and brings the reader up to date. *Conceptual framework* is a compact form of different concepts proposed in the study. Definitions of all-important terms are explained for the readers to understand the concepts. The adoption of *methodology* is essential part of research. It must be mentioned with full of explanation. This part describes, the research design used, the data collection methods employed, the manner of sampling (if any), how the work was carried out, the variables and controls employed, the reliability of instruments selected, the statistical tools and procedures used in the analysis. *Limitations* of the study are a sincere accountability of the researcher. The serious researcher faces the problem and makes accurate record carefully and honestly in introduction.

Main Body of the Report

The report must be made with a *statement of findings* along with recommendations in a simple language. It is required to understand easily by all concerned intellectuals.

The *result* is detailed presentation of the findings. It must be enriched with supportive data in the forms of tables, charts, photographs, etc. to establish validity of the result. The writing of the main text or illustration is the next part of the report and it would be arranged in different *chapters*. The chapterisation is primary requirement of the reader who wishes to make detailed study or a specific portion of the problem. The chapters should be organized systematically with appropriate headings.

Conclusion

The *summary* has become customary to conclude the research report. It has been written in brief the research problem, the methodology, the major findings, and the major conclusions drawn from the research results. Beside this the *recommendations* are expected from the study. Finally, the *suggestions* of the research worker must be practicable and based on logical reasoning.

Reference Materials

The *end matter* is the appendices. It should be enlisted in respect of all technical data. The *bibliography* is the list of sources consulted for the study. Lastly, the *index* is to be included in the report.

At last, the materials must be presented in a good binding form to the reader.

10

List of the Museums in India

1. **Academy of Fine Arts**
   2, Cathedral Road, Calcutta 700 071.
   Type: Private.
   Subordinate Unit of *Institute of Visual Art.*
   Opening Hours: 12:00 to 09:00, Monday Closed.
   Founded in: 1933.
   Subjects: Art, Crafts, and Personalia.
   Collections: Ancient Sculpture, Paintings, Miniature Paintings, Ivory, Wood, Textile, Personal Belongings.
   Services: Research, Library, Film Shows.
   Publications: Exhibit Catalogues.
   Contact Person: Head of the Organization.

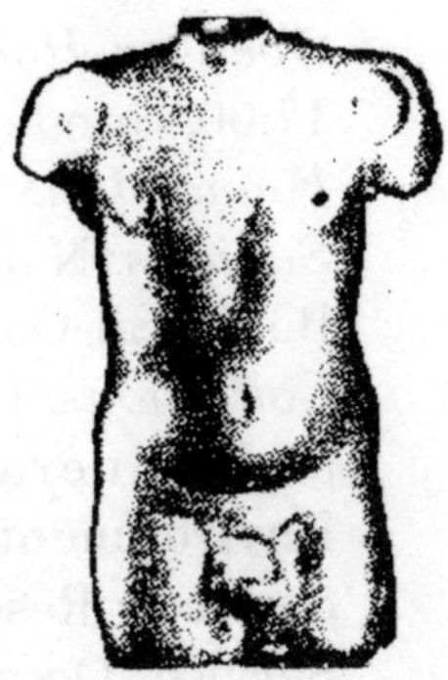

2. **Acharya Jogesh Chandra Purakriti Bhavan**
   P.O. Bishnupur, Dist. Bankura, West Bengal 722122.
   Type: Autonomous Organisation.
   Opening Hours: 08:00 to 19:00, Sunday, Tuesday, Thursday and Saturday Closed.
   Founded in: 1951.

Subjects: Archaeology, Art, Crafts, Tribal and Folk Art.
Collections: Prehistory, Ancient Sculpture, Brass, Copper, Bronze and Iron Objects, Arms and Weapons, Paintings, Miniature Paintings, Scrolls, Pata Chitra, Wood, Pottery, Terracotta, Tapestry/Carpet, Books, Films/Slides/Tapes, Dolls, Toys, Figurines, Musical Instruments.
Services: Research, Conservation, Guide Service, Occasional Temporary Exhibitions, Voluntary Services.
Publications: Guide Book, Exhibit Catalogues, and Journal.
Contact Person: Secretary.

3. **Aghar Kar Museum**
Botany Department, University of Allahabad, Allahabad 211002.
Type: University.
Subordinate Unit of *Botany Department,* University of Allahabad.
Opening Hours: 10:00 to 17:00, Sunday Closed.
Founded in: 1923.
Subjects: Natural History, Botanical Garden.
Collections: Fossils, Rocks and Minerals, Botany, Environment.
Services: Research, Guide Service, Occasional Temporary Exhibitions, Graduate and Post Graduate Classes.
Publications: Monographs, Seminar Proceedings.
Contact Person: Curator.

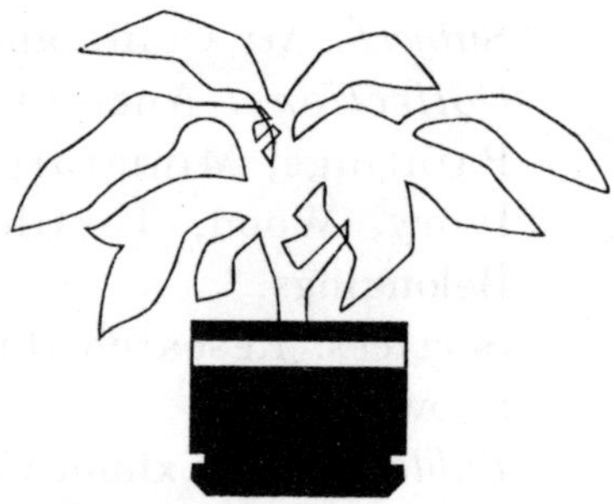

4. **Allahabad Museum**
Chandrasekhar Azad Park, Allahabad–211 002.
Type: Autonomous.
Subordinate unit of *Allahabad Museum Society.*

Opening Hours: 10:15 to 16:30, Sunday, Monday and second Saturday closed.
Founded in: 1931.
Subjects: Pre-history, Archaeology, Paintings, Art, Anthropology and Zoology.
Collections: Pre-historic tools, Archaeological objects of Harappan culture, Copper artifacts, Beads, Seals, Sculptures, Coins of gold, silver and copper, Paintings, Carvings on wood, ivory, metal, porcelain and Zoological and Anthropological objects.
Services: Library, Photographic laboratory, Conservation laboratory, Modeling section, Educational programmes, Guide tours, Slide and film shows and lectures.
Publications: Masterpieces of Allahabad Museum, Books on collections of stone sculptures, terracotta and paintings, Plastercast models and photography.
Contact Person: Director.

5. **Anand Bhawan**
Jawaharlal Nehru Memorial Fund,
Allahabad 211 002.
Type: Autonomous Organisation.
Subordinate Unit of *Jawaharlal Nehru Memorial Fund.*
Opening *Hours:* 09:30 to 17:30, Monday Closed.
Founded in: 1971.
Subjects: Personalia, Planetarium.
Collections: Books, Personal Belongings.
Services: Guide Service.
Publications: Picture Postcards, Books.
Contact Person: Controller.

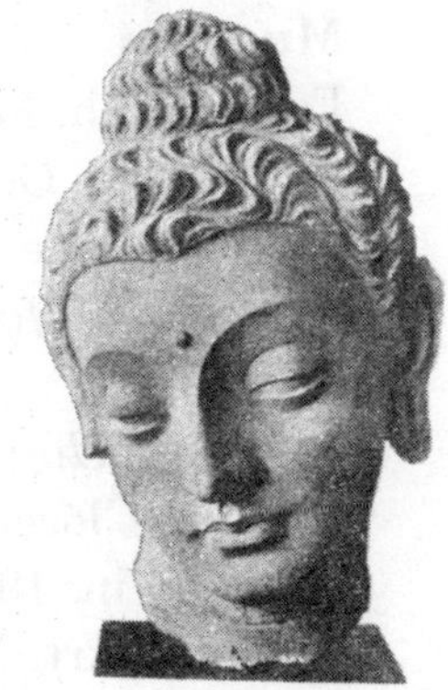

6. Anandaniketan Kirtishala

Anandaniketan, Bagnan, Howrah, West Bengal 711303.
Type: Private.
Subordinate Unit of *Anandaniketan Rural Upliftment Research Institute.*
Opening Hours: 11:00 to 17:00, Thursday Closed.
Founded in: 1962.
Subjects: Archaeology, Art, Crafts, Tribal and Folk Art, Natural History, Botanical Garden, Science and Technology, Local History.
Collections: Prehistory, Ancient Sculpture, Brass, Copper, Paintings, Scrolls, Pata Chitra, Wood, Pottery, Terracotta, Embroidery, Manuscript, Books, Fossils, Rocks and Minerals.
Services: Research, Occasional Temporary Exhibitions, Other Outreach Programme, Film Shows.
Publications: Guide Book, Monographs, Books.
Contact Person: Curator.

7. Anglo Sikh War Memorial Museum

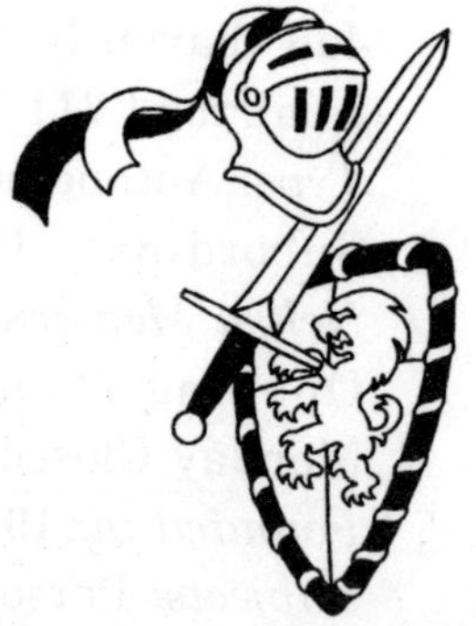

Ferozeshah, Ferozpur, Punjab.
Type: State Government.
Subordinate Unit of *Dept. of Cultural Affairs and Museums,* Punjab.
Opening Hours: 10:00 to 17:00, Monday Closed.
Founded in: 1976
Subjects: Art, Modern Painting on Anglo Sikh War Weapons.
Collections: Anus and Weapons, Paintings.
Services: Research, Guide Service, and Library.
Publications: Brochure.
Contact Person: Director.

8. Anthropology Museum

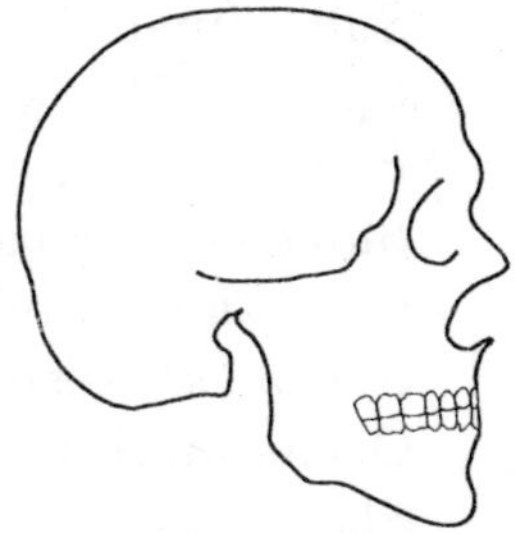

Department of Anthropology,
University of Delhi, Delhi 110 007.
Type: University.
Opening Hours: 09:00 to 17:30,
Sunday and Saturday Closed.
Founded in: 1948.
Subjects: Archaeology, Ethnography, Anthropology, Crafts, Tribal and Folk Art.
Collections: Prehistory, Arms and Weapons, Pottery, Terracotta, Baskets, Jewellery, Embroidery, Costumes, Textile, Musical Instruments.
Services: Research.
Contact Person: Head.

9. Archaeological Museum, Aihole

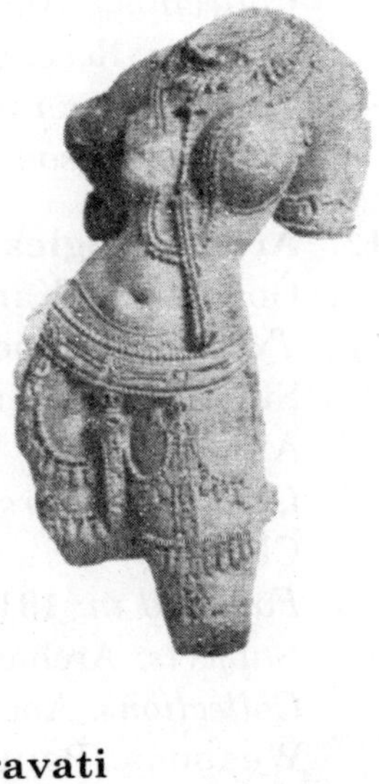

Dist. Bijapur, Karnataka 587 138.
Type: Government.
Subordinate Unit of *Museums Branch*, ASI, Calcutta.
Opening Hours: 10:00 to 17:00,
Friday Closed.
Founded in: 1985.
Subjects: Archaeology.
Collections: Ancient Sculpture.
Services: Research, Conservation, Guide Service, Occasional Temporary Exhibitions, Library, Film Shows.
Contact Person: Archaeologist.

10. Archaeological Museum, Amaravati
ASI, Dist. Guntur,
Andhra Pradesh 522 020.
Type: Government.

Subordinate Unit of *Museums Branch*, ASI Calcutta.
Opening Hours: 10:00 to 17:00.
Founded in: 1951.
Subjects: Archaeology.
Collections: Prehistory, Ancient Sculpture.
Services: Research, Conservation, Guide Service, Occasional Temporary Exhibitions, Library, Film Shows.
Publications: Guide Book, Picture Postcards.
Contact Person: Archaeologist.

11. **Archaeological Museum, Badami**
Dist. Bijapur, Karnataka, 587 201.
Type: Government.
Subordinate Unit of *Museums Branch*, ASI, Calcutta.
Opening Hours: 10:00 to 17:00, Friday Closed.
Founded in: 1985.
Subjects: Archaeology.
Collections: Ancient Sculpture.
Services: Research, Conservation, Guide Service, Occasional Temporary Exhibitions, Library, Film Shows.
Contact Person: Archaeologist.

12. **Archaeological Museum, Bijapur**
Golgumbaz, Karnataka 586 101.
Type: Government.
Subordinate Unit of *Museums Branch*, ASI, Calcutta.
Opening Hours: 10:00 to 17:00, Friday Closed.
Founded in: 1912.
Subjects: Archaeology.
Collections: Ancient Sculpture, Arms and Weapons, Paintings, Porcelain, Wood, Tapestry/Carpet, Manuscript.
Services: Research, Conservation, Guide Service, Occasional Temporary

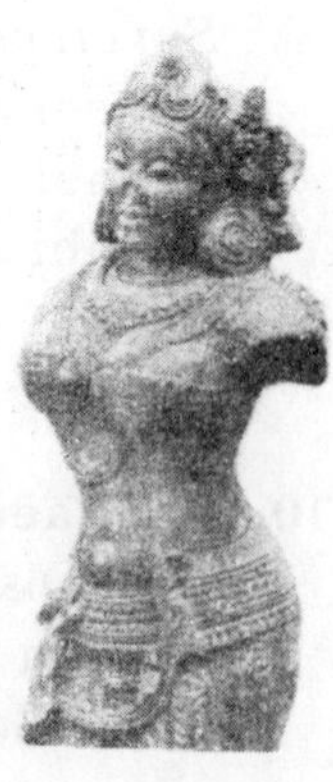

Exhibitions, Library, Film Shows.
Publications: Guide Book.
Contact Person: Archaeologist.

13. Archaeological Museum, Bodhgaya
Archaeological Survey of India, Gaya, Bihar 824 231.
Type: Government.
Subordinate Unit of *Museums Branch*, ASI, Calcutta.
Opening Hours: 10:00 to 17:00, Friday Closed.
Founded in: 1956.
Subjects: Archaeology.
Collections: Ancient Sculpture, Terracotta.
Services: Research, Conservation, Guide Service, Occasional Temporary Exhibitions, Library, Film Shows.
Contact Person: Archaeologist.

14. Archaeological Museum, Chandragiri
Raja Mahal Fort, Dist. Chittor, Andhra Pradesh 517 101.

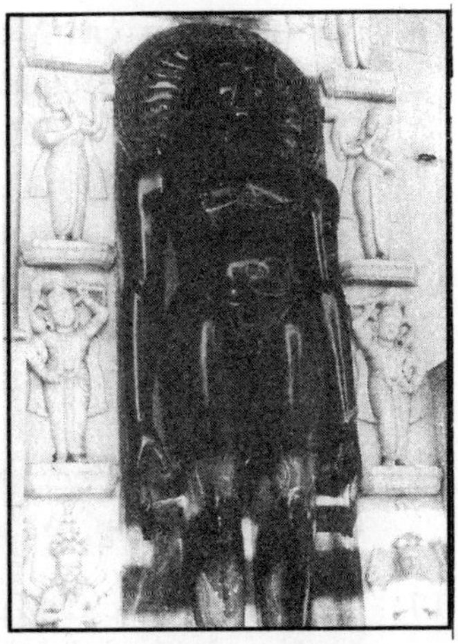

Type: Government.
Subordinate Unit of *Museums Branch*, A.S.I., Calcutta.
Opening Hours: 10:00 to 17:00, Friday Closed.
Founded in: 1988.
Subjects: Archaeology.
Collections: Arms and Weapons, Wood, Terracotta, Manuscript.
Services: Research, Conservation, Guide Service, Occasional Temporary Exhibitions, Library, Film Shows.
Contact Person: Archaeologist.

15. Archaeological Museum, Cochin
Mattaricherry Palace, Cochin 682 002.
Type: Government.
Subordinate Unit of *Archaeological Survey of India.*
Opening Hours: 10:00 to 17:00, Friday Closed.
Founded in: 1986.
Subjects: Art, Personalia related to Cochin Royal Family.
Collections: Ancient Sculpture, Brass, Copper, Bronze and Iron Objects, Arms and Weapons, Paintings, Ivory, Wood, Costumes, Textile, Tapestry/Carpet, Manuscript, Personal Belongings, Figurines.
Services: Research, Conservation, and Occasional Temporary Exhibitions, Library.
Publications: Guide Book, Picture Postcards, Monographs.
Contact Person: Archaeologist.

16. Archaeological Museum, Cuttack
ASI, Post Office-Ratnagiri, Dist. Cuttack, Orissa 754 236.
Type: Government.
Subordinate Unit of *Museums Branch,* Archaeological Survey.
Founded in: 1991.
Subjects: Archaeology.
Collections: Ancient Sculpture, Pottery, Jewellery, and Inscriptions.
Contact Person: Archaeologist.

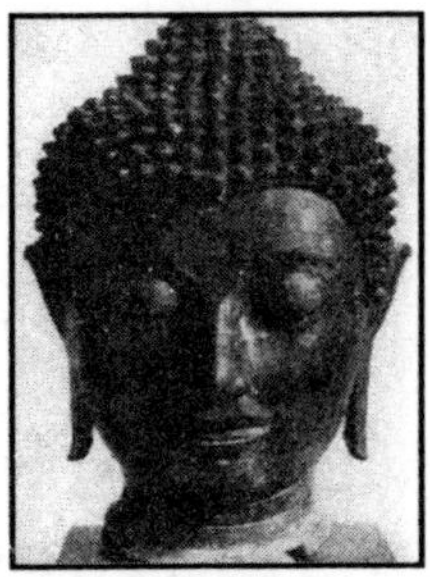

17. Archaeological Museum, Goa
Archaeological Survey of India, Western Region, Velha, Goa 403 402.
Type: Government.
Subordinate Unit of *Museums Branch,* Archaeological Survey of India.
Opening Hours: 10:00 to 17:00, Friday Closed.
Founded in: 1964.

Subjects: Archaeology.
Collections: Prehistory, Ancient Sculpture, Copper, Bronze and Iron Objects, Arms and Weapons, Paintings, Ivory, Wood.
Services: Research, Guide Service, and Occasional Temporary Exhibitions, Library.
Publications: Guide Book, Picture Postcards.
Contact Person: Archaeologist.

18. Archaeological Museum, Gwalior Fort

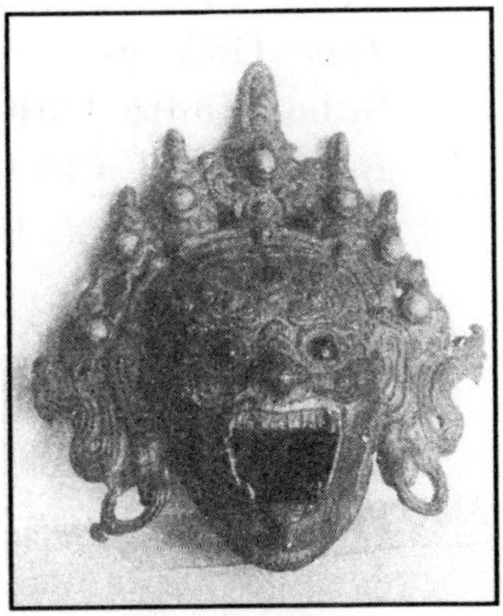

Archaeological Survey of India, Gwalior Fort, Madhya Pradesh 474 008.
Type: Government of India.
Subordinate Unit of *Museums Branch,* ASI, Calcutta.
Opening Hours: 10:00 to 17:00, Friday Closed.
Founded in: 1922.
Subjects: Archaeology.
Collections: Ancient Sculpture, Brass, Copper, and Terracotta.
Services: Research, Conservation, Guide Service, Occasional Temporary Exhibitions, Library, Film Shows.
Publications: Guide Book.
Contact Person: Archaeologist.

19. Archaeological Museum, Halebid
ASI, Dist. Hassan, Karnataka 573 121.
Type: Government.
Subordinate Unit of *Museums Branch,* ASI, Calcutta.
Opening Hours: 10:00 to 17:00, Friday Closed.
Founded in: 1962.
Subjects: Archaeology.

Collections: Ancient Sculpture, Wood.
Services: Research, Conservation, Guide Service, Occasional Temporary Exhibitions, Library, Film Shows.
Contact Person: Archaeologist.

20. Archaeological Museum, Hanipi
Karnalapur, P.O. Hospet, Dist. Bellary, Karnataka 583 221.
Type: Government.
Subordinate Unit of *Museums Branch*, ASI, Calcutta.
Opening Hours: 10:00 to 17:00, Friday Closed.
Founded in: 1953.
Subjects: Archaeology.
Collections: Ancient Sculpture, Paintings, Pottery, Terracotta, Jewellery, Manuscript.
Services: Research, Conservation, Guide Service, Occasional Temporary Exhibitions, Library, Film Shows.
Publications: Guide Book, Picture Postcards.
Contact Person: Archaeologist.

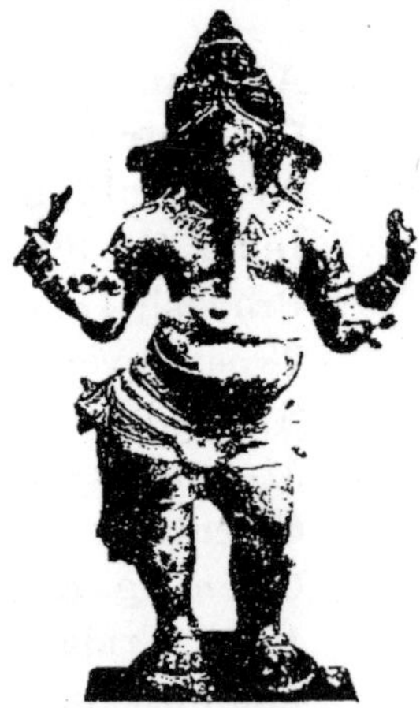

21. Archaeological Museum, Kalibangan
Archaeological Survey of India, Dist. Sri Ganganagar, Rajasthan 335 803.
Type: Government.
Subordinate Unit of *Museums Branch*, ASI, Calcutta.
Opening Hours: 10:00 to 17:00, Friday Closed.
Founded in: 1988.
Subjects: Archaeology.
Collections: Copper, Pottery, and Terracotta.
Services: Research, Conservation.

Publications: Guide Book.
Contact *Person*: Archaeologist.

22. **Archaeological Museum, Khajuraho**
Archaeological Survey of India, Dist. Chhatarpur, Madhya Pradesh 471606.
Type: Government.
Subordinate Unit of *Museums*.
Branch, ASI, Calcutta.
Opening Hours: 10:00 to 17:00, Friday Closed.
Founded in: 1910.
Subjects: Archaeology.
Collections: Ancient Sculpture.
Services: Research, Conservation, Guide Service, Occasional Temporary Exhibitions, Library, Film Shows.
Publications: Guide Book, Picture Postcards.
Contact Person: Archaeologist.

23. **Archaeological Muscum, Kondapur**
ASI, Via Nandi-Kandi, Dist. Medak, Andhra Pradesh 502 299.
Type: Government.
Subordinate Unit of *Museums Branch*, ASI, Calcutta.
Opening Hours: 10:00 to 17:00, Friday Closed.
Founded in: 1952.
Subjects: Archaeology.
Collections: Ancient Sculpture, Bronze and Iron Objects, Pottery, Terracotta.
Services: Research, Conservation, Guide Service, Occasional Temporary Exhibitions, Library, Film Shows
Publications: Guide Book.
Contact Person: Archaeologist.

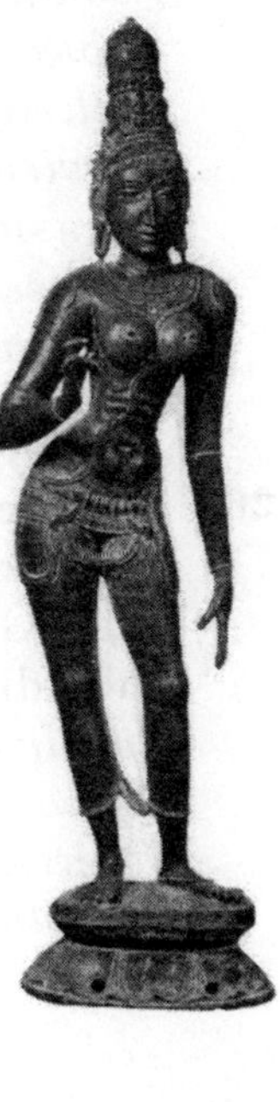

24. **Archaeological Museum, Lothal**
P.O. Lothal Bhurkhri, Dist. Ahmedabad, Gujrat 383231.
Type: Government.
Subordinate Unit of *Museums Branch*, ASI, Calcutta.
Opening Hours: 10:00 to 17:00, Friday Closed.
Founded in: 1984.
Subjects: Archaeology.
Collections: Pottery, Terracotta.
Services: Research, Conservation, Guide Service, Occasional Temporary Exhibitions, Library, Film Shows.
Publications: Guide Book, Picture Postcards.
Contact Person: Archaeologist.

25. **Archaeological Museum, Nagarjuna-Konda**
ASI, P.O. Vijayapuri South, Dist. Guntur, Andhra Pradesh 522 439.
Type: Government.
Subordinate Unit of *Museums Branch*, ASI, Calcutta.
Opening Hours: 10:00 to 17:00, Friday Closed.
Founded in: 1966.
Subjects: Archaeology.
Collections: Ancient Sculpture.
Services: Research, Conservation, Guide Service, Occasional Temporary Exhibitions, Library, Film Shows.
Publications: Guide Book, Picture Postcards.
Contact Person: Archaeologist.

26. **Archaeological Museum, Nalanda**
Archaeological Survey of India, Nalanda, Bihar 803 111.
Type: Government.
Subordinate Unit of *Museums Branch*, ASI, Calcutta.
Opening Hours: 10:00 to 17:00, Friday Closed.
Founded in: 1917.
Subjects: Archaeology.
Collections: Ancient Sculpture, Bronze and Iron Objects, Terracotta.

Services: Research, Conservation, Guide Service, Occasional Temporary Exhibitions, Film Shows.
Publications: Guide Book, Picture Postcards.
Contact Person: Head of the Museum.

27. Archaeological Museum, Purana Qila
Archaeological Survey of India, New Delhi 110 001.
Type: Government.
Subordinate Unit of *Museums Branch*, ASI, Calcutta.
Opening Hours: 10:00 to 17:00, Friday Closed.
Founded in: 1974.
Subjects: Archaeology.
Collections: Ancient Sculpture, Ivory, Pottery, Terracotta, and Technology.
Services: Research, Conservation, Guide Service, Occasional Temporary Exhibitions, Library, Film Shows.
Publications: Guide Book, Picture Postcards, and Seminar Proceedings.
Contact Person: Head of the Museum.

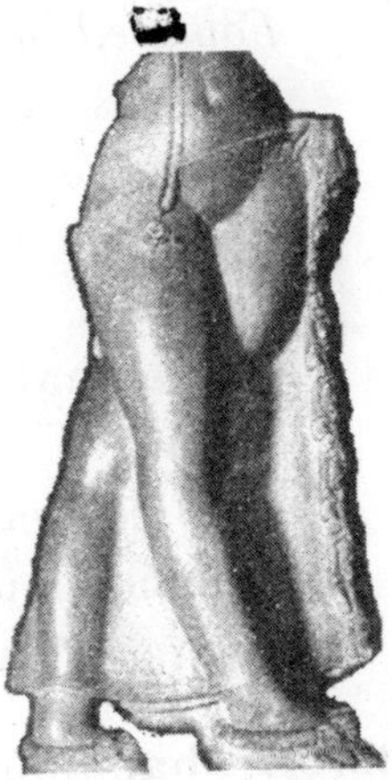

28. Archaeological Museum, Puri
Archaeological Survey of India, Dist. Puri, Orissa 752 111.
Type: Government.
Subordinate Unit of *Museums Branch,* ASI, Calcutta.
Opening Hours: 10:00 to 17:00, Friday Closed.
Founded in: 1968.
Subjects: Archaeology.
Collections: Ancient Sculpture.
Services: Research, Conservation, Guide Service, Occasional Temporary Exhibitions, Library, Film Shows.
Publications: Guide Book, Picture Postcards.
Contact Person: Archaeologist.

29. Archaeological Museum, Red Fort

Archaeological Survey of India, Red Fort, Northern Region, Delhi 110 006.

Type: Government.

Subordinate Unit of *Museums Branch,* ASI, Calcutta.

Opening Hours: 10:00 to 17:00, Friday Closed.

Founded in: 1909.

Subjects: Archaeology.

Collections: Ancient Sculpture, Arms and Weapons, Paintings, Costumes, Tapestry/Carpet, Manuscript.

Services: Research, Conservation, Guide Service, Occasional Temporary Exhibitions, Library, Film Shows.

Publications: Guide Book, Picture Postcards, and Exhibit Albums, Journals.

Contact Person: Archaeologist.

30. Archaeological Museum, Ropar

Archaeological Survey of India, Ropar, Punjab.

Type: Government.

Subordinate Unit of *Museums Branch*, ASI, Calcutta.

Opening Hours: 10:00 to 17:00, Friday Closed.

Founded in: 1988.

Subjects: Archaeology.

Collections: Ancient Sculpture, Terracotta.

Services: Research, Conservation.

Contact Person: Archaeologist.

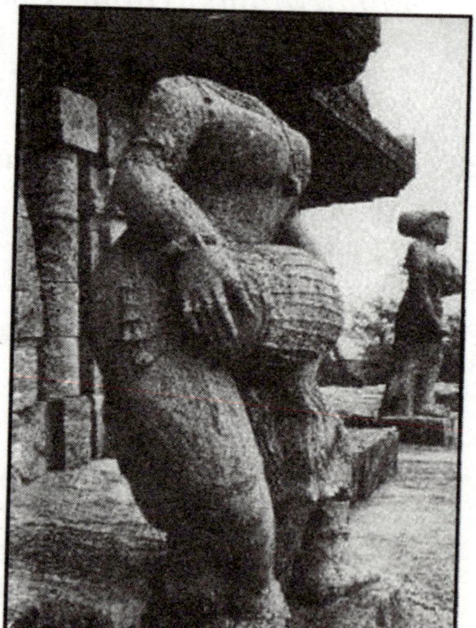

31. Archaeological Museum, Sanchi

Archaeological Survey of India, Dist. Raisen, Madhya Pradesh 464 661.
Type: Government.
Subordinate Unit of Museums Branch, ASI, Calcutta.
Opening Hours: 10:00 to 17:00, Friday Closed.
Founded in: 1966
Subjects: Archaeology.
Collections: Ancient Sculpture.
Services: Research, Conservation, Guide Service, Occasional Temporary Exhibitions, Library, Film Shows.
Publications: Guide Book, Picture Postcards, and Slides.
Contact Person: Archaeologist.

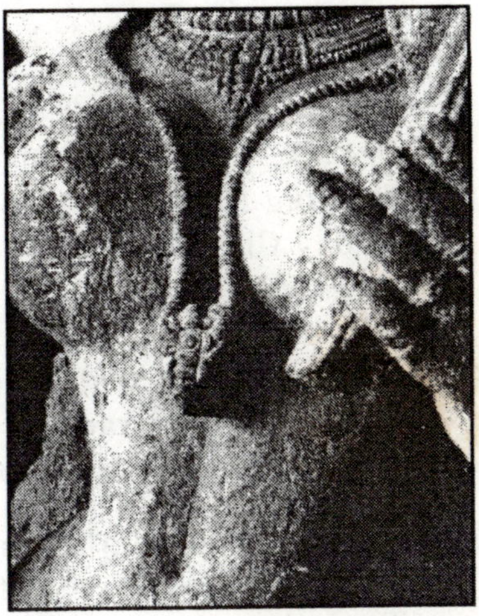

32. Archaeological Museum, Sanghol

Ucha Pind, Tehsil Samrala, Dist. Ludhiana, Punjab.
Type: State Government.
Subordinate Unit of *Dept. of Cultural Affairs and Museums*.
Opening Hours: 10:00 to 17:00, Monday Closed.
Founded in: 1990.
Subjects: Archaeology, Art.
Collections: Ancient Sculpture, Copper, Bronze and Iron Objects, Terracotta, Jewellery, Seal, Sealing and Coins.
Services: Research, Guide Service, Occasional Temporary Exhibitions.
Publications: Exhibit Catalogues, Monographs.
Contact Person: Director.

33. Archaeological Museum, Sarnath

Dist. Varanasi, Uttar Pradesh 221007.

Type: Government.

Subordinate Unit of *Museums Branch*, ASI, Calcutta.

Opening Hours: 10:00 to 17:00, Friday Closed.

Founded in: 1910.

Subjects: Archaeology.

Collections: Ancient Sculpture, Pottery, and Terracotta, Seal.

Contact Person: Archaeologist.

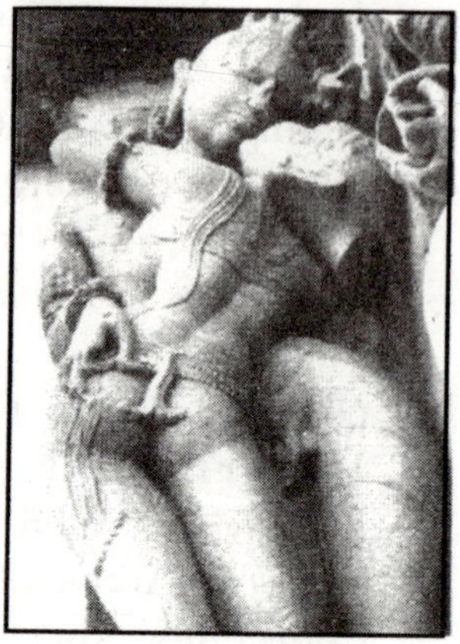

34. Archaeological Museum, Vaishali

Archaeological Survey of India, Dist. Vaishali.

Type: Government.

Subordinate Unit of Museums Branch, ASI, Calcutta.

Opening Hours: 10:00 to 17:00, Friday Closed.

Founded in: 1971.

Subjects: Archaeology.

Collections: Ancient Sculpture, Terracotta, Coin, Seal.

Services: Research, Conservation, Guide Service, Occasional Temporary Exhibitions, Library, Film Shows.

Contact Person: Archaeologist.

35. Archival Museum of Andhra Pradesh

Tarnaka, Hyderabad 500 007.

Type: Government.

Subordinate Unit of *State Archives and Research* Institute.

Opening Hours: 10:30 to 17:00, Sunday Closed.

Founded in: 1965.

Subjects: Archive History.

Collections: Manuscript, Books.

Services: Research, Guide Service, and Occasional Temporary Exhibitions.

Publications: Guide Book, Brochure.
Contact Person: Commissioner.

36. Arms and Chandeliers Gallery
Quila Mubarak Patiala, Punjab.
Type: State Government.
Subordinate Unit of *Dept. of Cultural Affairs* Archaeology and Museums.
Opening Hours: 10:00 to 17:00, Monday Closed.
Founded in: 1956.
Subjects: Art, History and Arms.
Collections: Arms and Weapons, Paintings, Chandeliers.
Services: Research, Guide Service.
Publications: Brochure.
Contact Person: Director.

37. Asutosh Museum of Indian Art
Centenary Building, Calcutta University, College Street, Calcutta 700 012.
Type: University.
Subordinate Unit of *Calcutta University.*
Opening Hours: 10:30 to 17:30, Sunday and Saturday Closed.
Founded in: 1937.
Subjects: Archaeology, Art, Crafts, Tribal and Folk Art.
Collections: Prehistory, Ancient Sculpture, Brass, Copper, Bronze and Iron Objects, Paintings, Miniature Paintings, Scrolls, Pata Chitra, Ivory, Wood, Pottery, Terracotta, Textile, Manuscript, Books, Films/Slides/Tapes, Dolls, Toys.
Services: Conservation, Guide Service, and Occasional Temporary Exhibitions, Library.
Publications: Guide Book, Picture Postcards, and Monographs.
Contact Person: Curator.

38. Bal Bhavan and National Children's Museum

Kotla Road, New Delhi 110002.

Type: Autonomous Organisation. Subordinate Unit of *Bal Bhavan Society India.*

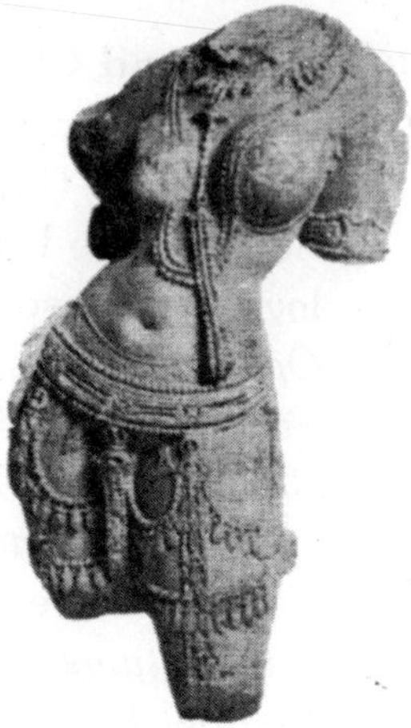

Opening Hours: 09:00 to 17:30.

Founded in: 1956.

Subjects: Art, Crafts, Science and Technology.

Collections: Paintings, Toys, Figurines, Musical Instruments, Fossils, Rocks and Minerals, Economic, Geology, Earth Science, Zoology, Botany, Environment, Physical Science, Technology.

Services: Research, Occasional Temporary Exhibitions, Travelling Exhibition, Library, Photography.

Publications: Slides, Exhibit Albums.

Contact Person: Director.

39. Bangiya Sahitya Parishad Chitrasala

243/1, Acharya Prafulla Chandra Road, Calcutta 700 006.

Type: Autonomous Organisation.

Opening Hours: 13:00 to 19:00, Thursday Closed.

Founded in: 1910.

Subjects: Archaeology, Art.

Collections: Ancient Sculpture, Brass, Copper, Bronze and Iron Objects, Arms and Weapons, Paintings, Pata Chitra, Terracotta, Manuscript, Personal Belongings.

Services: Research, Guide Service, Occasional Temporary Exhibitions, Library.

Publications: Books.

Contact Person: Secretary.

40. Bharat Kala Bhavan

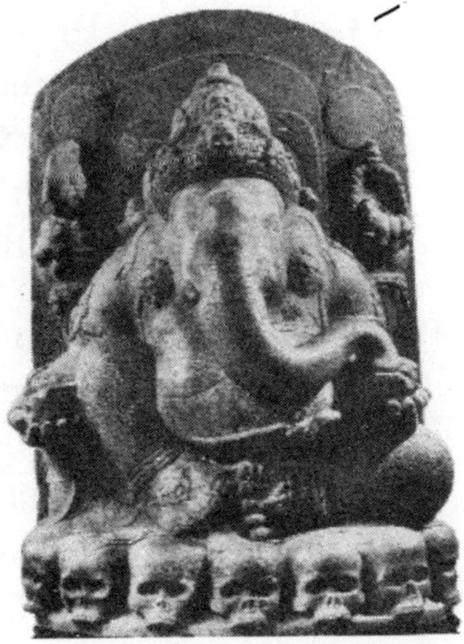

Benaras Hindu University,
Varanasi 221005.
Type: University.
Subordinate Unit of *Benaras Hindu University.*
Founded in: 1920.
Subjects: Archaeology, Art, Historical Records, Literary Materials, and Philately.
Collections: Prehistory, Ancient Sculpture, Brass, Copper, Bronze and Iron Objects, Arms and Weapons, Paintings, Miniature Paintings, Scrolls, Pata Chitra, Modern Sculpture, Porcelain, Glass, Ivory, Wood, Pottery, Terracotta, Leather Work, Jewellery, Embroidery, Costumes, Textile, Tapestry/Carpet, Manuscript, Books, Films/Slides/Tapes, Personal Belongings, Dolls, Toys, Musical Instruments, Coins, Philately.
Services: Research, Conservation, Guide Service, Occasional Temporary Exhibitions, Library, Film Shows, Workshop, Seminar, Lecture.
Publications: Exhibit Catalogues, Picture Postcards, Slides, Exhibit Albums, Monographs, Books, Block Prints, Seminar Proceedings.
Contact Person: Head.

41. Bharathiar Memorial Museum/Research Centre

No. 20, Eswaran Dharmaraja Koli Street, Pondicherry 605 001.
Type: State Government.
Opening Hours: 09:00 to 17:45, Monday Closed.
Founded in: 1972.
Subjects: Archaeology, Art, Tribal and Folk Art, Personalia.

Collections: Prehistory, Copper, Bronze and Iron Objects, Porcelain, Ivory, Wood, Pottery, Terracotta, Jewellery, Personal Belongings.
Services: Research, Guide Service, and Library.
Contact Person: Officer-in-Charge.

42. **Bharathidasan Memorial Museum-Research Centre**
95, Perumol Koli Street, Pondicherry 605 001.
Type: State Government.
Opening Hours: 09:00 to 17:45, Monday Closed.
Founded in: 1971.
Subjects: Personalia.
Collections: Personal Belongings.
Services: Research, Guide Service, and Library.
Contact Person: Officer-in-Charge.

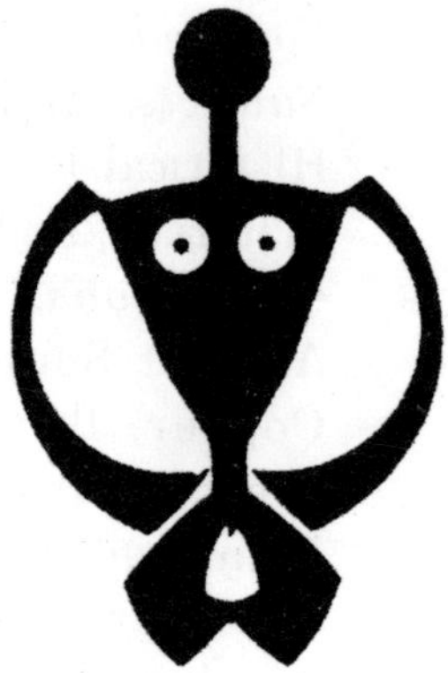

43. **Birla Academy of Art and Culture**
108, Southern Avenue, Calcutta 700 029.
Type: Private.
Subordinate Unit of *Birla Education Trust.*
Opening Hours: 16:00 to 19:00, Monday Closed.
Founded in: 1966.
Subjects: Archaeology, Art, Crafts, Tribal and Folk Art.
Collections: Ancient Sculpture, Brass, Bronze and Iron Objects, Paintings, Miniature Paintings, Scrolls, Pata Chitra, Modern Sculpture, Porcelain, Ivory, Wood, Terracotta, Textile, Manuscript, Books.
Services: Research, Guide Service, Occasional Temporary Exhibitions, Travelling Exhibition, Other Outreach Programme, Library, Film Shows.
Publications: Exhibit Catalogues.
Contact Person: Director.

44. Birla Industrial and Technological Museum

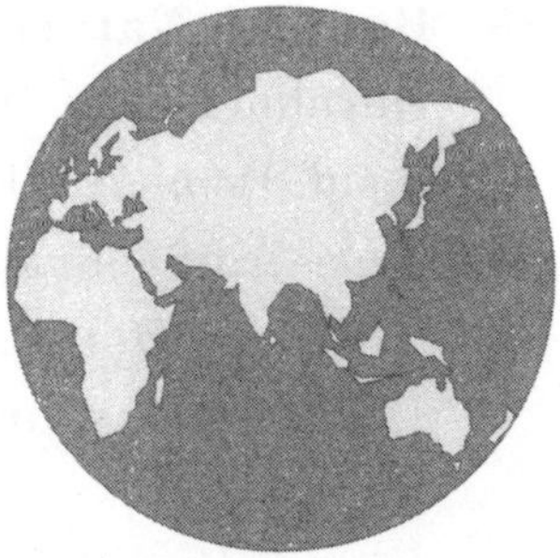

19A, Gurusaday Road, Calcutta 700 019.
Type: Autonomous Organisation.
Subordinate Unit of *National Council of Science Museums.*
Opening Hours: 10:00 to 17:30, Monday Closed.
Founded in: 1959.
Subjects: Industrial/Commercial, Children's, Science and Technology.
Collections: Working and Participatory Exhibits on Earth Science, Physical Science, Industrial Products and Processes, Scientific and Technological Artifacts, Coal Mine Objects, Children's Exhibits, Books, Films, Slides, Tapes.
Services: Research, Guide Service, Travelling Exhibition, Other Outreach Programme, Library, Film Shows, Television Shows.
Publications: Guide Book, Exhibit Catalogues, Books, Pamphlets, Brochures, Souvenirs, Folders, and Programme of Events, Annual Reports.
Contact Person: Director.

45. Birla Museum
Vidya Vihar, Pilani, Rajasthan 333 031.
Type: Autonomous Organisation.
Opening Hours: 09:00 to 17:00, Monday Closed.
Founded in: 1954.
Subjects: Science and Technology.
Collections: Physical Science, Technology, Industrial Products and Processes.
Services: Guide Service, Occasional Temporary Exhibitions, Library, Film Shows.
Publications: Slides, Exhibit Albums, Books.
Contact Person: Director.

46. Bombay Natural History Society

Hornbill House, Opp. Lion Gate, Shaheed Bhagat Singh Road, Bombay 400 023.

Type: Autonomous Organisation.

Opening Hours: 10:00 to 17:00, Sunday and Saturday Closed.

Founded in: 1883.

Subjects: Natural History.

Collections: Zoology, Birds, Mammals, Reptiles, Butterflies, and Insects.

Services: Research, Conservation, Occasional Temporary Exhibitions, Library, Film Shows.

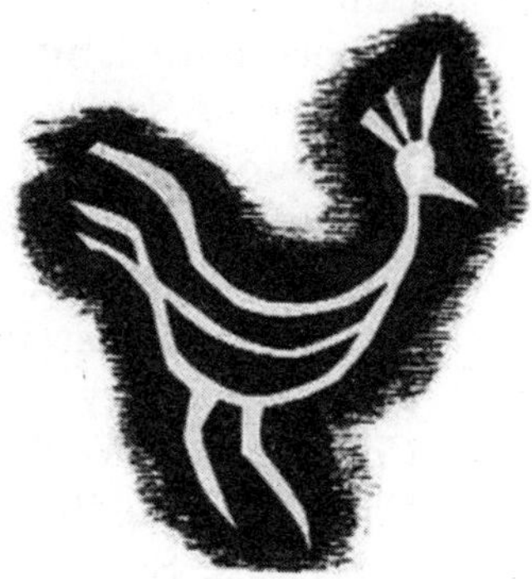

Publications: Mono-graphs, Books, Journals, Newsletter.

Contact Person: Curator.

47. Botanical Survey of India, Jodhpur

Arid Zone Circle, D-7 Shastri Nagar, Jodhpur 342003.

Type: Government.

Subordinate Unit of *Botanical Survey of India.*

Opening Hours: 09:00 to 17:30, Sunday and Saturday Closed.

Founded in: 1972.

Subjects: Tribal and Folk Art, Botanical Garden.

Collections: Wood, Botany, lndustrial Products and Processes.

Services: Research, Conservation, Library.

Publications: Monographs, Books, Journals, Newsletter.

Contact Person: Head / Scientist.

48. Burdwan Science Centre

Ramna Maidan, Baburbagh, P.O. Rajbati, Dist. Burdwan - 713104.

Type: Autonomous.

Subordinate Unit of *National Council of Science Museums.*

Opening Hours: 10.00 to 17.30, Monday closed.

Founded in: 1992.

Subjects: Children's and Popular Science.

Collections: Park exhibits and participatory type exhibits on popular science.

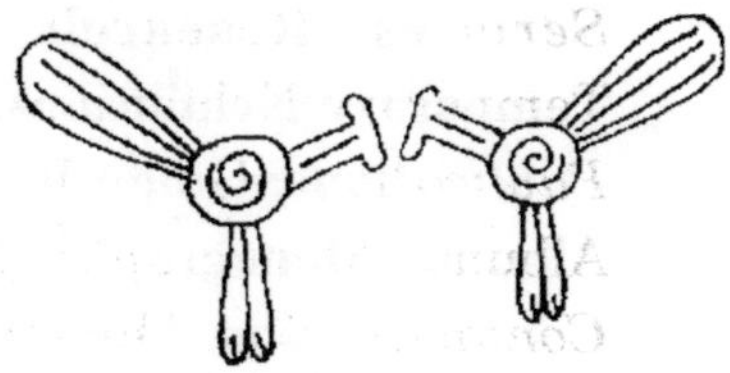

Services: Inflated dome planetarium, library, video shows, science demonstration, popular lectures, mobile exhibition and community programme.

Contact Person: Curator.

49. Carey Museum

Serampore College, P.O. Serampore, Dist. Hooghly, West Bengal 712 201.

Type: Autonomous Organisation.

Opening Hours: 10:00 to 17:00, Sunday Closed.

Founded in: 1800.

Subjects: Educational and Memorial.

Collections: Paintings, Manuscript, Books, Films/Slides/Tapes/Personal Belongings, Rocks and Minerals, Zoology.

Services: Research, Library.

Publications: Picture Postcards, Seminar Proceedings.

Contact Person: Head of the Organization.

50. Central Museum, Calcutta

Anthropological Survey of India, 2, Ripon Street, Calcutta 700 016.

Type: Government. of India.

Opening Hours: 10:30 to 17:30, Sunday and Saturday Closed.
Subjects: Art, Ethnography, Anthropology, Crafts, Tribal.
Collections: Toys, Figurines, Musical Instruments, Environment, Physical Science, Technology, Industrial Products and Processes.
Services: Research, Guide Service, Occasional Temporary Exhibitions, Film Shows.
Publications: Guide Book, Exhibit Catalogues, Exhibit Albums, Monographs, Newsletter.
Contact Person: Director General.

51. Central Museum, Nagpur
Nagpur, Maharashtra 44001.
Type: State Government.
Opening Hours: 10:00 to 17:00, Monday Closed.
Founded in: 1863.
Subjects: Archaeology, Art, Anthropology, Crafts, Tribal and Folk Art, Natural History.
Collections: Prehistory, Copper, Bronze and Iron Objects, Arms and Weapons, Paintings, Miniature Paintings, Porcelain, Ivory, Wood, Pottery, Terracotta, Textile, Manuscript, Books, Musical Instruments, Geological Specimens.

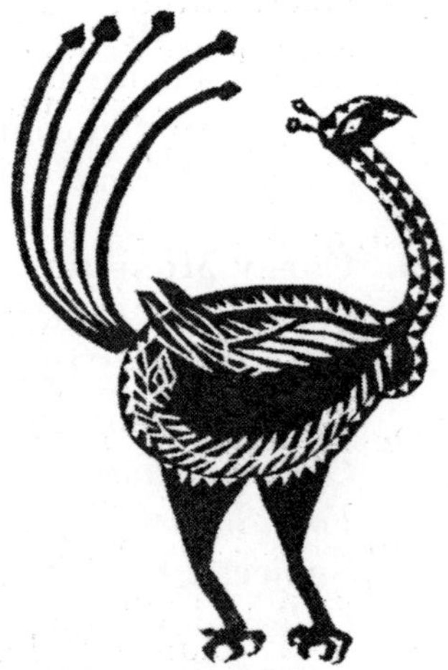

Services: Research, Conservation, Guide Service, Occasional Temporary Exhibitions, Library, Film Shows.
Publications: Picture Postcards.
Contact Person: Curator.

52. Central Research and Training Laboratory
Sector-V, Block-GN, Bidhan Nagar, Calcutta 700 091.
Type: Autonomous Organisation.
Subordinate Unit of National *Council of Science Museums.*
Founded in: 1988.
Subjects: Planetarium, Children's, Science and Technology.
Collections: Working and Animated Exhibits on Physical Science, Technology, Industry, Fun Science Exhibits and Outdoor Scientific Exhibits.
Services: Research, Library.
Contact Person: Director.

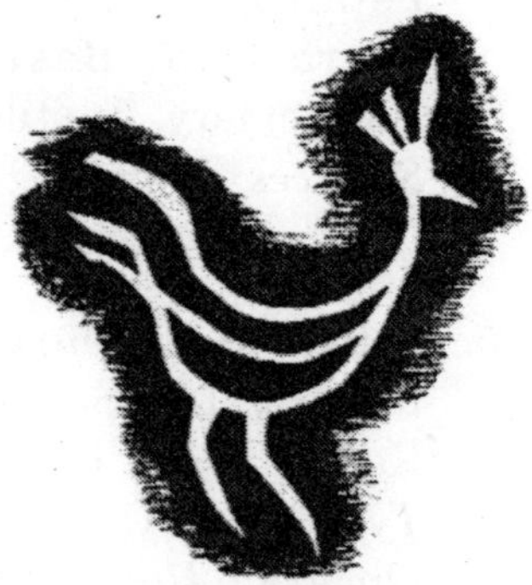

53. Commercial Museum
Arts and Commerce Building, Guwahati University, Guwahati, Assam 781014.
Type: University.
Opening Hours: 12:30 to 18:30, Sunday Closed.
Founded in: 1956.
Subjects: Art, Crafts, and Industrial/Commercial.
Collections: Brass, Ivory, Wood, Baskets, Leather-work, Embroidery, Costumes, Textile, Tapestry/Carpet, Personal Belongings, Dolls, Toys, Musical Instruments, Rocks and Minerals, Economic, Geology, Industrial Products and Processes, Cane and Bamboo, Forest Products, Horns.
Services: Occasional Temporary Exhibitions.
Publications: Guide Book.
Contact Person: Curator.

54. Crafts Museum, Art in Industry Museum
9-12, Old Court House Street, Calcutta 700 001.

Type: Government.
Opening Hours: 11:00 to 17:30, Sunday and Saturday Closed.
Founded in: 1947.
Subjects: Art, Crafts, Tribal and Folk Art.
Collections: Ancient Sculpture, Brass, Copper, Bronze and Iron Objects, Arms and Weapons, Paintings, Scrolls, Pata Chitra, Porcelain, Glass, Ivory, Wood, Pottery, Terracotta, Baskets, Leather Work, Jewellery, Embroidery, Textile, Musical Instruments.
Services: Library.
Contact Person: Deputy Director.

55. Cultural Research Institute
P-1/4, C.I.T. Scheme, VIP Road, Kankurgachi, Calcutta 700054.
Type: State Government.
Opening Hours: 10:30 to 17:30, Sunday and Saturday Closed.
Founded in: 1955.
Subjects: Ethnography, Anthropology, Crafts, Tribal and Folk Art.
Collections: Books, Figurines, Musical Instruments, Material and Cultural Artifacts of Tribal Community.
Services: Research, Conservation, Guide Service, Occasional Temporary Exhibitions.
Publications: Exhibit Catalogues, Exhibit Albums, and Monographs.
Contact Person: Director.

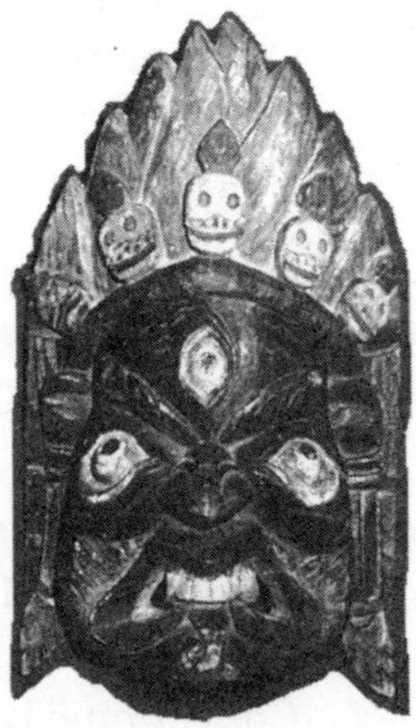

56. Darbar Hall Museum
Janta Chowk, Junagadh, Gujarat 362 001.
Type: State Government.
Opening Hours: 09:00 to 18:00, Wednesday Closed.
Founded in: 1947.

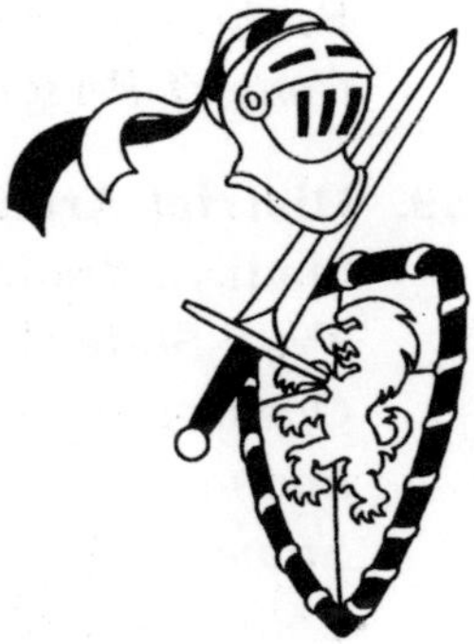

Subjects: Art, Personalia, Local History.
Collections: Personal Belongings, Royal Thrones, Chairs, Clocks, Oil Paintings, Photographs, Palanquins, Textiles, Arms and Weapons, Chandeliers.
Services: Research, Guide Service, Occasional Temporary Exhibitions, Other Outreach Programme, Library, Film Shows.
Publications: Guide Book, Exhibit Catalogues, Picture, Postcards, Monographs, Books.
Contact Person: Curator.

57. Department of Archaeology and Museums
Archaeological Site Museum, Dist. Mahabubnagar, Alampur 509 152.
Type: State Government.
Subordinate Unit of *Archaeology and Museums Dept.*, Govt. of Andhra Pradesh.
Opening Hours: 10:30 to 17:00, Friday Closed.
Founded in: 1952.
Subjects: Archaeology, Art.
Collections: Ancient Sculpture.
Services: Guide Service.
Publications: Monographs.
Contact Person: Guide Lecturer.

58. Department of Zoology, Madras Christian College
Tambaram, Madras 600 059.
Type: Autonomous Organisation.
Subordinate Unit of *Madras Christian College.*
Opening Hours: 08:00 to 17:00, Sunday Closed.
Founded in: 1889.
Subjects: Natural History, Aquarium.
Collections: Zoology.

Services: Occasional Temporary Exhibitions.
Contact Person: Professor.

59. District Archaeological Museum, Vidisha
Madhya Pradesh.
Type: State Government.
Opening Hours: 10:00 to 17:00, Monday Closed.
Founded in: 1964.
Subjects: Archaeology.
Collections: Prehistory, Ancient Sculpture, Copper, 5ronze and Iron Objects, Pottery, Terracotta.
Services: Research, Conservation, Guide Service, Occasional Temporary Exhibitions, Library.
Contact Person: Curator.

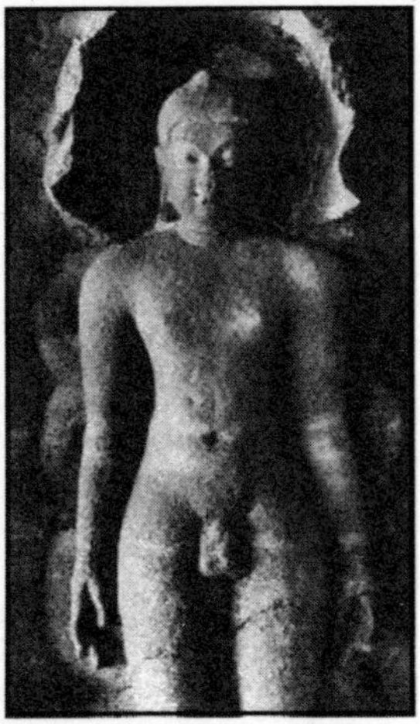

60. District Museum, Bomdila
DRO's Office, Bomdila, Dist. West Kameng, Arunachal Pradesh 790 001.
Type: State Government.
Founded in: 1956.
Subjects: Ethnography.
Collections: Brass, Copper, Bronze and Iron Objects, Arms and Weapons, Paintings, Miniature Paintings, Scrolls, Glass, Ivory, Wood, Pottery, Terracotta, Baskets, Leather work, Jewellery, Embroidery, Costumes, Textile, Tapestry/Carpet, Manuscript, Books, Films/ Slides/Tapes, Personal Belongings, Dolls, Toys, Musical Instruments.
Services: Research, Conservation, Guide Service, Travelling Exhibition, Film Shows.
Publications: Monographs, Journals, Seminar Proceedings, Newsletter.
Contact Person: DRO.

61. District Museum, Sangrur
Banasur Bagh, Sangrur, Punjab.
Type: State Government.
Subordinate Unit of *Dept. of Cultural Affairs and Museums,* Punjab.
Opening Hours: 10:00 to 17:00, Monday Closed.
Founded in: 1972.
Subjects: Art, Crafts, Tribal and Folk Art, Children's.
Collections: Brass, Copper, Bronze and Iron Objects, Arms and Weapons, Paintings, Porcelain, Glass, Ivory, Wood, Pottery, Terracotta, Jewellery, Embroidery, Costumes, Textile, Tapestry/Carpet.

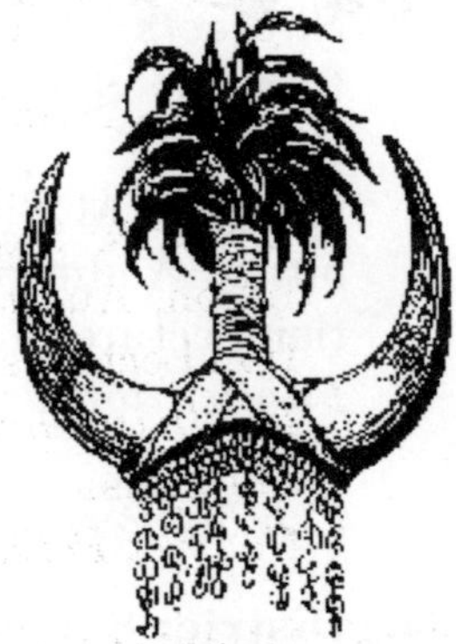

Services: Research, Conservation, Occasional Temporary Exhibitions.
Contact Person: (IAS) Director.

62. District Science Centre, Dharampur
Garden Road, Dist. Valsad, Dhararnpur, Gujarat 396 050.
Type: Autonomous Organisation.
Subordinate Unit of *National Council of Science Museums.*
Founded in: 1984.
Subjects: Children's, Science and Technology.
Collections: Working and Participatory Exhibits on Physical Science, Health, Hygiene and Agriculture, Books, Films, Slides, Tapes.
Services: Guide Service, Occasional Temporary Exhibitions, Other Outreach Programme, Library, Film Shows.
Publications: Pamphlet.
Contact Person: District Science Officer.

63. District Science Centre, Digha
Foreshore Road, Dist. Midnapore, New Digha-721428.
Type: Autonomous.
Subordinate Unite of *National Council of Science Museums.*
Subjects: Physical Science, Popular Science and Marine Biology.
Services: Mobile Science Exhibition, Auditorium, Demonstration Lectures for General Public.
Publications: Guide Book and Manuals.
Contact Person: Curator.

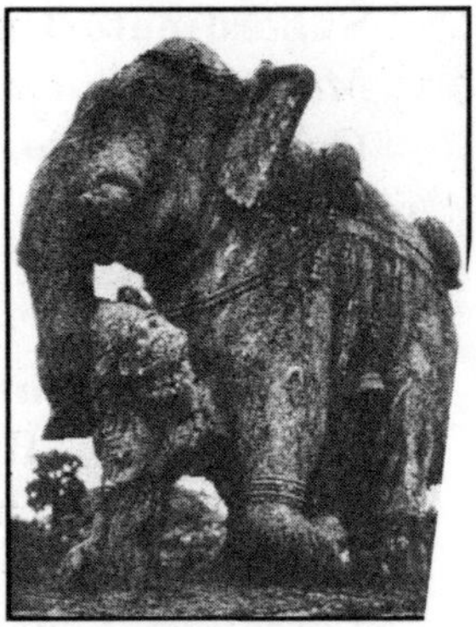

64. District Science Centre, Gulbarga
Municipal Garden, Gulbarga 585 103.
Type: Autonomous Organisation.
Subordinate Unit of *National Council of Science Museums.*
Opening Hours: 11:30 to 19:00, Monday Closed.
Founded in: 1984.
Subjects: Children's, Science and Technology.
Collections: Working and Participatory Exhibits on Agriculture, Physical Science, Energy and Industry.
Services: Guide Service, Occasional Temporary Exhibitions, Other Outreach Programme, Film Shows.
Publications: Pamphlet.
Contact Person: District Science Officer.

65. District Science Centre, Purulia
North Lake Road, Purulia, West Bengal 723 101.
Type: Autonomous Organisation.
Subordinate Unit of *National Council of Science Museums.*
Opening Hours: 11:00 to 18:30, Monday Closed.
Founded in: 1982.

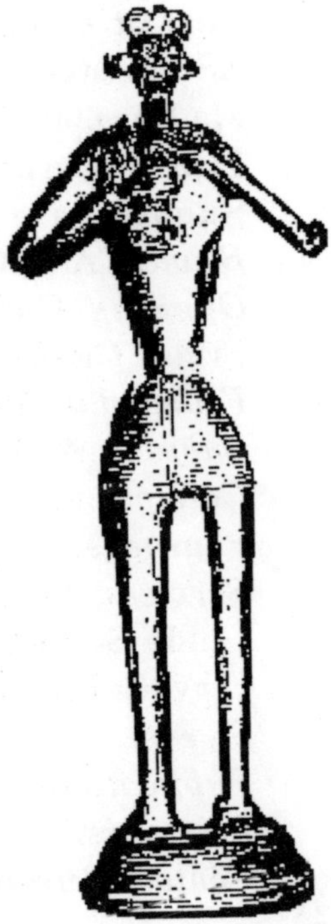

Subjects: Ethnography, Children's, Science and Technology.
Collections: Working and Participatory Exhibits on Industry, Agriculture, Environment and Physical Science, Economic Geology, Films/Slides/Tapes.
Services: Guide Service, Occasional Temporary Exhibitions, Other Outreach Programme, Library, Film Shows.
Publications: Guide Book.
Contact Person: District Science Officer.

66. District Science Centre, Tirunelveli
National Highway No. 7,
Kokkirakulain, Tirunelveli
627 009.
Type: Autonomous Organisation.
Subordinate Unit of *National Council of Science Museums.*
Opening Hours: 11:30 to 19:00, Monday Closed.
Founded in: 1987.
Subjects: Children's, Science and Technology.
Collections: Working and Participatory Exhibits on Ocean, Environment, Physical Science and Marine Aquarium, Books, Films, Slides, Tapes.
Services: Guide Service, Occasional Temporary Exhibitions, Travelling Exhibition, Other Outreach Programme, Library, Film Shows.
Publications: Pamphlet.
Contact Person: Education Officer.

67. Fort St. George Museum, Madras
ASI, Southern Region, Tamil Nadu, Madras 600 009.
Type: Government.
Subordinate Unit of *Museums Branch,* ASI, Calcutta.
Opening Hours: 10:00 to 17:00, Friday Closed.
Founded in: 1948.
Subjects: Archaeology.
Collections: Arms and Weapons, Paintings.
Services: Research, Conservation, Guide Service, Occasional Temporary Exhibitions, Library, Film Shows.
Publications: Guide Book, Picture Postcards.
Contact Person: Archaeologist.

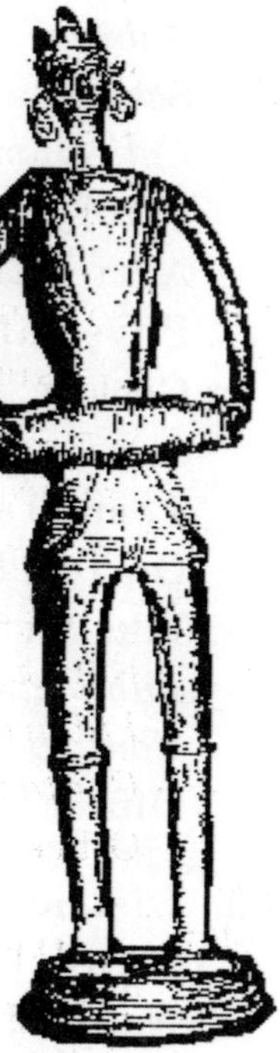

68. Gandhi Memorial Museum
Gandhi Museum Road, Madurai, Tamilnadu 625 020.
Type: Autonomous Organisation.
Opening Hours: 10:00 to 17:30.
Founded in: 1959.
Subjects: Crafts, Personalia.
Collections: Bronze and Iron Objects, Paintings, Ivory, Wood, Leather Work, Textile, Books, Films/Slides/Tapes, Personal Belongings, Photographs Relics of Mahatma Gandhi.
Services: Research, Guide Service, Occasional Temporary Exhibitions, Library, Film Shows, Educational Programmes.
Publications: Guide Book, Exhibit Catalogues, and Picture Postcards, Books, Seminar Proceedings.
Contact Person: Secretary.

69. Gandhi Smarak Sangrahalaya

Harijan Ashram, Ahmedabad, Gujarat 380 027.
Type: Public Trust.
Opening Hours: 08:30 to 18:30.
Founded in: 1952.
Subjects: Personalia.
Collections: Paintings, Manuscript, Books, Films/Slides/Tapes, Personal Belongings.

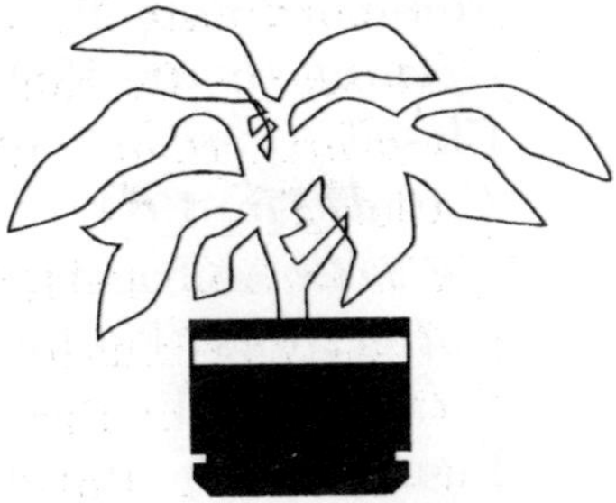

Services: Research, Library, Film Shows.
Publications: Exhibit Catalogues, Picture Postcards, and Books.
Contact Person: Director.

70. Gass Forest Museum

Institute of Forest, Genetics and Tree Breeding, Forest Campus, R.S. Puram, Coimbatore 641002.
Type: Government.
Subordinate Unit of *Institute of Forest, Genetics and Tree Breeding*.
Opening Hours: 09:00 to 17:30, Sunday and Saturday Closed.
Founded in: 1902.
Subjects: Forestry.
Collections: Arms and Weapons, Ivory, Wood, Jewellery, Rocks and Minerals, Zoology, Botany, Environment, Minor Forest Product, Forest Utilization, Mycology, Entomology, Precious and Ornamental Stones, Silviculture, Wildlife.
Services: Teaching in Forestry.
Publications: Guide Book, Monographs.
Contact Person: Head of the Institute.

71. Government Archaeological Museum

Sadbu Ashram, Hoshairpur, Punjab 146 021.

Type: State Government.
Subordinate Unit of *Dept. of Cultural Affairs and Museums,* Punjab.
Opening Hours: 10:00 to 17:00, Sunday and Saturday Closed.
Founded in: 1971.
Subjects: Archaeology, Art.
Collections: Prehistory, Ancient Sculpture, Pottery, Terracotta, Figurines, Photographs.
Services: Research, Guide Service.
Publications: Brochure.
Contact Person: (IAS), Director.

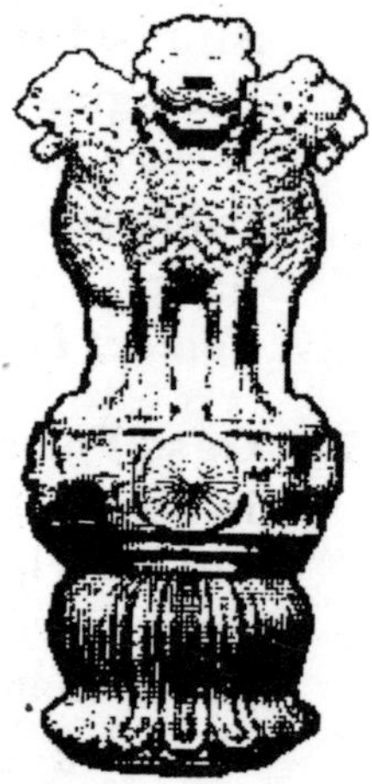

72. **Government Industrial and Commercial Museum**
45, Ganesh Chandra Avenue, Calcutta 700 013.
Type: State Government.
Opening Hours: 10:00 to 17:30, Sunday and Saturday Closed.
Founded in: 1939.
Subjects: Art, Crafts, Tribal and Folk Art.
Collections: Paintings, Miniature Paintings, Scrolls, Pata Chitra, Ivory, Wood, Terracotta, Baskets, Leatherwork, Textile, Dolls, Toys, Musical Instruments, Rocks and Minerals.
Services: Guide Service, Occasional Temporary Exhibitions, Library.
Contact Person: Officer-in-Charge.

73. **Government Museum, Madras**
Pantheon Road, Egmore, Madras 600008.
Type: State Government.
Opening Hours: 09:00 to 17:00, Friday Closed.
Founded in: 1851.

Subjects: Archaeology, Art, Ethnography, Anthropology, Crafts, Tribal and Folk Art, Industrial /Commercial, Natural History, Children's.

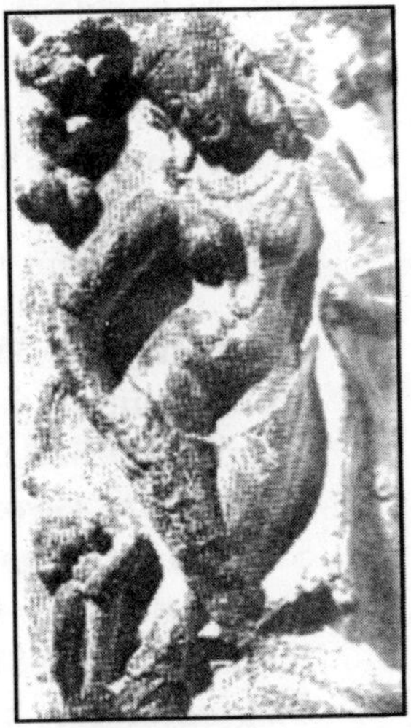

Collections: Prehistory, Ancient Sculpture, Brass, Copper, Bronze and Iron Objects, Arms and Weapons, Paintings, Miniature Paintings, Modern Sculpture, Porcelain, Glass, Ivory, Wood, Pottery, Terracotta, Baskets, Leatherwork, Jewellery, Embroidery, Costumes, Textile, Tapestry/Carpet, Manuscript, Books, Films/Slides/Tapes, Personal Belongings, Dolls, Toys, Figurines, Musical Instruments, Fossils, Rocks and Minerals, Economic Geology, Earth Science, Zoology, Botany, Physical Science, Industrial Products and Processes.

Services: Research, Conservation, Guide Service, Occasional Temporary Exhibitions, Library, Film Shows, Lectures.

Publications: Guide Book, Exhibit Catalogues, Picture Postcards, Slides, Exhibit Albums, and Monographs, Book, Journals, Newsletter.

Contact Person: Director.

74. Government Museum, Pudukkottai

Pudukkottai, Tamil Nadu 622 002.

Type: State Government.

Opening Hours: 09:00 to 17:00, Friday Closed.

Founded in: 1910.

Subjects: Archaeology, Art, Ethnography, Anthropology, Crafts, Natural History.

Collections: Prehistory, Ancient Sculpture Brass, Copper, Bronze and Iron Objects, Arms and Weapons, Paintings, Miniature Paintings, Ivory, Wood, Pottery,

Baskets, Jewellery, Embroidery, Textile, Manuscript, Books, Dolls, Toys, Musical Instruments, Fossils, Rocks and Minerals, Economic Geology, Zoology, Botany.
Services: Research, Conservation, Guide Service, Occasional Temporary Exhibitions, Other Outreach Programme, Library, Film Shows, Lectures.
Publications: Guide Book.
Contact Person: Curator.

75. Government Museum, Tiruchirapalli
19/2 Promenade Road, Cantonment, Tiruchirapalli, Tamilnadu 620 001.
Type: State Government.
Subordinate Unit of *Government. Museum,* Madras.
Opening Hours: 09:00 to 17:00, Friday Closed.
Founded in: 1982.
Subjects: Archaeology, Art, Ethnography, Anthropology, Crafts, Tribal and Folk Art, Industrial/Commercial, Natural History, Botanical Garden.
Collections: Prehistory, Ancient Sculpture, Brass, Bronze and Iron Objects, Arms and Weapons, Paintings, Modern Sculpture, Wood, Pottery, Terracotta, Costumes, Textile, Toys, Musical Instruments, Fossils, Rocks and Minerals, Zoology, Botany.

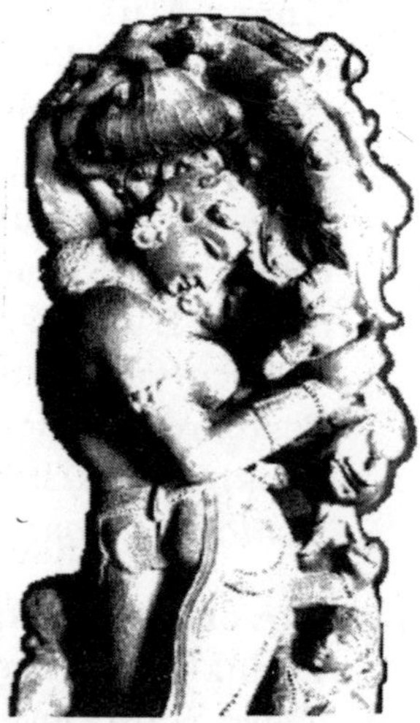

Services: Research, Guide Service, Library, Film Shows, and Lectures.
Contact Person: Curator.

76. Government Museum, Vellore
Lakshmanaswamy Town Hall, Vellore, Fort 632 004, Tamil Nadu.

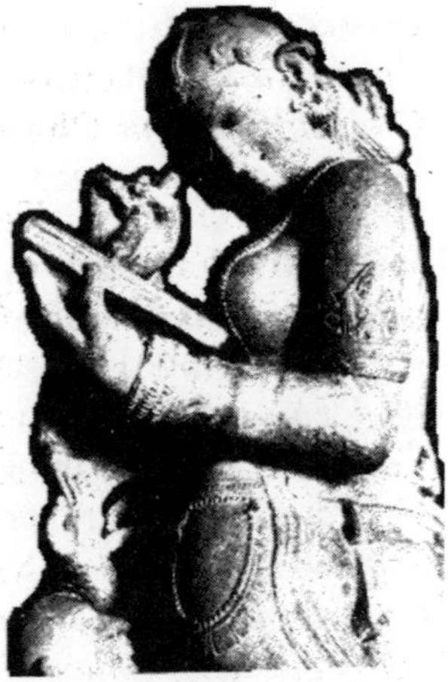

Type: State Government.
Opening Hours: 09:00 to 17:00, Friday Closed.
Founded in: 1985.
Subjects: Archaeology, Art, Ethnography, Anthropology, Crafts, Tribal and Folk Art, Natural History, Botanical Garden, Sculpture Garden.
Collections: Prehistory, Ancient Sculpture, Brass, Copper, Bronze and Iron Objects, Arms and Weapons, Paintings, Glass, Wood, Pottery, Terracotta, Baskets, Costumes, Manuscript, Books, Films/Slides/Tapes, Musical Instruments, Fossils, Rocks and Minerals, Economic Geology, Zoology, Botany, Environment.
Services: Research, Conservation, Guide Service, Occasional Temporary Exhibitions, Other Outreach Programme, Library, Film Shows, Seminars, Art Competitions, Lectures.
Contact Person: Curator.

77. Gurusaday Museum
Bratacharigram, P.O. Joka, Dist. 24 Parganas (South), West Bengal 743 512.
Type: Autonomous Organisation.
Opening Hours: 11:00 to 17:00, Monday Closed.
Founded in: 1963.
Subjects: Archaeology, Art, Ethnography, Anthropology, Crafts, Tribal and Folk Art.
Collections: Ancient Sculpture, Brass, Copper, Bronze and Iron Objects, Arms and Weapons, Paintings, Miniature Paintings, Scrolls, Pata Chitra, Wood, Pottery, Terracotta, Baskets, Embroidery, Textile, Manuscript, Books, Personal Belongings, Dolls, Toys, Figurines, Musical Instruments, Fossils.

Services: Research, Guide Service, Occasional Temporary Exhibitions, Library.
Publications: Picture Postcards, Folder.
Contact Person: Chairman.

78. Hall of Science, Technology and Energy

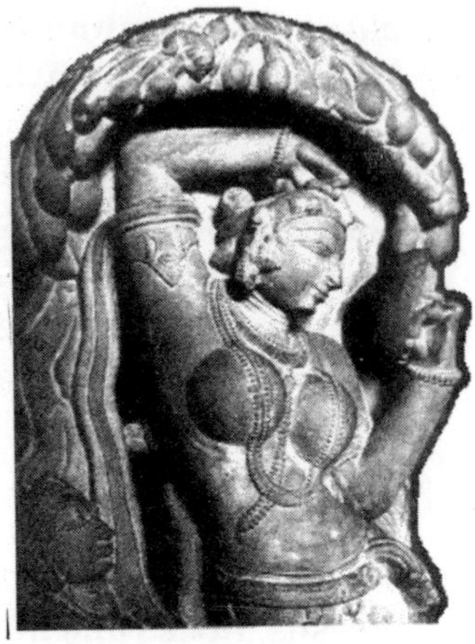

C/o National Science Centre, Pragati Maidan, Bhairon Road, New Delhi 110 001.
Type: Autonomous Organisation.
Subordinate Unit of *National Council of Science Museums.*
Subjects: Children's, Science and Technology.
Collections: Working Models and Exhibits on Physical Science, Energy and Industry.
Services: Guide Service, Occasional Temporary Exhibitions, Travelling Exhibition, Other Outreach Programme, Library, Film Shows.
Contact Person: Curator.

79. Hazarduari Palace Museum

ASI, P.O. Lalbagh, Dist. Murshidabad, West Bengal 742 149.
Type: Government.
Subordinate Unit of *Museums Branch,* ASI, Calcutta.
Opening Hours: 10:00 to17:00, Friday Closed.
Founded in: 1963.
Subjects: Archaeology.
Collections: Ancient Sculpture, Copper, Bronze and Iron Objects, Arms and Weapons, Paintings, Porcelain, Glass, Ivory, Musical Instruments.
Services: Research, Conservation, Guide Service, Occasional Temporary Exhibitions, Library, Film Shows.
Contact Person: Archaeologist.

80. Heras Institute of Indian History and Culture
St. Xavier's College, 5, Mahapalika Marg, Bombay 400 001.
Type: Unit of College.
Subordinate Unit of *St. Xavier's College.*
Opening Hours: 11:30 to 17:00, Sunday, Tuesday, Wednesday and Saturday Closed.
Founded in: 1922.
Subjects: Archaeology, Art.
Collections: Ancient Sculpture, Brass, Copper, Bronze and Iron Objects, Arms and Weapons, Paintings, Ivory, Wood, Pottery, Books.

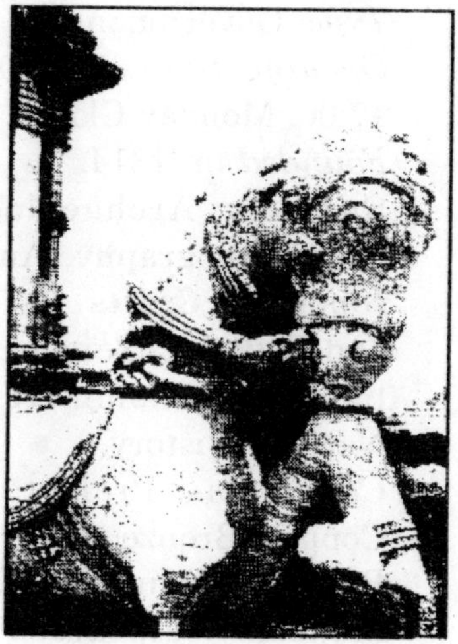

Services: Research, Occasional Temporary Exhibitions, Library.
Publications: Exhibit Catalogues, Picture Postcards, Books, Journals.
Contact Person: Director.

81. Himalayan Mountaineering Institute
Darjeeling, West Bengal 734 101.
Type: Autonomous Organisation.
Opening Hours: 09:30 to 17:00.
Founded in: 1954.
Subjects: Tribal and Folk AM Natural History, Mountaineering.
Collections: Brass, Bronze and Iron Objects, Paintings, Personal Belongings, Figurines, Rocks and Minerals, Botany, Environment.
Services: Film Shows.
Publications: Journals.
Contact Person: Head of the Institute.

82. Indian Museum

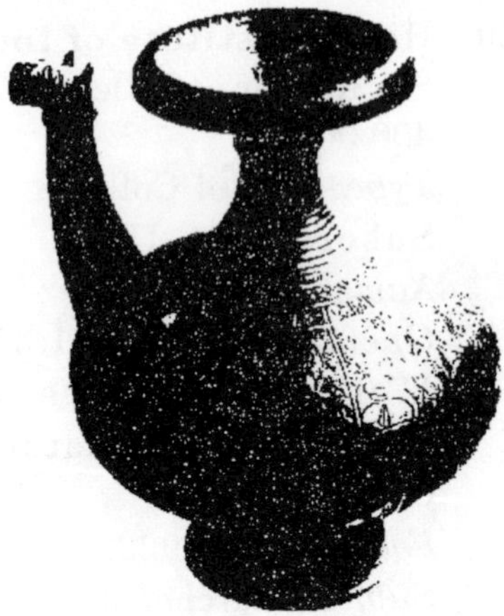

27, Jawaharlal Nehru Road, Calcutta 700 016.
Type: Government.
Opening Hours: 10:00 to 17:00, Monday Closed.
Founded in: 1814.
Subjects: Archaeology, Art, Ethnography, Anthropology, Crafts, Tribal and Folk Art, Personalia, Industrial /Commercial, Natural History.
Collections: Prehistory, Ancient Sculpture, Brass, Copper, Bronze and Iron Objects, Arms and Weapons, Paintings, Miniature Paintings, Scrolls, Pata Chitra, Modern Sculpture, Porcelain, Glass, Ivory, Wood, Pottery, Terracotta, Baskets, Leather Work, Jewellery, Embroidery, Costumes, Textile, Tapestry/Carpet, Manuscript, Books, Films/Slides/Tapes, Personal Belongings, Dolls, Toys, Musical Instruments, Fossils, Rocks and Minerals, Economic Geology, Zoology, Botany, Industrial Products and Processes.
Services: Research, Conservation, Guide Service, Occasional Temporary Exhibitions, Other Outreach Programme, Library, Film Shows.
Publications: Guide Book, Exhibit Catalogues, Picture Postcards, Slides, Exhibit Albums, Monographs, Books, Journals, Seminar Proceedings, Workshop Proceedings, Newsletter.
Contact Person: Director.

83. Indian War Memorial Museum, Red Fort

Archaeological Survey of India, Red Fort, Delhi 110 006.
Type: Government.
Subordinate Unit of *Museums Branch,* ASI, Calcutta.
Opening Hours: 10:00 to 17:00, Friday Closed.

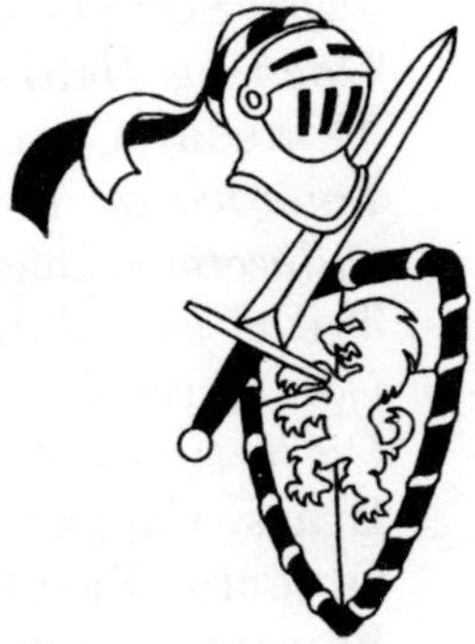

Founded in: 1982.
Subjects: Archaeology.
Collections: Arms and Weapons, Wood, Costumes, Textile.
Services: Research, Conservation, Guide Service, Occasional Temporary Exhibitions, Library, Film Shows.
Publications: Slides, Exhibit Albums, and Seminar Proceedings.
Contact Person: Archaeologist.

84. Indira Gandhi Rashtriya Manav Sangrahalaya
Shamla Hills, Bhopal 462 016.
Type: Autonomous Organisation.
Opening Hours: 10:00 to 17:00.
Founded in: 1977.
Subjects: Archaeology, Ethno-graphy, Anthropology, Crafts, Tribal and Folk Art, Children's.
Collections: Prehistory, Bronze and Iron Objects, Arms and Weapons, Pottery, Terracotta, Baskets, Leather Work, Costumes, Textile, Personal Belongings, Toys, Figurines, Musical Instruments, Fossils, Environment, Rock Art.
Services: Research, Conservation, Guide Service, Occasional Temporary Exhibitions, Travelling Exhibition, Other Outreach Programme, Library, Film Shows, Tribal Technology, Popular Lectures.
Publications: Guide Book, Exhibit Catalogues, and Picture Postcards, Slides, Books, Workshop Proceedings.
Contact Person: Director.

85. Institute De Chandernagor
The Residency, Strand Road, P.O. Chandernagor, Dist. Hooghly 712 136.

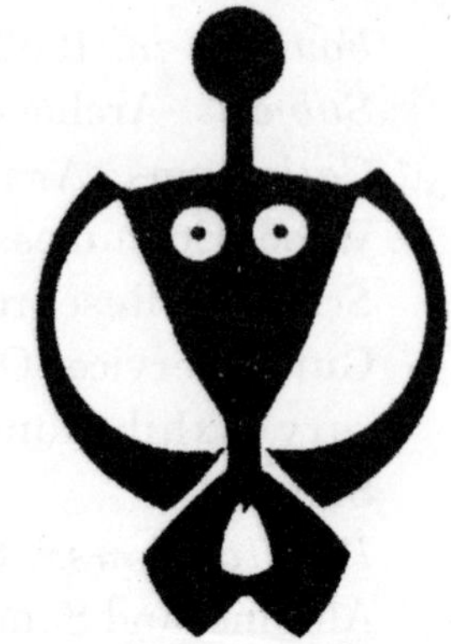

Type: State Government.
Opening Hours: 11:00 to 18:00, Thursday Closed.
Founded in: 1951.
Subjects: Archaeology, Art, Crafts, Tribal and Folk Art, Industrial/ Commercial.
Collections: Ancient Sculpture, Brass, Copper, Bronze and Iron Objects, Paintings, Miniature Paintings, Scrolls, Pata Chitra, Porcelain, Glass, Ivory, Wood, Pottery, Terracotta, Textile, Manuscript, Books, Dolls, Toys, Industrial Products and Processes, Coins.
Services: Research, Conservation, Guide Service, Occasional Temporary Exhibitions, Library, Film Shows.
Publications: Folder.
Contact Person: Director.

86. Jawahar Toy Museum
1, Rue D'Eveche, Pondicherry 605 001.
Type: State Government.
Opening Hours: 10:00 to 17:00, Monday Closed.
Founded in: 1987.
Subjects: Toys.
Collections: Dolls, Toys.
Services: Guide Service.
Contact Person: Curator.

87. Junagadh Museum
Sakkar Baug, Junagadh, Gujarat 362 001.
Type: State Government.
Opening Hours: 09:00 to 18:00, Wednesday Closed.
Founded in: 1901.
Subjects: Archaeology, Art, Crafts, Tribal and Folk Art, Natural History.
Collections: Prehistory, Ancient Sculpture, Copper, Bronze and Iron Objects, Paintings, Miniature

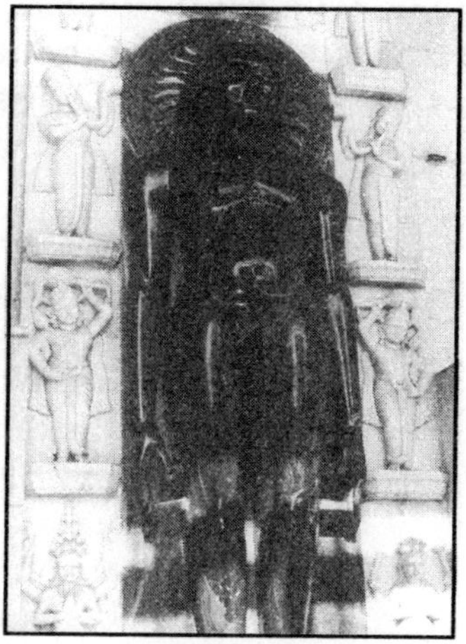

Paintings, Modern Sculpture, Porcelain, Glass, Ivory, Wood, Pottery, Terracotta, Jewellery, Embroidery, Costumes, Textile, Manuscript, Books, Zoology, Marble Work, Silver Art, Carpet, and Inscriptions.
Services: Research, Guide Service, Occasional Temporary Exhibitions, Other Outreach Programme, Library, Film Shows.
Publications: Guide Book, Exhibit Catalogues, and Picture Postcards.
Contact Person: Curator.

88. Kachchh Museum
Bhuj, Gujarat 370 001.
Type: State Government.
Opening Hours: 09:00 to 17:45, Sunday and Wednesday Closed.
Founded in: 1877.
Subjects: Archaeology, Art, Anthropology, Crafts, and Tribal and Folk Art, Personalia, Natural History.
Collections: Paintings, Books, Musical Instruments, Rocks and Minerals, Anthropological and Archaeological Minor Arts and Crafts, Shipping, Numismatics.
Services: Research, Conservation, Guide Service, Occasional Temporary Exhibitions, Travelling Exhibition, Library, Film Shows.
Publications: Guide Book, Picture Postcards, and Books.
Contact Person: Curator.

89. Lady Wilson Museum
Dharampur, Dist. Valsad, Gujarat 396 050.
Type: State Government.
Opening Hours: 10:15 to 17:30, Wednesday Closed.

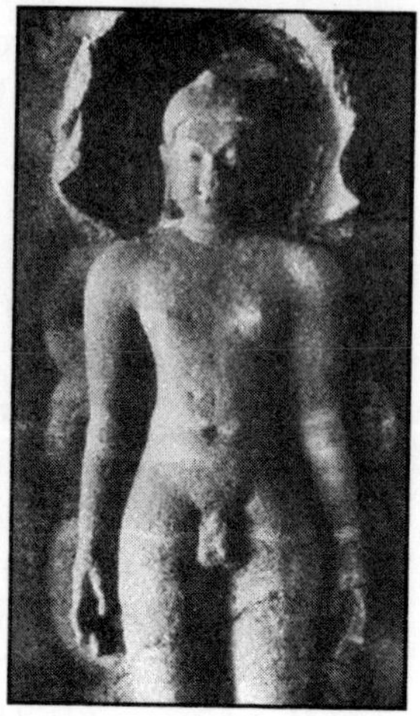

Founded in: 1928.
Subjects: Archaeology, Art, Anthropology, Crafts, Tribal and Folk Art, Natural History, Children's.
Collections: Prehistory, Ancient Sculpture, Arms and Weapons, Paintings, Miniature Paintings, Porcelain, Glass, Wood, Pottery, Terracotta, Baskets, Leatherwork, Jewellery, Embroidery, Costumes, Textile, Tapestry/Carpet, Manuscript, Books, Dolls, Toys, Musical Instruments, Rocks and Minerals, Economic Geology, Earth Science, Zoology, Botany.
Services: Research, Conservation, Occasional Temporary Exhibitions, Library, Film Shows.
Publications: Guide Book.
Contact Person: Curator.

90. Lala Lajpat Rai Museum cum Library
Tagroan, Dist. Ludhiana, Punjab.
Type: State Government.
Subordinate Unit of *Dept. of Cultural Affairs and Museums,* Punjab.
Opening Hours: 10:00 to 17:00, Monday Closed.
Founded in: 1989.
Subjects: Personalia.
Collections: Books, Personal Belongings.
Services: Research, Library.
Contact Person: Director.

91. Lalbhai Dalpatbhai Museum
Near Gujarat University, Ahmedabad, Gujarat 380 009.
Type: Trust.
Subordinate Unit of *L. D. Institute of Indology.*
Opening Hours: 10:30 to 17:30, Monday Closed.
Founded in: 1984.

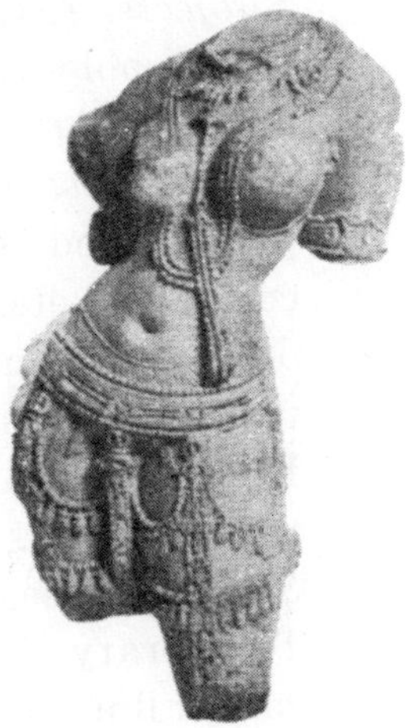

Subjects: Archaeology, Art.
Collections: Prehistory, Ancient Sculpture, Brass, Copper, Bronze and Iron Objects, Paintings, Miniature Paintings, Scrolls, Pata Chitra, Ivory, Wood, Terracotta, Manuscript, Books.
Services: Research, Conservation, Guide Service, Occasional Temporary Exhibitions, Other Outreach Programme, Library, Film Shows, Lectures.
Publications: Picture Postcards, Slides, Books, and Journals.
Contact Person: Director.

92. Local Antiquities Museum, Chitradurga
Chitradurga, Karnataka 577 501.
Type: State Government.
Opening Hours: 09:00 to 17:00, Monday Closed.
Founded in: 1952.
Subjects: Archaeology, Art.
Collections: Prehistory, Ancient Sculpture, Brass, Copper, Bronze and Iron Objects, Arms and Weapons, Paintings, Modern Sculpture, Glass, Ivory, Pottery, Terracotta, Manuscript.
Services: Library, Film Shows.
Publications: Guide Book, Exhibit Catalogues.
Contact Person: Curator.

93. M.P. State Tribal Museum
Circular Road, Chhindwara, Madhya Pradesh 480 001.
Type: State Government.
Subordinate Unit of *Dept. of Tribal, Harijan and Backward Classes.*
Opening Hours: 10:30 to 17:30, Sunday Closed.
Founded in: 1954.

Subjects: Art, Ethnography, Anthropology, Crafts, Tribal and Folk Art.

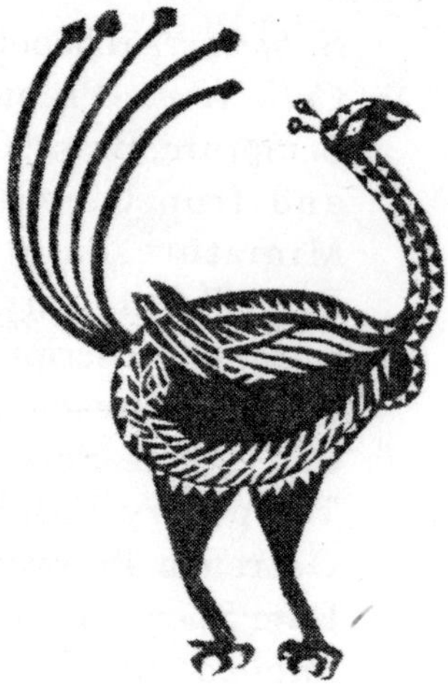

Collections: Arms and Weapons, Wood, Pottery, Terracotta, Baskets, Leather Work, Jewellery, Embroidery, Costumes, Films/Slides/Tapes, Figurines, Musical Instruments, Fossils.

Services: Research, Occasional Temporary Exhibitions, Library, Film Shows.

Publications: Monographs.

Contact Person: Director.

94. Magan Sangraralaya Samiti

Dr. J.C. Kumarappa Road, Maganwadi, Wardha 442 201.

Type: Autonomous Organisa-tion.

Opening Hours: 08:30 to 17:50, Sunday Closed.

Founded in: 1938.

Subjects: Crafts, Personalia, Industrial/Commercial, Aqua-rium, Children's, Awareness of Science.

Collections: Brass, Copper, Ivory, Wood, Pottery, Terracotta, Baskets, LeatherWork, Costumes, Textile, Tapestry/Carpet, Dolls, Toys, Fossils, Technology, Industrial Products and Processes.

Services: Research, Occasional Temporary Exhibitions, Travelling Exhibition, Library, Film Shows, Seminars and Conference.

Publications: Slides, Journals.

Contact Person: Chairman.

95. Maharaja Fatesingh Museum

Laxmi Vilas Palace Compound, Jawaharlal Nehru Marg, Baroda 390 001.

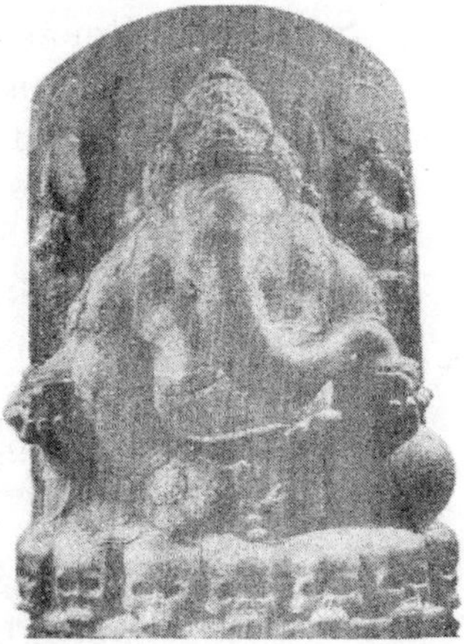

Type: Public Trust.
Subordinate Unit of *Board of Trustees,* Fatesingh Museum.
Opening Hours: 09:00 to 18:30, Monday Closed.
Founded in: 1961.
Subjects: Archaeology, Art, Ethnography, Anthropology, Crafts, Tribal and Folk Art.
Collections: Ancient Sculpture, Bronze and Iron Objects, Arms and Weapons, Paintings, Modern Sculpture, Porcelain, Glass, Ivory, Pottery, Embroidery.
Services: Guide Service.
Publications: Exhibit Catalogues.
Contact Person: Managing Trustee.

96. Maharaja Museum and Picture Gallery
16, Manidip Society, Jivraj Park, Ahmedabad 380051.
Type: State Government.
Opening Hours: 10:00 to 17:00, Monday Closed.
Founded in: 1894.
Subjects: Archaeology, Ethnography, Anthropology, Crafts, Tribal and Folk Art, Personalia, Industrial/Commercial, Natural History, Children's, Science and Technology.
Collections: Prehistory, Ancient Sculpture, Brass, Copper, Bronze and Iron Objects, Arms and Weapons, Paintings, Miniature Paintings, Scrolls, Pata Chitra, Porcelain, Glass, Ivory, Wood, Pottery, Terracotta, Leather Work, Jewellery, Embroidery, Costumes, Textile, Tapestry/Carpet, Manuscript, Books, Film/Slides/Tapes, Personal Belongings, Musical Instruments, Fossils, Rocks and Minerals, Economic Geology, Zoology, Botany.

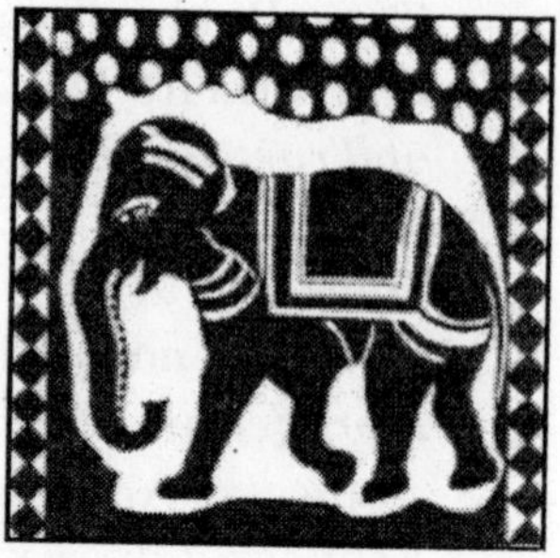

Services: Research, Guide Service, Occasional Temporary Exhibitions, and Travelling Exhibition, Other Outreach Programme, Film Shows.
Publications: Guide Book, Exhibit Catalogues, Picture Postcards, Slides, Exhibit Albums, Monographs.
Contact Person: Head.

97. **Maharaja Ranjit Singh Museum**
Amritsar, Ranibagh, Punjab 143001.
Type: State Government.
Subordinate Unit of *Dept. of Cultural Affairs Arch. and Museums*
Opening Hours: 10:00 to 17:00, Monday Closed.
Founded in: 1977.
Subjects: Art, Personalia.
Collections: Arms and Weapons, Paintings, Miniature Paintings, Manuscript.
Services: Research, Guide Service.
Contact Person: Director.

98. **Marbel Palace Art Gallery and Zoo Garden**
46, Muktaram Babu Street, Calcutta 700 007.
Type: Autonomous Organisation.
Opening Hours: 10:00 to 16:00, Monday and Thursday Closed.
Founded in: 1835.
Subjects: Art.
Collections: Bronze and Iron Objects, Paintings, Modern Sculpture, Embroidery, Musical Instruments.
Services: Research.
Contact Person: Head of the Organization.

99. **Mattancherry Palace Museum, Cochin**
Archaeological Survey of India, Cochin, Kerala 682 002.

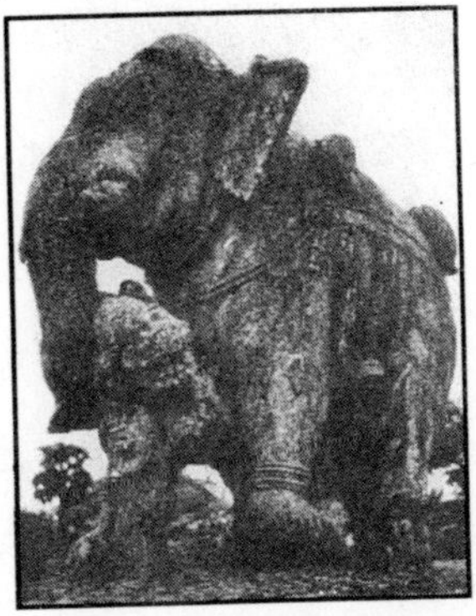

Type: Government.
Subordinate Unit of *Museums Branch,* ASI, Calcutta.
Opening Hours: 10:00 to 17:00, Sunday and Friday Closed.
Founded in: 1912.
Subjects: Archaeology.
Collections: Arms and Weapons, Paintings, Glass, Ivory, Wood, Embroidery, Costumes, Textile.
Services: Conservation, Guide Service, Occasional Temporary Exhibitions, Library, Film Shows.
Publications: Picture Postcards.
Contact Person: Archaeologist.

100. Municipal Museum, Gwalior
Motimahal Campus, Gwalior 474 007.
Type: Municipality.
Opening Hours: 10:30 to 16:30, Monday Closed.
Founded in: 1922
Subjects: Archaeology, Art, Anthropology, Crafts, Tribal and Folk Art, Natural History, Armory, Coins, Textile.
Collections: Prehistory, Ancient Sculpture, Brass, Copper, Bronze and Iron Objects, Arms and Weapons, Paintings, Miniature Paintings, Modern Sculpture, Porcelain, Glass, Ivory, Wood, Costumes, Textile, Tapestry/Carpet, Manuscript, Personal Belongings, Musical Instruments, Fossils, Rocks and Minerals.

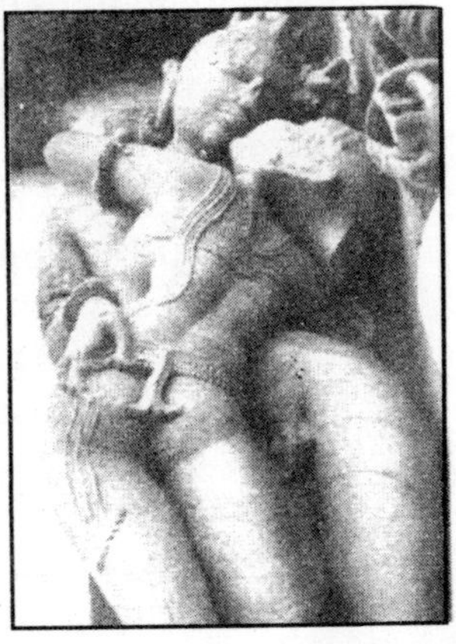

Services: Research, Guide Service, Occasional Temporary Exhibitions, Library, Film Shows.
Publications: Exhibit Catalogues, Monographs, Journals.
Contact Person: Head of the Institute.

101. **Museum of Art and Archaeology, University of Mysore**
Manasa Gangotri, Mysore, Karnataka 570 006.
Type: University.
Opening Hours: 10:30 to 17:00, Sunday Closed.
Founded in: 1973.
Subjects: Archaeology, Art, Anthropology.
Collections: Prehistory, Ancient Sculpture, Brass, Copper, Bronze and Iron Objects, Arms and Weapons, Paintings, Miniature Paintings, Pata Chitra, Ivory, Wood, Pottery, Terracotta, Jewellery, Manuscript, Films/Slides/Tapes, Musical Instruments, Fossils.
Services: Research, Conservation, Guide Service, Occasional Temporary Exhibitions, Library, Film Shows.
Publications: Guide Book, Slides, Books, Journals, and Seminar Proceedings.
Contact Person: Chairman.

102. **Museums and Zoos Department**
Museums and Zoos, Thiruvananthapuram 695 033.
Type: State Government.
Opening Hours: 13:00 to 17:00, Monday Closed.
Subjects: Archaeology, Art, Ethnography, Anthropology, Crafts, Tribal and Folk Art, Natural History, Botanical Garden, Zoo Garden, Art Gallery.
Collections: Ancient Sculpture, Brass, Copper, Bronze and Iron Objects, Arms and Weapons, Paintings, Miniature Paintings, Modern Sculpture, Porcelain, Glass, Ivory, Wood, Pottery, Jewellery, Costumes, Manuscript, Books, Films/Slides/Tapes, Personal Belongings, Dolls, Fossils, Rocks and Minerals, Zoology, Botany, Industrial Products and Processes.

Services: Conservation, Guide Service, Occasional Temporary Exhibitions, Library, Film Shows.
Publications: Guide Book, Monographs.
Contact Person: Director.

103. Naradah Museum, Nawadah
Post Nawadah, Dist. Nawadah, Bihar 805 110.
Type: State Government.
Opening Hours: 10:30 to 16:30, Monday Closed.
Founded in: 1973.
Subjects: Archaeology, Art, Crafts, Tribal and Folk Art, Natural History, Aquarium, Children's, Zoo Garden.
Collections: Ancient Sculpture, Brass, Copper, Bronze and Iron Objects, Arms and Weapons, Paintings, Modern Sculpture, Porcelain, Wood, Pottery, Terracotta, Embroidery, Textile, Manuscript, Coins, and Natural History.
Services: Research, Conservation, Guide Service, Occasional Temporary Exhibitions, Library, Film Shows, Children's Competition.
Publications: Books, Journals, Seminar Proceedings.
Contact Person: Curator.

104. National Centre for the Performing Arts
Dorabji Tata Road, Nariman Point, Bombay 400 021.
Type: Public Trust.
Opening Hours: 11:00 to 19:00, Sunday Closed.
Founded in: 1966.
Subjects: Art, Tribal and Folk Art.
Collections: Ancient Sculpture, Paintings, Miniature Paintings, Modern Sculpture, Porcelain, Books, Films/Slides/Tapes, Musical Instruments.

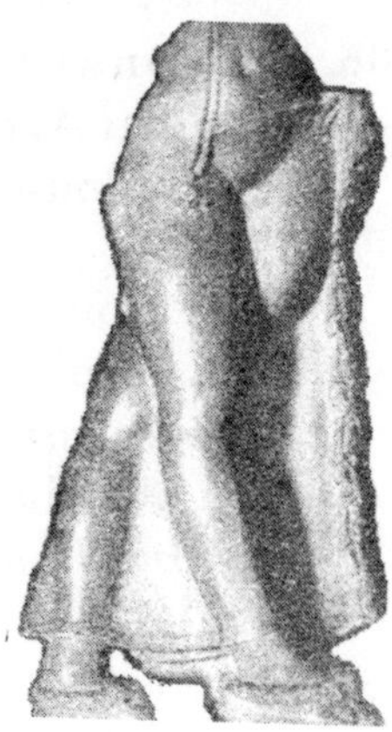

Services: Research, Conservation, Occasional Temporary Exhibitions, Travelling Exhibition, Library, Film Shows.
Publications: Exhibit Catalogues, Slides.
Contact Person: Chairman.

105. National Council of Science Museums
Sector V, Block GN, Bidhan Nagar, Calcutta 700 091.
Type: Autonomous Organisation.
Founded in: 1978.
Subjects: Children's, Science and Technology.
Collections: Working and Participatory Exhibits on Physical Science, Environment, Earth Science, Geology, Health, Energy, Outdoor Science Exhibits, Fun Science Exhibits, Scientific Artifacts, Cultural Heritage, Books, Films, Slides, Tapes.
Services: Research, Occasional Temporary Exhibitions, Travelling Exhibition, Other Outreach Programme, Library, Educational Kits, School Science Centres, Inflatable. Planetarium, Training Programme, Workshop, Seminars.
Publications: Guide Book, Exhibit Catalogues, Exhibit Albums, Books, Journals, Seminar Proceedings, and Newsletter.
Contact Person: Director General.

106. National Gallery of Modern Art
Jaipur House, New Delhi 110003.
Type: Government.
Subordinate Unit of *Department of Culture,* Govt.of India.
Opening Hours: 10:00 to 17:00.
Founded in: 1954.

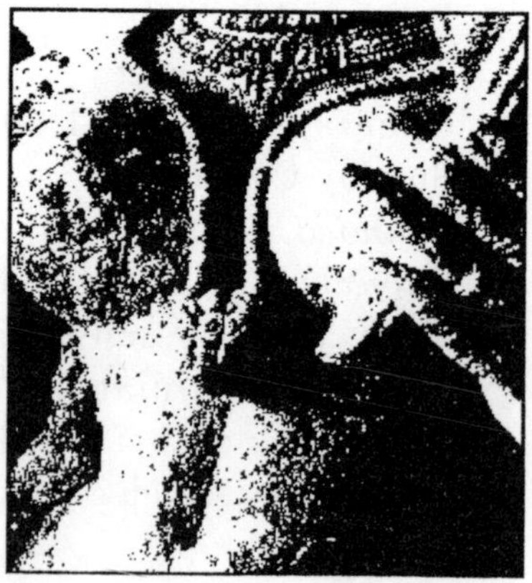

Subjects: Art, Paintings.
Collections: Paintings, Modern Painting, Sculpture and Graphics.
Services: Research, Conservation, Guide Service, Occasional Temporary Exhibitions, Travelling Exhibition, Library, Film Shows, Training.
Publications: Guide Book, Exhibit Catalogues, Picture Postcards, Slides, Monographs.
Contact Person: Director.

107. National Gandhi Museum
Rajghat, New Delhi 110 002.
Type: Private
Opening Hours: 09:30 to 17:30, Monday Closed.
Founded in: 1951.
Subjects: Personalia.
Collections: Personal Belongings, Photographs, Documents, Books, and Manuscripts.
Services: Research, Occasional Temporary Exhibitions, Travelling Exhibition, Library, Film Shows, Seminars.
Publications: Guide Book, Picture Postcards.
Contact Person: Director.

108. National Handicrafts and Handlooms Museum
Pragati Maidan, Bhairon Road, New Delhi 110 001.
Type: Government.
Subordinate Unit of *Ministry of Textiles,* Govt. of India.
Opening Hours: 10:00 to 18:00.
Founded in: 1956.
Subjects: Art, Ethnography, Anthropology, Crafts, Tribal and Folk Art, Traditional Crafts.
Collections: Ancient Sculpture, Brass, Copper, Bronze and Iron Objects, Paintings, Miniature Paintings,

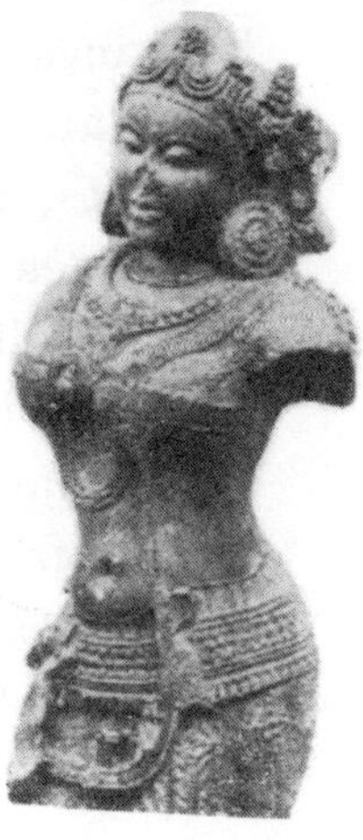

Scrolls, Pata Chitra, Glass, Ivory, Wood, Pottery, Terracotta, Baskets, Leather Work, Jewellery, Embroidery, Costumes, Textile, Tapestry/Carpet, Manuscript, Books, Films/Slides/Tapes, Dolls, Toys, Figurines, and Musical Instruments.

Services: Research, Conservation, Guide Service, Occasional Temporary Exhibitions, Other Outreach Programme, Library, Film Shows, Non-formal Education through Crafts.

Publications: Exhibit Catalogues, Picture Postcards, Monographs, Books.

Contact Person: Director.

109. National Museum

Janpath, New Delhi 110 011.

Type: Government.

Opening Hours: 10:00 to 17:00, Monday Closed.

Founded in: 1949.

Subjects: Archaeology, Art, Ethnography, Anthropology, Crafts, Tribal and Folk Art, Personalia.

Collections: Prehistory, Ancient Sculpture, Brass, Copper, Bronze and Iron Objects, Arms and Weapons, Paintings, Miniature Paintings, Scrolls, Pata Chitra, Porcelain, Glass, Ivory, Wood, Pottery, Terracotta, Baskets, Leather Work, Jewellery, Embroidery, Costumes, Textile, Tapestry/Carpet, Manuscript, Books, Dolls, Musical Instruments.

Services: Research, Conservation, Guide Service, Occasional Temporary Exhibitions, Travelling Exhibition, Library, Film Shows.

Publications: Guide Book, Exhibit Catalogues, Picture Postcards, Slides, and Monographs.

Contact Person: Director General.

110. National Museum of Natural History
FICCI Building, Barakhamba Road, New Delhi 110 001.
Type: Government.
Subordinate Unit of *Ministry of Environment and Forest.*
Opening Hours: 10:00 to 17:00, Monday Closed.
Founded in: 1978.
Subjects: Natural History, Ecology, Conservation, Biodiversity Human Biology.

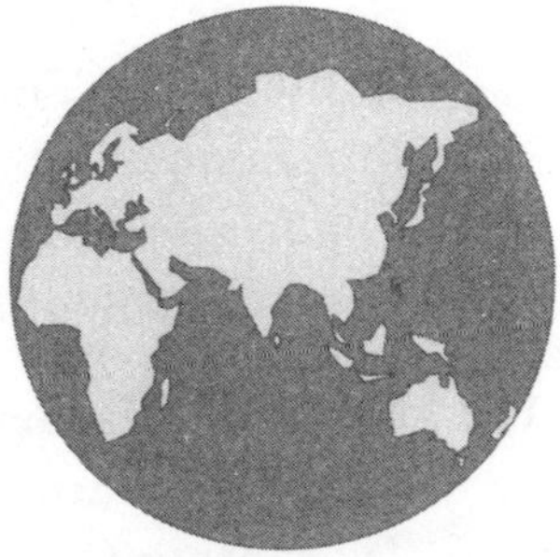

Collections: Books, Films/Slides/Tapes, Fossils, Rocks and Minerals, Economic Geology, Earth Science, Zoology, Botany, Environment, Natural History, Photographs.
Services: Research, Conservation, Guide Service, Occasional Temporary Exhibitions, Travelling Exhibition, Other Outreach Programme, Library, Film Shows, School Loan Service, Discovery Room, and Activity Room.
Publications: Guide Book, Exhibit Catalogues, Monographs, Books, Seminar Proceedings, Newsletter, Workbooks, Take-home Labels.
Contact Person: Director.

111. National Science Centre
Pragati Maidan, Near Gate No. 1, Bhairon Road, New Delhi 110 001.
Type: Autonomous Organisa-tion.
Subordinate Unit of *National Council of Science Museums.*
Founded in: 1992.
Subjects: Children's, Science and Technology.
Collections: Working and Participatory Exhibits on the History of Indian

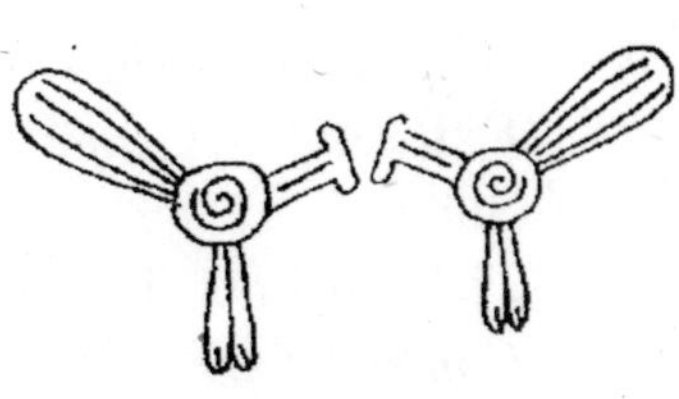

Science, Technology and Culture, Exhibits on Fun Science, Books, Films, Slides, Tapes.
Services: Guide Service, Occasional Temporary Exhibitions, Travelling Exhibition, Other Outreach Programme, Library, Film Shows.
Publications: Guide Book, Exhibit Catalogues. Slides.
Contact Person: Director.

112. Natural History Museum
Zoological Garden, Stadium Road, Punjab.
Type: State Government.
Subordinate Unit of *Education Department,* Govt. of Punjab.
Opening Hours: 07:00 to 19:00.
Subjects: Natural History.
Collections: Natural History Objects.
Services: Guide service.
Contact Person: Head of the Organization.

113. Nehru Children's Museum
94/1 Chowringhee Road, Calcutta 700 020.
Type: Autonomous Organisation.
Subordinate Unit of *National Cultural Organisation.*
Opening Hours: 11:00 to 19:00, Monday Closed.
Founded in: 1972.
Subjects: Children's, Science and Technology, Dolls and Toys, Miniature Models, Aquarium, Crafts.
Collections: Films/Slides/Tapes, Dolls, Toys, Figurines, Paintings, Miniature Paintings, Environment, Physical Science, Technology.
Services: Guide Service, Occasional Temporary Exhibitions, Other Outreach Programme, Library, Film Shows.
Publications: Pamphlets.
Contact Person: Director.

114. Nehru Memorial Museum and Library
Teen Murti House, New Delhi 110011.
Type: Autonomous Organisation.
Opening Hours: 09:30 to 17:00, Monday Closed.
Founded in: 1964.
Subjects: Personalia.

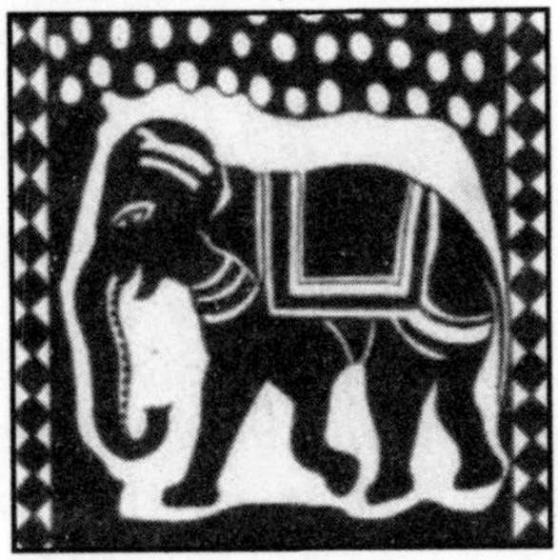

Collections: Paintings, Miniature Paintings, Scrolls, Modern Sculpture, Porcelain, Glass, Ivory, Wood, Textile, Tapestry/Carpet, Manuscript, Books, Films./Slides/Tapes, Personal Belongings, Photographs, Documents, Presented Materials to Jawaharlal Nehru.
Services: Research, Guide Service, Occasional Temporary Exhibitions.
Publications: Guide Book, Picture Postcards.
Contact Person: Director.

115. Nehru Planetarium
Teen Murti Bhavan, New Delhi 110 011.
Type: Autonomous Organisation.
Opening Hours: 10:00 to 16:45, Monday Closed.
Founded in: 1984.
Subjects: Planetarium, Space Science.
Collections: Films/Slides/Tapes, Books, Prints, Planetarium Projectors.
Services: Occasional Temporary Exhibitions, Library, Film Shows, Planetarium Programmes.
Publications: Slides, Newsletter.
Contact Person: Director.

116. Nehru Science Centre, Bombay
Dr E Moses Road, Worli, Bombay 400 018.
Type: Autonomous Organisa-tion.
Subordinate Unit of *National Council of Science Museums.*

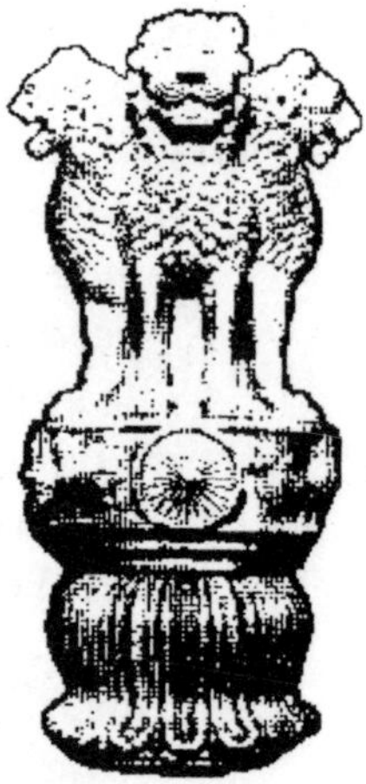

Opening Hours: 11:30 to 19:00, Monday Closed.
Founded in: 1985.
Subjects: Children's, Science and Technology.
Collections: Working and Participatory Exhibits on Physical Science, Scientific and Technological Artifacts, Open-air Science Exhibits, Children's Exhibits, Vintage Car, Books, Films, Slides, Tapes.
Services: Research, Guide Service, Occasional Temporary Exhibitions, and Travelling Exhibition, Other Outreach Progra-mme, Library, Film Shows.
Publications: Guide Book, Exhibit Catalogues, Slides, Seminar Proceedings, Workshop Proceedings, Pamphlets, Folders.
Contact Person: Director.

117. Nehru Science Centre, Pondicherry
52, Sardar Vallabbhai Patel Salai, Pondicherry 605 0101.
Type: Government.
Opening Hours: 10:00 to 17:00, Monday Closed.
Founded in: 1988.
Subjects: Science and Technology, Physical Science, Technology.
Services: Guide Service, Occasional Temporary Exhibitions.
Publications: Books.
Contact Person: Curator.

118. Netaji Museum-Netaji Research Bureau
38/2, Lala Lajpat Rai Sarani, Calcutta 700 020.
Type: Trust.
Opening Hours: 10:00 to 17:00, Monday Closed.
Founded in: 1957.
Subjects: Personalia.

Collections: Costumes, Books, Letters, Photographs, Documents.
Services: Research, Film Shows.
Publications: Books, Journals, Seminar Proceedings.
Contact Person: Director.

119. Patna Museum

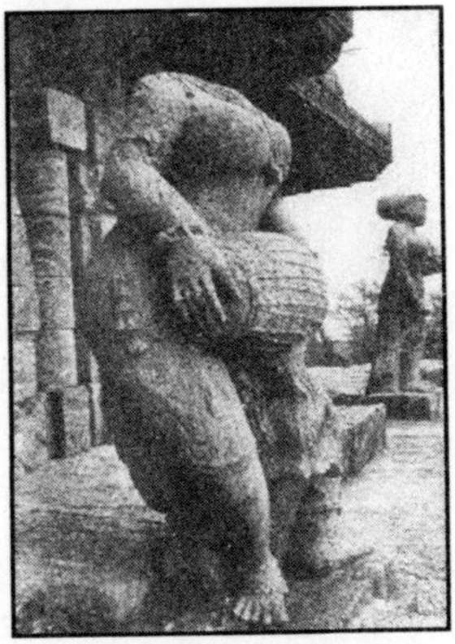

Buddha Marg, Patna, Bihar 800 001.
Type: Government.
Subordinate Unit of *Directorate of Museums,* Govt. of Bihar.
Opening Hours: 10:30 to 16:30, Monday Closed.
Founded in: 1917.
Subjects: Archaeology, Art, Ethnography, and Natural History.
Collections: Ancient Sculpture, Bronze and Iron Objects, Arms and Weapons, Paintings, Terracotta, Fossils, War Trophies, Antiquities, Coins, East Asian Art Objects.
Services: Research, Conservation, Guide Service, Occasional Temporary Exhibitions, Library.
Publications: Guide Book, Picture Postcards.
Contact Person: Director.

120. Pondicherry Museum

1, Rue Romain Rolland, Pondicherry 605 001.
Type: State Government.
Opening Hours: 10:00 to 17:00, Monday Closed.
Founded in: 1983.
Subjects: Archaeology, Art, Crafts.
Collections: Prehistory, Copper, Bronze and Iron Objects, Arms and Weapons, Paintings, Miniature Paintings, Modern Sculpture, Porcelain, Glass, Ivory,

Wood, Pottery, Terracotta, Jewellery, Embroidery, Tapestry/Carpet, Manuscript, Books, Fossils, Rocks and Minerals, Sea Shells.
Services: Research, Guide Service, Library.
Publications: Exhibit Catalogues, Books.
Contact Person: Curator.

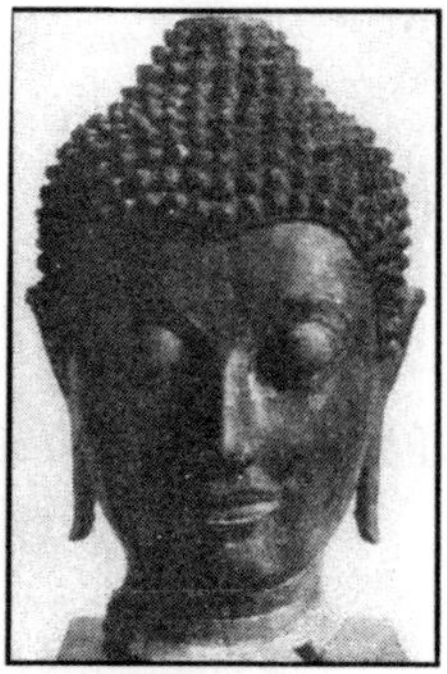

121. Prince of Wales Museum of Western India
159/161 M.G. Road, Fort, Bombay 400 023.
Type: Autonomous Organisation.
Opening Hours: 10:15 to 18:00, Sunday, Monday Closed.
Founded in: 1905.
Subjects: Archaeology, Art, and Natural History.
Collections: Prehistory, Ancient Sculpture, Brass, Copper, Bronze and Iron Objects, Arms and Weapons, Paintings, Miniature Paintings, Scrolls, Porcelain, Glass, Ivory, Wood, Pottery, Terracotta, Jewellery, Embroidery, Textile, Tapestry/Carpet, Manuscript, Books, Films/Slides/Tapes, Musical Instruments, Zoology.
Services: Research, Guide Service, and Library.
Publications: Guide Book, Exhibit Catalogues, and Picture Postcards.
Contact Person: Director.

122. Purulia Zilla Samgrahasala
C/O Haripada Sahitya Mandir, Post Box 6, Purulia, West Bengal 723 101.
Type: Voluntary.
Opening Hours: 15:00 to 18:00, Monday, Tuesday, Thursday, Friday and Saturday Closed.
Founded in: 1960.
Subjects: Archaeology.

Collections: Ancient Sculpture, Arms and Weapons, Pottery, Terracotta, Manuscript.
Services: Guide Service, Occasional Temporary Exhibitions, Library, Film Shows.
Publications: Exhibit Catalogues.
Contact Person: Convener.

123. **R.K. Mission Institute of Culture (Museum)**
Gol Park, Calcutta 700 029.
Type: Voluntary Organisation.
Opening Hours: 10:00 to 18:30, Sunday Closed.
Founded in: 1938.
Subjects: Art, Crafts, Tribal and Folk Art.
Collections: Prehistory, Ancient Sculpture, Brass, Copper, Bronze and Iron Objects, Paintings, Miniature Paintings, Scrolls, Pata Chitra, Modern Sculpture, Ivory, Wood, Terracotta, Jewellery, Embroidery, Textile, Tapestry/Carpet, Manuscript.
Services: Occasional Temporary Exhibitions.
Publications: Guide Book, Picture Postcards.
Contact Person: Head of the Institute.

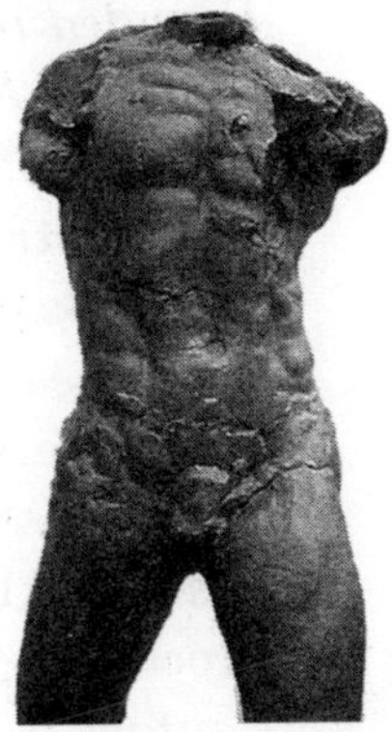

124. **R P Arts and K B Commerce College Museum**
B.D.Rao College, Cambay, Khambbat, Dist.Kheda, Gujarat 388 620.
Type: College Museum.
Founded in: 1960.
Subjects: Archaeology, History.
Services: Research, Guide Service.

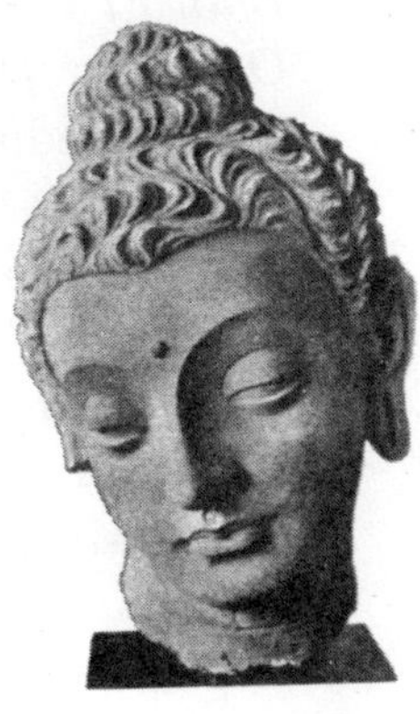

Publications: Guide Book, Exhibit Catalogues, Monographs, Books.
Contact Person: Director.

125. Rabindra Bharati Museum
6/4, Dwarkanath Tagore Lane, Calcutta 700 007.
Type: University.
Subordinate Unit of *Rabindra Bharati University.*
Opening Hours: 10:00 to 17:00, Sunday Closed.
Founded in: 1961.
Subjects: Art, Personalia.
Collections: Paintings, Miniature Paintings, Scrolls, Pata Chitra, Modern Sculpture, Porcelain, Glass, Ivory, Wood, Baskets, Leather Work, Jewellery, Embroidery, Costumes, Textile, Manuscript, Books, Films/Slides/Tapes, Personal Belongings, and Musical Instruments.
Publications: Exhibit Catalogues, Picture Postcards, Exhibit Albums, Monographs, Books, and Seminar Proceedings.
Contact Person: Curator.

126. Rabindra Bhavana
P.O. Santiniketan, Bolpur, West Bengal 731235.
Type: University.
Subordinate Unit of *Visva Bharati University.*
Opening Hours: 10:30 to 16:30, Wednesday Closed.
Founded in: 1942.
Subjects: Personalia.
Collections: Brass, Copper, Bronze and Iron Objects, Arms and Weapons, Paintings, Miniature Paintings, Scrolls, Porcelain, Ivory, Wood, Leather Work, Jewe-

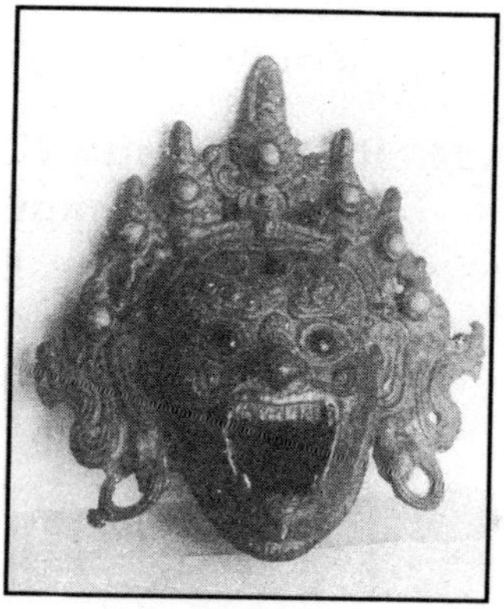

llery, Costumes, Textile, Manuscript, Books, Films/Slides/Tapes, Personal Belongings, and Musical Instruments.
Services: Research, Conservation, Occasional Temporary Exhibitions, Library, Film Shows.
Publications: Guide Book, Picture Postcards, Exhibit Albums, Monographs, Newsletter.
Contact Person: Director.

127. **Rail Transport Museum**
Chanakyapuri, New Delhi 110 021.
Type: Government.
Subordinate Unit of *Ministry of Railway.*
Opening Hours: 09:30 to 17:30, Monday Closed.
Founded in: 1977.
Subjects: Science and Technology, Historical and Technical Development of Indian Railways.
Collections: Brass, Bronze and Iron Objects, Paintings, Porcelain, Wood, Manuscript, Books, Films/Slides/Tapes, Personal Belongings.
Services: Research, Conservation, Guide Service, Occasional Temporary Exhibitions, Library, Film Shows.
Publications: Guide Book, Exhibit Catalogues, Picture Postcards, Monographs, and Books.
Contact Person: Joint Director.

128. **Raja Dinkar Kelkar Museum**
Raja Kelkar Museum, Karnalkunj, 1378 Shukravar, Natu Bag, Pune 411002.
Type: Autonomous Organisation.
Opening Hours: 08:30 to 18:00.
Founded in: 1962.
Subjects: Archaeology, Art, Ethnography, Anthropology, Crafts, Tribal and Folk Art, Children's.

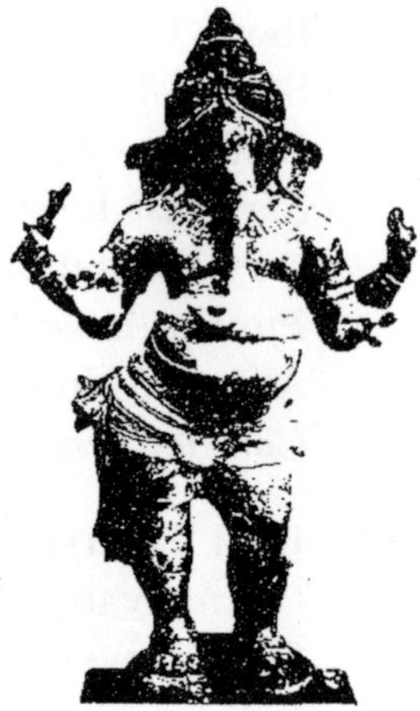

Collections: Ancient Sculpture, Brass, Copper, Bronze and Iron Objects, Arms and Weapons, Paintings, Miniature Paintings, Scrolls, Pata Chitra, Porcelain, Glass, Ivory, Wood, Pottery, Terracotta, Baskets, Leather Work, Jewellery, Embroidery, Costumes, Textile, Tapestry/ Carpet, Manuscript, Books, Figurines, Musical Instruments, Fossils.
Services: Occasional Temporary Exhibitions, Library.
Publications: Exhibit Catalogues, Picture Postcards.
Contact Person: Head of the Organization.

129. Rajwade Museum
Rajwade Path, Lane No. 1, Dhule (M.S) 424 001.
Type: Autonomous Organisation.
Subordinate Unit of *I.V.K Rajwade Sanshodhan Mandal.*
Opening Hours: 09:30 to 19:30, Sunday Closed.
Founded in: 1932.
Subjects: Archaeology, Art, Ethnography, Crafts, and Tribal and Folk Art, Personalia.
Collections: Ancient Sculpture, Brass, Copper, Bronze and Iron Objects, Arms and Weapons, Paintings, Miniature Paintings, Scrolls, Ivory, Wood, Pottery, Terracotta, Jewellery, Musical Instruments.
Services: Research, Conservation, Guide Service, Occasional Temporary Exhibitions, Library, Film Shows, Seminar, Symposium Conference.
Publications: Guide Book, Exhibit Catalogues, Picture Postcards, Journals, Seminar Proceedings, and Workshop Proceedings.
Contact Person: Curator.

130. Raman Science Centre

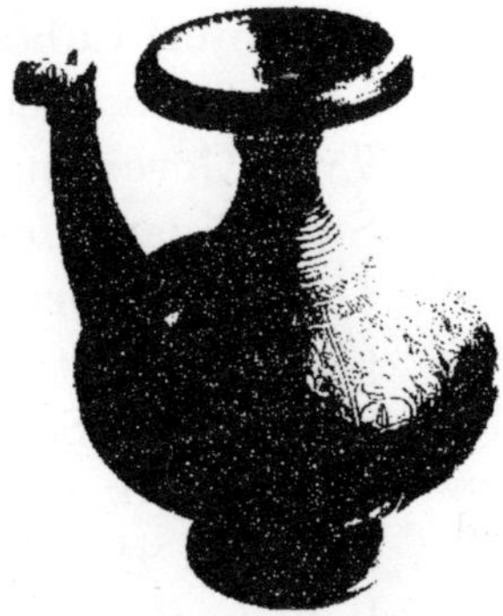

Opposite Gandhisagar, Near Phule Market, Nagpur 440 018.
Type: Autonomous Organisation.
Subordinate Unit of *National Council of Science Museums.*
Opening Hours: 11:30 to 19:00, Monday Closed.
Founded in: 1978.
Subjects: Children's, Science and Technology.
Collections: Working and Participatory Exhibits on Physical Science, Fun Science, Atmosphere, Books, Films, Slides, Tapes.
Services: Guide Service, Occasional Temporary Exhibitions, Travelling Exhibition, Library, Film Shows.
Publications: Pamphlet.
Contact Person: Project Co-ordinator.

131. Rashtrakavi Govind Pai Memorial Museum

M.G.M. College, Udupi, Karnataka 576 102.
Type: Autonomous Organisation.
Subordinate Unit of *Mahatma Gandhi Memorial College.*
Opening Hours: Sunday Closed.
Founded in: 1970.
Subjects: Archaeology, Art, Tribal and Folk Art.
Collections: Ancient Sculpture, Brass, Copper, Bronze and Iron Objects, Wood, Manuscript, Books, Films/ Slides/Tapes.
Services: Research, Conserva-tion.
Publications: Exhibit Catalogues, Picture Postcards, Slides, Exhibit Albums, Monographs, Books, Journals.
Contact Person: Director.

132. Regional Labour Institute

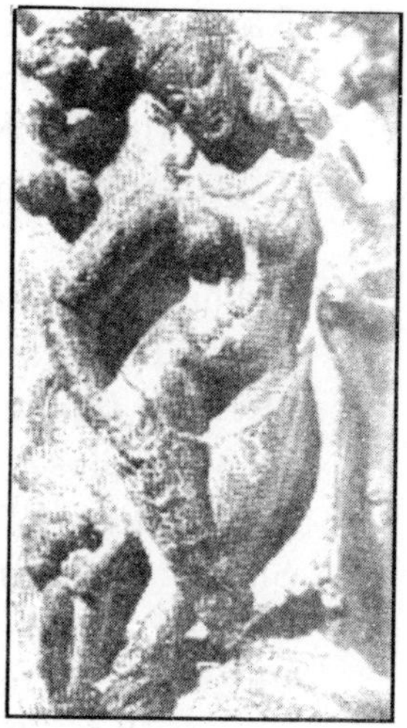

Lake Town, Calcutta 700 089.
Type: Government.
Subordinate Unit of *Ministry of Labour,* Government of India.
Opening Hours: 09:30 to 18:00, Sunday and Saturday Closed.
Founded in: 1965.
Subjects: Health and Safety of Industrial Workers.
Collections: Films/Slides/Tapes, Technology, Industrial Products and Processes, Models on Safety and Health.
Services: Guide Service.
Publications: Guide Book, Slides, and Seminar Proceedings.
Contact Person: Director.

133. Regional Science Centre, Bhopal
Banganga Road, Shamla Hills, Bhopal 462 002.
Type: Autonomous Organisation.
Subordinate Unit of *National Council of Science Museums.*
Subjects: Children's, Science and Technology.
Collections: Working and Participatory Exhibits on Inventions, Physical Science, Inflatable Dome Interactive Planetarium, Books, Films, Slides, Tapes.
Services: Travelling Exhibition.
Contact Person: Curator.

134. Regional Science Centre, Bhubaneswar
Pandit Jawaharlal Nehru Marg, Bhubaneswar 751013.
Type: Autonomous Organisation.
Subordinate Unit of *National Council of Science Museums.*

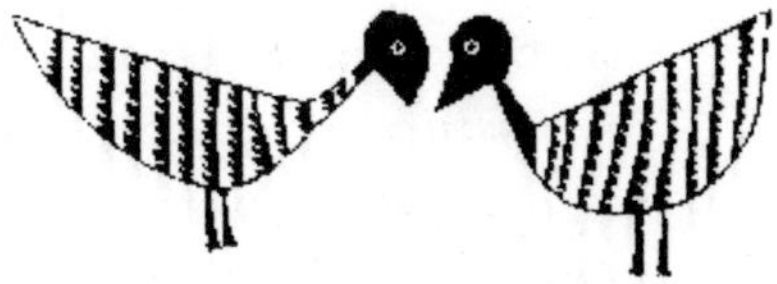

Opening Hours: 11:30 to 19:00, Monday Closed.
Founded in: 1989.
Subjects: Children's, Science and Technology.
Collections: Working and Participatory Exhibits on Universe; Physical Science, Environment, Inflatable Dome Interactive Planetarium, Books, Films, Slides, and Tapes.
Services: Guide Service, Occasional Temporary Exhibitions, Travelling Exhibition, and Other Outreach Programme, Library, Film Shows.
Publications: Pamphlet.
Contact Person: Curator.

135. Regional Science Centre, Calicut
C/o Calicut Development Authority,
Post Box 142, G H Road, Calicut 673 001.
Type: Autonomous Organisation.
Subordinate Unit of *National Council of Science Museums.*
Opening Hours: 11:30 to 19:00, Monday Closed.
Founded in: 1978.
Subjects: Planetarium, Children's, Science and Technology.
Collections: Working and Participatory Exhibits on Physical Science, Planetarium, Books, Films, Slides, Tapes.
Services: Travelling Exhibition.
Contact Person: Curator.

136. Regional Science Centre, Guwahati
Jawaharnagar, Near Mugafirtn, Khanapara, Guwahati 781022.
Type: Autonomous Organisation.

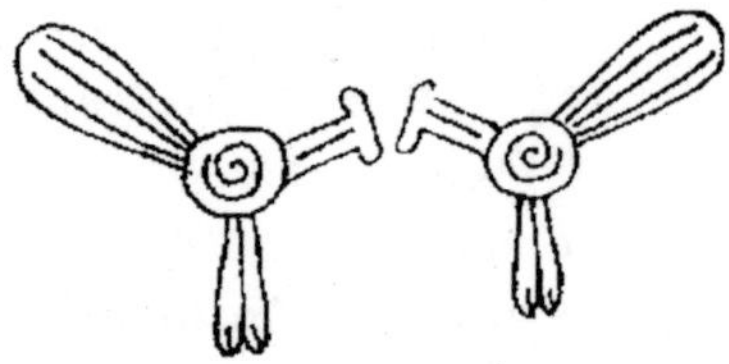

Subordinate Unit of *National Council of Science Museums.*
Opening Hours: 11:30 to 19:00, Monday Closed.
Founded in: 1978.
Subjects: Children's, Science and Technology.
Collections: Working and Participatory Exhibits on Earth Science, Nature, Environment, Agriculture, Energy, Physical Science, Children's Exhibits, Inflatable Dome Interactive Planetarium, Books, Films, Slides, Tapes.
Services: Guide Service, Occasional Temporary Exhibitions, Travelling Exhibition, Other Outreach Programme, Library, Film Shows.
Contact Person: Curator.

137. Regional Science Centre, Lucknow
Aliganj Extension, Sector-E, Green Belt, Lucknow 226 020.
Type: Autonomous Organisation.
Subordinate Unit of *National Council of Science Museums.*
Opening Hours: 11:30 to 19:00, Monday Closed.
Founded in: 1989.
Subjects: Children's, Science and Technology.
Collections: Working and Participatory Exhibits on Water, Astronomy, Physical Science, Inflatable Dome Interactive Planetarium, Books, Films, Slides, Tapes.
Services: Guide Service, Occasional Temporary Exhibitions, Travelling Exhibition, Other Outreach Programme, Library, Film Shows.
Publications: Pamphlet.
Contact Person: Curator.

138. Regional Science Centre, Tirupati

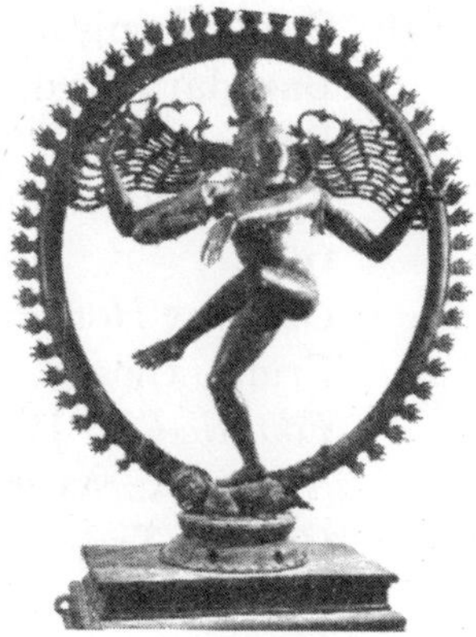

Qtr. No. 66, University Qtr. Prakasam Nagar, University Campus, Tirupati 517 502.
Type: Autonomous Organisation.
Subordinate Unit of *National Council of Science Museums.*
Collections: Working and Participatory Exhibits on Motion, Physical Science, Inflatable Dome Interactive Planetarium, Books, Films, Slides, Tapes.
Services: Travelling Exhibition.
Contact Person: Curator.

139. S.R.C. Museum of Indology

24, Gangwal Park, Prachya Vidya Path, Jaipur 302 004.
Type: Autonomous Organization.
Opening Hours: 10:00 to 20:00, Thursday Closed.
Founded in: 1960.
Subjects: Archaeology, Art, Ethnography, Crafts, and Tribal and Folk Art, Personalia, Natural History, Ayurved and Alchemy, Numismatics, Philately and Fiscals, Astronomy.
Collections: Prehistory, Ancient Sculpture, Brass, Copper, Bronze and Iron Objects, Arms and Weapons, Paintings, Miniature Paintings, Scrolls, Pata Chitra, Porcelain, Glass, Ivory, Wood, Pottery, Terracotta, Baskets, Leather Work, Costumes, Textile, Manuscript, Books, Fossils, Rocks and Minerals, Technology, Tantra Yantra.
Services: Guide Service, Occasional Temporary Exhibitions.
Publications: Exhibit Catalogues, Picture Postcards, Slides, Monographs, Folder.
Contact Person: Founder Chairman.

140. Salar Jung Museum

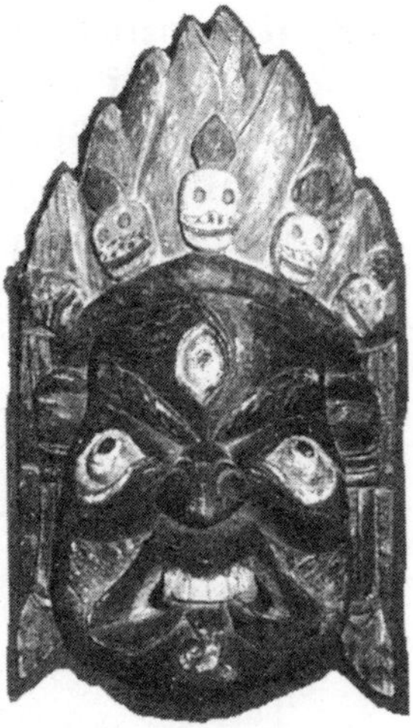

Baradari, Hyderabad, Andhra Pradesh 500 002.
Type: Autonomous Organisation.
Opening Hours: 10:00 to 17:00, Friday Closed.
Founded in: 1951.
Subjects: Archaeology, Art, Crafts, Tribal and Folk Art, Children's.
Collections: Ancient Sculpture, Brass, Copper, Bronze and Iron Objects, Arms and Weapons, Paintings, Miniature Paintings, Scrolls, Pata Chitra, Modern Sculpture, Porcelain, Glass, Ivory, Wood, Pottery, Jewellery, Embroidery, Costumes, Textile, Tapestry/Carpet, Manuscript, Books, Personal Belongings.
Services: Research, Conservation, Guide Service, Occasional Temporary Exhibitions, Library, Film Shows, Seminar, Workshop.
Publications: Guide Book, Exhibit Catalogues, Picture Postcards, Slides, Monographs, Books, Journals, Seminar Proceedings.
Contact Person: Director.

141. Science City, Calcutta

Park Circus Connector, G.K. Road, Calcutta-700046.
Type: Autonomous.
Subordinate Unit of *National Council of Science Museums.*
Opening Hours: 09.00 to 21.00.
Founded in: Formal Opening Scheduled-1998.
Subjects: Science of Perception, Classical Indian Concepts of Basic Elements of Matter, Evolution of life, Environment and Ecology of India, Mysteries of Life

in India, Awareness of Natural Disaster, Unity and Diversity of Cultures.
Services: Monorail, Ropeway for transport within the campus, Large scale people movers for indoor exhibitions, Space theatre with sophisticated planetarium and large films format projection on hemispherical dome, Open air science park with interactive games, Water body exhibits and Energy park, Convention centre of International standards with Main Auditorium for 2000 and Mini Auditorium for 400 with high-tech projection facilities, Multi-lingual simulation translation facilities. Twelve storied tower with revolving Restaurant at the top.
Contact Person: Director General.

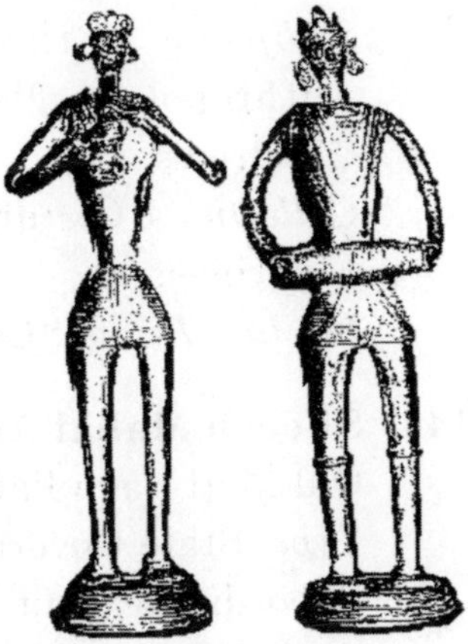

142. **Shaheed-e-Azam, S. Bhagat Singh Museum**
Khatkar Kalan, Dist. Jullundar, Punjab.
Type: State Government.
Subordinate Unit of *Dept. of Cultural Affairs and Museums,* Punjab.
Opening Hours 10:00 to 17:00, Monday Closed.
Founded in: 1980.
Subjects: Personalia, Freedom Struggle Movement.
Collections: Costumes, Manuscript, Books, Personal Belongings, Photographs.
Services: Research, Guide Service, Occasional Temporary Exhibitions.
Publications: Exhibit Catalogues, Brochure.
Contact Person: Director.

143. **Shankar's International Dolls Museum**
Nehru House, 4, Bahadur Shah Zafar Marg, New Delhi 110002.

Type: Government.
Subordinate Unit of *Children's Book Trust.*
Opening Hours: 10:00 to 18:00, Monday and Friday Closed.
Founded in: 1965.
Subjects: Ethnography, Anthropology, Personalia, Children's.
Collections: Costumes, Dolls, Figurines.
Contact Person: Curator.

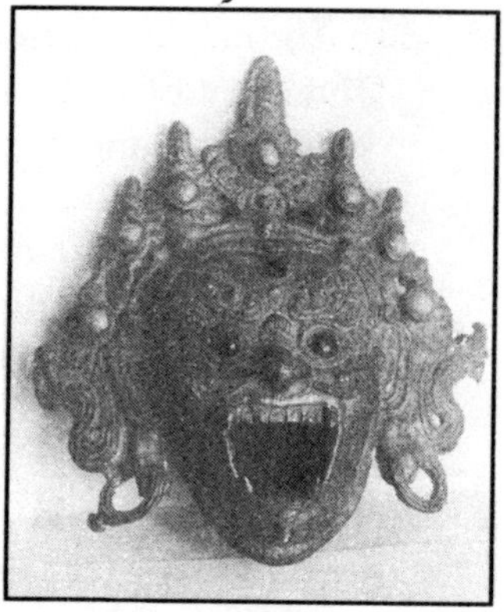

144. Sheesh Mahal Art Gallery
Old Moti Bagh Palace, Patiala, Punjab.
Type: State Government.
Subordinate Unit of *Department of Cultural Affairs, Archaeology and Museums,* Chandigarh.
Opening Hours: 10:00 to 17:00, Monday Closed.
Founded in: 1972.
Subjects: Archaeology, Art, Anthropology, Crafts, Tribal and Folk Art, Personalia, Industrial/ Commercial, Natural History.
Collections: Ancient Sculp-ture, Brass, Copper, Bronze and Iron Objects, Paintings, Miniature Paintings, Scrolls, Pata Chitra, Glass, Ivory, Wood, Pottery, Terracotta, Leather Work, Jewellery, Embroidery, Costumes, Textile, Tapestry/Carpet, Manuscript, Personal Belongings, Figurines, Musical Instruments, Fossils, Rocks and Minerals, Coins, Medals.
Services: Research, Occasional Temporary Exhibitions.
Publications: Picture Postcards, Brochure.
Contact Person: Director.

145. Shri Girdharbrai Sangrahalaya Children Museum

Amreli, Gujarat 364 601.
Type: Public Trust.
Subordinate Unit of *Bal Bhavan,* Amreli.
Opening Hours: 08:30 to 18:30, Wednesday Closed.
Founded in: 1955.
Subjects: Archaeology, Art, Crafts, Tribal and Folk Art, Personalia, Natural History, Health and Medical, Planetarium, Science and Technology, Zoo Garden, Kathi House, Ramayan Section, Toys House, International Dolls.

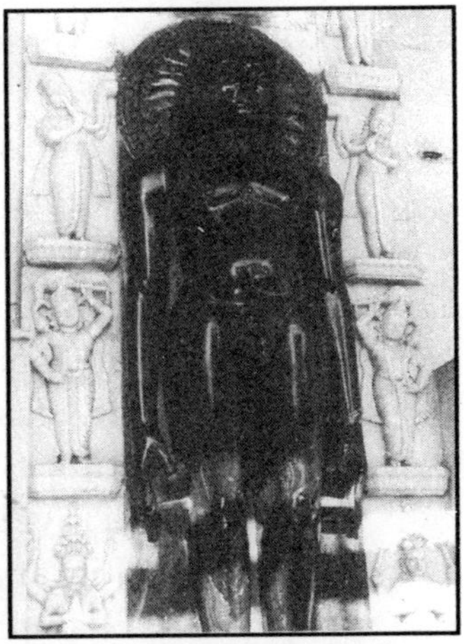

Collections: Prehistory, Ancient Sculpture, Brass, Copper, Bronze and Iron Objects, Arms and Weapons, Paintings, Miniature Paintings, Pata Chitra, Modern Sculpture, Glass, Ivory, Wood, Pottery, Terracotta, Baskets, Jewellery, Embroidery, Costumes, Textile, Tapestry/Carpet, Films/Slides/Tapes, Personal Belongings, Dolls, Toys, Figurines, Musical Instruments, Earth Science, Botany, Environment, Physical Science, Technology, Industrial Products and Processes, Coins.
Services: Conservation, Guide Service, Occasional Temporary Exhibitions, Travelling Exhibition, Other Outreach Programme, Library, Film Shows, Birds Exhibition, Science Corner, Sports, Paintings, Environment Education Camps.
Publications: Guide Book, Exhibit Catalogues, Picture Postcards, Slides, Exhibit Albums, Monographs, Books, Seminar Proceedings, Workshop Proceedings, Newsletter.
Contact Person: Director.

146. Shrikrishna Science Centre

Chajju Bagh, West Gandhi Maidan, Patna 800 001.
Type: Autonomous Organisation.
Subordinate Unit of *National Council of Science Museums.*
Opening Hours: 11:30 to 19:00, Monday Closed.
Founded in: 1978.
Subjects: Children's, Science and Technology.

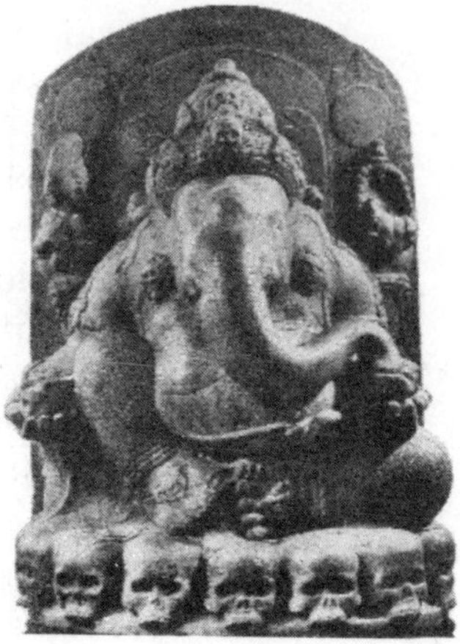

Collections: Working and Participatory Exhibits on Physical Science, Evolution, Inflatable Dome Interactive Planetarium, Photographs, Books, Films, Slides, Tapes.
Services: Guide Service, Occasional Temporary Exhibitions, Travelling Exhibition, Other Outreach Programme, Library, Film Shows.
Publications: Pamphlets, Folders.
Contact Person: Curator.

147. Sibsagar College Museum

P.O. Joysagar, Dist. Sibsagar, Assam 785 665.
Type: Private.
Subordinate Unit of *Sibsagar College.*
Opening Hours: 09:00 to 16:00, Sunday Closed.
Founded in: 1949.
Subjects: Archaeology, Art, Crafts, Tribal and Folk Art.

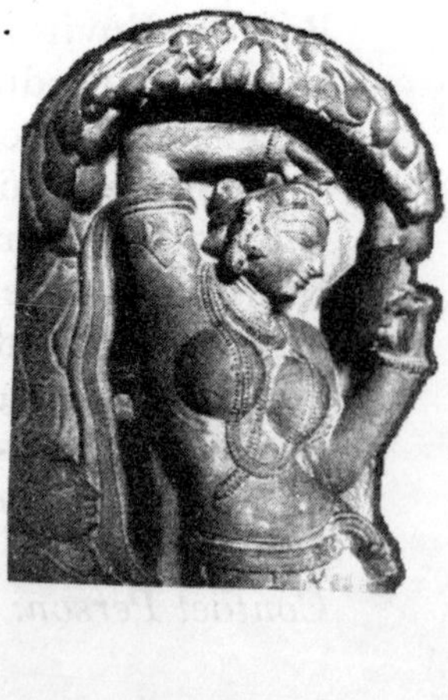

Collections: Ancient Sculpture, Brass, Copper, Bronze and Iron Objects, Arms and Weapons, Paintings, Miniature Paintings, Modern Sculpture, Wood, Pottery, Terracotta, Baskets, Jewellery, Embroidery, Costumes, Textile, Tapestry/Carpet, Manuscript, Books, Films/ Slides/Tapes, Musical Instruments.
Services: Research, Conservation, Guide Service, Occasional Temporary Exhibitions, Library.
Publications: Exhibit Catalogues.
Contact Person: Principal.

148. Singhpur Palace Museum, Chanderi
Archaeological Survey of India, Dist. Guna, Madhya Pradesh.
Type: Government.
Subordinate Unit of *Museums* Branch, ASI, Calcutta.
Founded in: 1986.
Subjects: Archaeology.
Collections: Ancient Sculp-ture.
Services: Research, Con-servation.
Contact Person: Archaeo-logist.

149. Site Museum Dholbaha
Hoshiarpur, Punjab.
Type: State Government.
Subordinate Unit of *Department of Cultural Affairs, Archaeology &Museums,* Punjab.
Opening Hours: 10:00 to 17:00, Monday Closed.
Founded in: 1978.
Subjects: Archaeology.
Collections: Ancient Sculpture.
Services: Research, Guide Service.
Contact Person: Director.

150. Sri Guru Teg Bahadur Museum

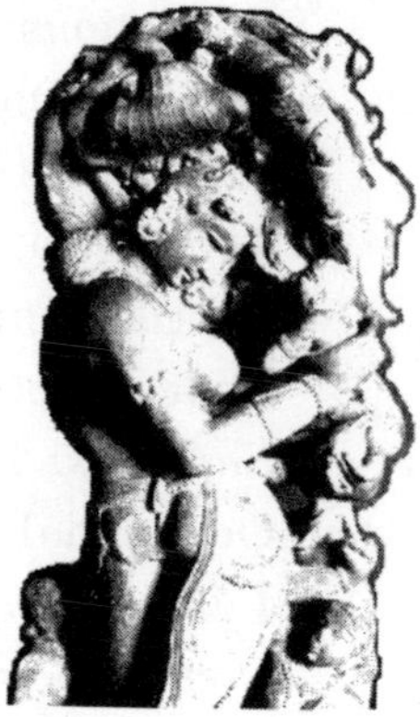

Anandapur Sahib, Dist, Roper, Punjab.

Type: State Government.

Subordinate Unit of *Dept. of Cultural Affairs, Archaeo-logy and Museums.*

Opening Hours: 10:00 to 17:00, Monday Closed.

Founded in: 1983.

Subjects: Art.

Collections: Paintings.

Services: Research, Guide Service.

Publications: Monographs, Brochure.

Contact Person: Director.

151. State Archaeological Museum

1, Satyen Ray Road, Behala, Calcutta 700 034 West Bengal.

Type: State Government.

Subordinate Unit of *Directorate of Archaeology.*

Opening Hours: 11:00 to 16:00, Sunday Closed.

Founded in: 1980.

Subjects: Archaeology, Art.

Collections: Prehistory, Ancient Sculpture, Copper, Bronze and Iron Objects, Arms and Weapons, Paintings, Miniature Paintings, Scrolls, Pata Chitra, Ivory, Wood, Pottery, Terracotta, Embroidery, Textile, Manuscript, Dolls, Toys, Fossils.

Services: Guide Service.

Publications: Picture Postcards.

Contact Person: Director.

152. State Museum, Bhopal

Banganga Road, Bhopal.
Type: State Government.
Opening Hours: 10:00 to 17:00, Monday Closed.
Founded in: 1971.
Subjects: Archaeology, Art.
Collections: Prehistory, Ancient Sculpture, Brass, Copper, Bronze and Iron Objects, Paintings, Miniature Paintings, Jewellery.
Services: Guide Service.
Publications: Picture Postcards.
Contact Person: Curator.

153. State Museum, Goa

1st Floor, Ashirvad Building, St. Inez, Panaji, Goa 403 001.
Type: Public Trust.
Subordinate Unit of *Directorate of Archives, Archaeology and Museums.*
Opening Hours: 10:00 to 17:30, Sunday Closed.
Founded in: 1978.
Subjects: Archaeology, Art, Ethnography, Anthro-pology, Crafts, Tribal and Folk Art, Natural History, Geology, Christian Art.

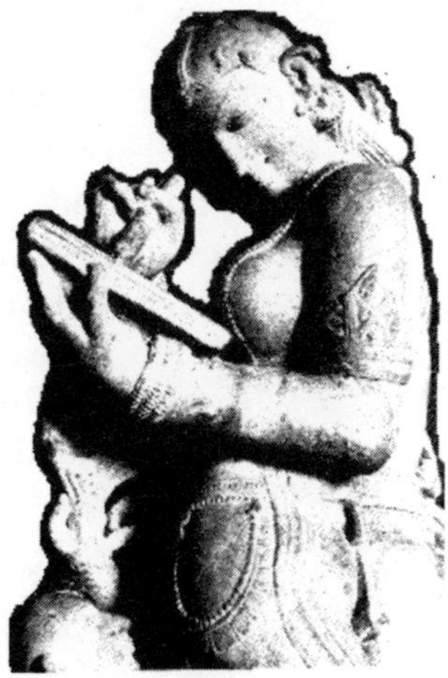

Collections: Prehistory, Ancient Sculpture, Brass, Copper, Bronze and Iron Objects, Arms and Weapons. Paintings, Miniature Paintings, Porcelain, Glass, Ivory Wood, Pottery, Terracotta Costumes, Textile, Manuscript, Musical Instruments Fossils, Rocks and Minerals, Coins, Currency Notes and Blocks.

Services: Research, Conservation, Guide Service, Occasional Temporary Exhibitions, Library, Film Shows.
Publications: Journals, Information Booklet.
Contact Person: Director.

154. State Museum, Hyderabad
Public Gardens, Hyderabad 500 004.
Type: State Government.
Subordinate Unit of *Dept. of Archaeology and Museums,* Govt. of A.P.
Opening Hours: 10:30 to 17:00, Friday Closed.
Founded in: 1930.
Subjects: Archaeology, Art, Personalia, Paintings, Coins, Contemporary Arts, Ornaments.

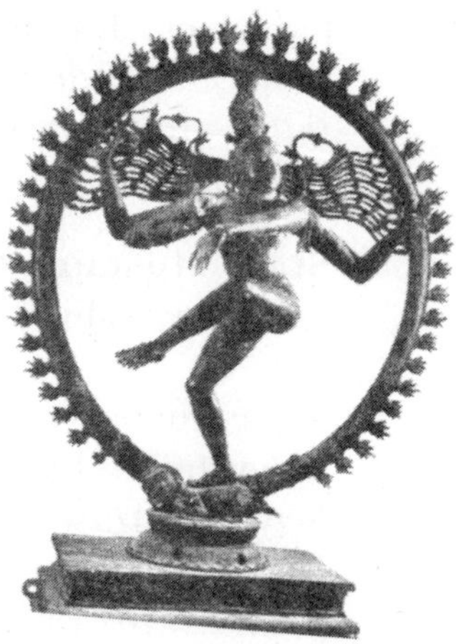

Collections: Prehistory, Ancient Sculpture, Brass, Copper, Bronze and Iron Objects, Arms and Weapons, Paintings, Miniature Paintings, Scrolls, Pata Chitra, Modern Sculpture, Porcelain, Glass, Ivory, Wood, Pottery, Terracotta, Leather Work, Jewellery, Embroidery, Costumes.
Services: Research, Conservation, Guide Service, Occasional Temporary Exhibitions, Travelling Exhibition Library.
Publications: Guide Book, Exhibit Catalogues, and Picture Postcards, Monographs.
Contact Person: Head of the Organization.

155. State Museum, Lucknow
Banarasi Bag, Lucknow 226001.
Type: State Government.
OpeningHours: 10:30 to 16:30, Monday Closed.
Founded in: 1863.

Subjects: Archaeology, Art, Ethnography, Anthropology, Tribal and Folk Art, Natural History.
Collections: Prehistory, Brass, Copper, Bronze and Iron Objects, Arms and Weapons, Paintings, Miniature Paintings, Scrolls, Pata Chitra, Modern Sculpture, Ivory, Wood, Terracotta, Jewellery, Textile, Manuscript, Musical Instruments, Ancient Sculptures, Embroidery.
Services: Travelling Exhibition, Guide Service.
Publications: Exhibit Catalogues.
Contact Person: Director.

156. State Tribal Museum
Circular Road, Chhindwada, Madhya Pradesh 480 001.
Type: Public Trust.
Subordinate Unit of *Ethnological Museum* (Tribal Research Institute).
Opening Hours: 10:30 to 17:30, Sunday Closed.
Founded in: 1954.
Subjects: Ethnography, Tribal and Folk Art.
Collections: Bronze and Iron Objects, Arms and Weapons, Wood, Pottery, Terracotta, Baskets, Leather Work, Jewellery, Embroidery, Costumes, Musical Instruments, Fossils.
Services: Research, Guide Service, Occasional Temporary Exhibitions.
Contact Person: Research Officer.

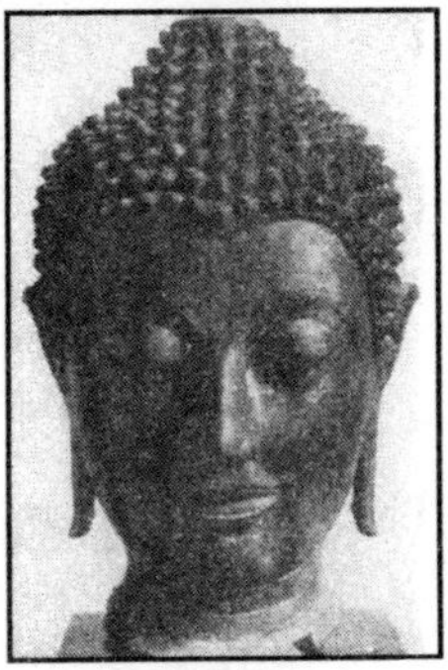

157. Taj Museum, Taj Mahal, Agra
Archaeological Survey of India, Agra, Uttar Pradesh 282 001.
Type: Government.
Subordinate Unit of *Museums Branch,* ASI, Calcutta.
Opening Hours: 10:00 to 17:00, Friday Closed.
Founded in: 1982.

Subjects: Archaeology.
Collections: Arms and Weapons, Paintings, Porcelain, Ivory, Manuscript.
Services: Research, Conservation, Guide Service, Occasional Temporary Exhibitions, Library, Film Shows.
Publications: Guide Book, Picture Postcards.
Contact Person: Archaeologist.

158. Thanjavur Art Gallery
Palace Complex, Thanjavur, Tamil Nadu 613 009.
Type: Autonomous Organisation.
Opening Hours: 09:00 to 18:00.
Founded in: 1951.
Subjects: Archaeology, Art, Crafts, Natural History, World Famous Icons in Bronzes.
Collections: Ancient Sculpture, Brass, Copper, Bronze and Iron Objects, Paintings.
Services: Research, Conservation, Guide Service.
Publications: Guide Book, Exhibit Catalogues, Picture Postcards.
Contact Person: Head of the Organization.

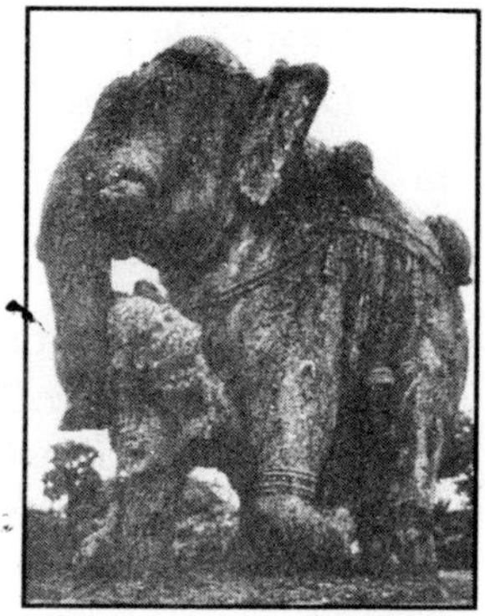

159. The Asiatic Society
1, Park Street, Calcutta 700 016.
Type: Autonomous Organization.
Opening Hours: 09.45 to 06:15, Sunday and Saturday Closed.
Founded in: 1784.
Subjects: Archaeology, Art, History.
Collections: Paintings, Sculpture, Documents, Manuscripts, Coins, Books.
Services: Reprography, Photography, Lectures, Library.

Publications: Books, Journals.
Contact Person: General Secretary.

160. Tibet House
1, Institutional Area, Lodhi Road, New Delhi 110 003.
Type: Autonomous Organisation.
Opening Hours: 09:00 to 17:00, Sunday Closed.
Founded in: 1965.
Subjects: Art, Anthropology, Crafts, Tribal and Folk Art.
Collections: Ancient Sculpture, Bronze and Iron Objects, Paintings, Miniature Paintings, Scrolls, Jewellery, Embroidery, Manuscript, Books, Dolls.
Services: Research, Guide Service, Occasional Temporary Exhibitions, Film Shows.
Publications: Exhibit Catalogues, Picture Postcards, Books, Seminar Proceedings.
Contact Person: Director.

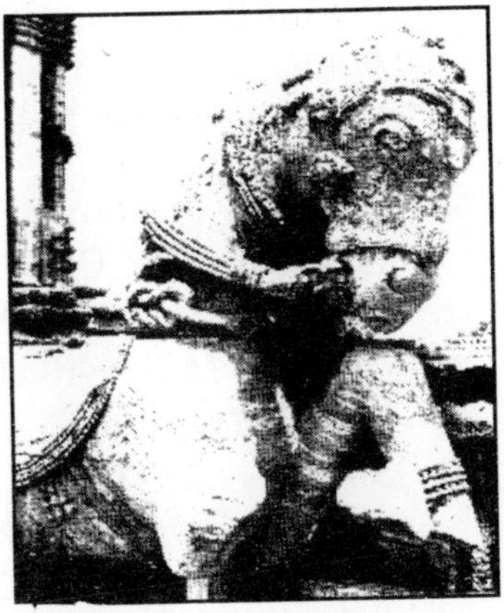

161. Tipu Sultan Museum, Srirangapatnam
Archaeological Survey of India, Srirangapatnam, Dist. Mandya, Karnataka 571438.
Type: Government.
Subordinate Unit of *Museums Branch,* ASI, Calcutta.
Opening Hours: 10:00 to 17:00, Friday Closed.
Founded in: 1959.
Subjects: Archaeology.
Collections: Bronze and Iron Objects, Arms and Weapons, Paintings, Porcelain, Jewellery, Manuscript.
Services: Research, Conservation, Guide Service,

Occasional Temporary Exhibitions, Library, Film Shows.
Contact Person: Archaeologist.

162. Tribal Welfare Museum

Tribal Research and Training Institute, 28 Queen's Garden, Pune 411001.
Type: State Government.
Opening Hours: 10:00 to 17:00, Sunday Closed.
Founded in: 1962.
Subjects: Ethnography, Crafts, Tribal and Folk Art.
Collections: Ancient Sculpture, Brass, Copper, Bronze and Iron Objects, Arms and Weapons, Paintings, Wood, Pottery, Terracotta, Baskets, Jewellery, Costumes, Books, Films/Slides/'Tapes, Musical Instruments.
Services: Guide Service, Occasional Temporary Exhibitions, Library, Film Shows.
Publications: Monographs, Journals.
Contact Person: Director.

163. Victoria Memorial

1, Queensway, Calcutta 700 071.
Type: Autonomous Organisation.
Opening Hours: 10:00 to 17:00, Monday Closed.
Founded in: 1903.
Subjects: Art, Crafts, Personalia, History.
Collections: Bronze and Iron Objects, Arms and Weapons, Paintings, Miniature Paintings, Scrolls, Pata Chitra, Modern Sculpture, Porcelain, Ivory, Wood, Terracotta, Costumes, Textile, Manuscript, Books, Personal Belongings, Documents, Artifacts.
Services: Research, Conservation, Guide Service. Other Outreach Programme, Library, Film Shows.
Publications: Guide Book, Picture Postcards. Journals. Seminar Proceedings, Workshop Proceedings.
Contact Person: Curator.

164. Vijaywada Science Centre

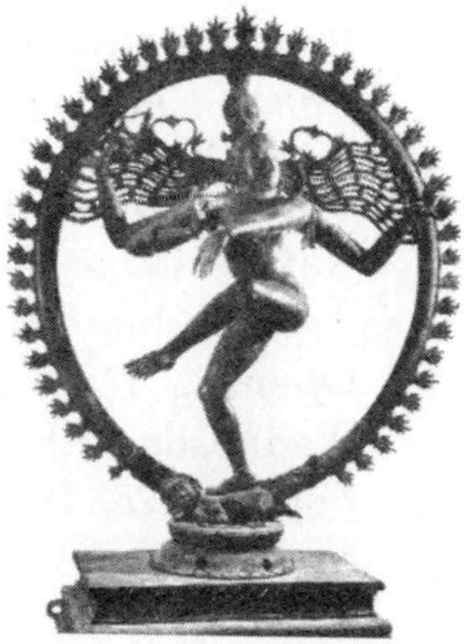

Gandhi Hill, Vijaywada-
520 001, Andhra Pradesh.
Type: Autonomous.
Subordinate Unit of *National Council of Science Museums.*
Opening Hours: 11:30 to 19:00, Monday Closed.
Founded in: 1992.
Subjects: Science and Technology.
Collections: Working and Participatory Exhibits on the History of Indian Science, Technology and Culture.
Services: Guide Service, Occasional Temporary Exhibitions.
Publications: Guide Book.
Contact Person: Project Co-ordinator.

165. Visvesvaraya Industrial and Technological Museum

Kasturba Road, Bangalore-560 001.
Type: Autonomous Organisa-tion.
Subordinate Unit of *National Council of Science Museums.*
Opening Hours: 10:00 to 17:30, Monday Closed.
*Subjects:*Industrial/Commer-cial, Children's, Science and Technology.
Collections: Working and Participatory Exhibits on Environment, Physical Science, Industrial Products and Processes, Timber and Paper, Scientific and Technological Artifacts, Children's Exhibits, Books, Films, Slides, Tapes, Interactive Planetarium Inflatable Dome.
Services: Research, Guide Service, Occasional Temporary Exhibitions, Travelling Exhibition, Other Outreach Programme, Library, Film Shows.

Publications: Guide Book, Exhibit Catalogues, Books, Seminar Proceedings, Pamphlets.
Contact Person: Director.

166. Watson Museum
Rajkot, Gujarat 360 001.
Type: Public Trust.
Opening Hours: 09:00 to 17:45, Wednesday Closed.
Founded in: 1888.
Subjects: Archaeology, Art, Anthropology, Crafts, Tribal and Folk Art, Natural History.
Collections: Prehistory, Ancient Sculpture, Copper, Bronze and Iron Objects, Arms and Weapons, Paintings, Miniature Paintings, Modern Sculpture, Glass, Ivory, Wood, Pottery, Leather Work, Embroidery, Textile, Tapestry/ Carpet, Musical Instruments, Zoology, Industrial Products and Processes.

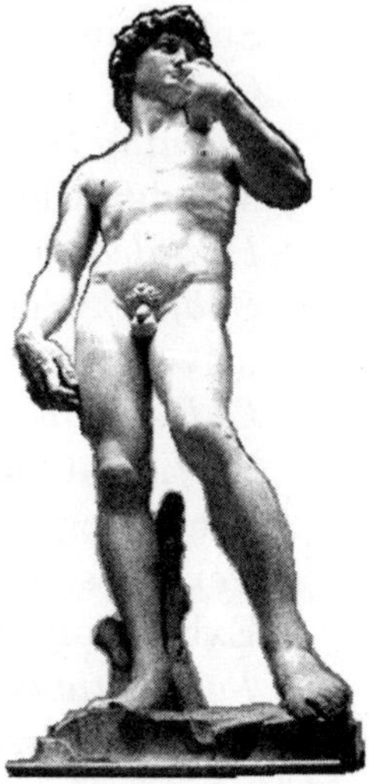

Services: Conservation, Guide Service, Library, Film Shows.
Publications: Guide Book, Picture Postcards, Books.
Contact Person: Director.

Appendix–I

A List of Required Items for Preservation and Conservation Work

Acetic acid (Glacial): It is corrosive organic acid with a specific gravity of 1.05 when the melting point is 16.7°C and boiling point 118°C. The pure acid or glacial and its liquids containing various percentages of acid (40%, 80%, etc.) are available in the market. This acid is soluble in water and alcohol.

Acetone: Colourless organic chemical in liquid form to the group of compounds known as "ketones". The specific gravity is 0.79 and boiling point is 56.5°C. It is a good solvent of celluloid.

Alcohol: This term commonly signifies spirits of wine of various strength.

Absolute alcohol (same as ethyl alcohol) is alcohol without any water, but as it absorbs water from the atmosphere, the strength of commercial absolute alcohol rarely exceeds 98 per cent. Rectified spirits are rendered pure and strong by redistillation (about 95% strong).

Ammonia: It is used as a good washing agent for neutralizing any acid that might have formed on a mineral.

Ammonium Phosphate: It is a good fire protecting material for wood.

Amyl Acetate: It is colourless organic liquid with an aromatic smell with specific gravity 0.875 and boiling point 140°C–148°C. We can find three varieties of amyl acetate of which "common amyl acetate", is the compound "iso-amyl acetate". It is a solvent of cellulose and also used along with acetone for preparing celluloid varnish, cement, etc.

Ascu: This is the trade name of a preparation containing copper, arsenic and chromium salts in the proportions, which are most resistant to bleaching. It is extensively used as a wood preservative.

Bees wax: Bees wax is a yellow, tough solid of complex composition. It is soluble in ether and chloroform with melting point ranges from 60°C.

Benzene (Benzol): It is a colourless, inflammable organic liquid with boiling point of 80°C; and an excellent solvent of resin, fats, etc.

Benzine (Petrol, Petroleum spirit): Benzine is not synonymous with benzene. The name is given to a light petroleum oil with a boiling point between 120°C–150°C.

Bibulous paper: This is capable of absorbing moisture. Any paper possessing this property, can be used in drying plants. It is also commonly known as "blotting paper".

Bleaching powder: It is also known as the "chloride of lime". This is white powder containing 35 to 40 per cent of available *chlorine*, as its name indicates. It is mainly used for bleaching the paper, textile, etc.

Calcium Hydroxide: It is also known as Calcium Hydroxide.

Carbon Tetrachloride: This is used in fumigation while mixed with ethylene-dichloride in the ratio of 1:3.

Caustic Potash: Chemical name is Potassium hydroxide. It is white deliquescent and caustic substance. When it is dissolved in water then great heat is produced.

Caustic Soda: Chemical name is Sodium hydroxide. It is white, highly deliquescent and caustic substance. This chemical is marketed in several forms–flakes, sticks, pellets, etc. It produces much heat at the time of dissolve in water.

Celluloid: It is good, transparent sheets are available in the market. Old photographic films may also be used, though this is not advisable when dealing with works of art. The sheets cut in small bits to put in equal parts of acetone and amyl acetate solution for easy dissolve to form "Celluloid cement". It consists of dissolved celluloid in a suitable solvent (acetone) to give a thick syrupy liquid (about 10%).

Celluloid Acetate: It is non-inflammable substance. Soluble in acetone and this solution can be used for preservative coatings. It is more stable compound than celluloid and so it is superior to celluloid solutions for treating old fabrics.

Chloral-hydrate: This is crystalline substance with a melting point of 57°C. Soluble in water and alcohol.

Chloramine-T: It is a dull white substance, which is capable of generating chlorine. It must be kept in a well-stoppered bottle.

Chloroform: This is a volatile, anaesthetic liquid with a boiling points 60°C. Good solvent for fat and other substance.

Clay: It is fine-grained kaolin, which should not crack when dried. It is used for purposes of modelling.

Corrosive Sublimate: It is chemically known as mercuric chloride. This is highly virulent poison. If any metal is allowed to come in contact with it, the solution is not only gets itself stained but also stains the specimens.

Ether: This liquid is highly volatile and inflammable.

Ethylene Dichloride: It is employed in fumigation mixed with carbon tetra-chloride in the ratio of 3:1.

Formalin: This is a commercial aqueous solution containing 40 per cent of the compound "formaldehyde".

Formic Acid: It is a colourless liquid when it is pure with a boiling point 101°C. It is a powerful antiseptic, very corrosive, and mixes with water in all proportions. Solutions of various strengths (50%, 25%, etc) are available in the market.

Glue: This is an impure form of gelatin and a good adhesive for wood. Fish glue, which is commonly sold in the market but effect, is unsatisfactory. Good quality glue should be light coloured and free from smell. It is prepared for use by breaking it into small pieces and soaking in cold water tills the pieces become soft and swollen. The excess water is poured off and the substance is heated in a glue pot below 80°C. The glue is applied with a brush when it is hot.

Bibliography

Basu, M.N. and Malay Nath Basu (1976): "Museum and its Role in Anthropology" published in *The Eastern Anthropologist*; Vol. 29, No. 1, Jan-Mar., 1976.

Basu Roy, Indrani (1993): *Kalighat–Its Impact on Socio-Cultural Life of Hindus*; published by Gyan Publishing House, New Delhi.

Basu Roy, Indrani (1995): "The Chitrakar Women of Kalighat" in the Book *The Necessity of Craft* edited by Lorna Kaino, published by UWA Press, Perth, Australia.

Basu Roy, Indrani (2003): *Anthropology: The Study of Man*; published by S. Chand & Co. Ltd., New Delhi.

Campbell, Joseph ed. (1964): *The Art of Indian Asia*, Vol. I & II; published by Bollingen Foundation, New York.

Ghosh, A.K. (1976): "Ethnographi museum–a design on human integration" published in *The Eastern Anthropologist*; Vol. 29, No. 1, Jan-Mar., 1976.

Hudson, Kenneth (1975): *A Social History of Museums*, published by Macmillion Press, London.

Morley, Grace (1976): "Museums of Anthropology: their role in East, South and Southeast Asia" published in *The Eastern Anthropologist*; Vol. 29, No. 1, Jan-Mar., 1976.

Roy, D. K. (1987): "Ethnographic Museum and Photography–A Design on Communication" published in the *Bulletin of C.R.I.*, Vol. XVII, No. 1 & 2.

Roy, D.K. (1988): "Ecology, Economy, Technology and Settled Cultivation in Eastern India" published in the *Bulletin of C.R.I.*, Vol. XVIII, No. 1 & 2.

Roy, D.K. (1990): *"Alankar-O-Adibasi Ramani"* (article on Ornaments in Tribal Women in Bengali) published in the Book Paschimbanger Adibasi Nari, (in Bengali) ed. By R.Gupta, Special Series No. 33., *C.R.I.*, Calcutta.

Roy, D.K. and M.K. Chowdhury (1997): "Modern Management of a Small Museum" published in the *Bulletin of C.R.I.*, Govt. of West Bengal, Vol. XIX, No. 4.

Wittlin, Alma S. (1949): *The Museum–Its History and Its Tasks in Education*; published by Routledge and Kegan Paul Limited, London.

Index

B

H

I

P

R

S

T